THE BATTLES OF
ARMAGEDDON

THE BATTLES OF
ARMAGEDDON

Megiddo and the Jezreel Valley from the
Bronze Age to the Nuclear Age

ERIC H. CLINE

Ann Arbor

THE UNIVERSITY OF MICHIGAN PRESS

2003   2002   2001   4   3   2

A CIP catalog record for this book is available from the British Library.

Library of Congress Cataloging-in-Publication Data

Cline, Eric H.
   The battles of Armageddon : Megiddo and the Jezreel valley from
the bronze age to the nuclear age / Eric H. Cline.
     p. cm.
   Includes bibliographical references (p.) and index.
   ISBN 0-472-09739-3 (cloth)
    1. Palestine—History, Military. 2. Bible. O.T.—History of
Biblical events. 3. Megiddo (Extinct city) I. Title.
DS119.2.C55   2000
355'.0095694—dc21   00-08539

For Diane, Hannah, and Joshua

Acknowledgments

For assistance with bibliography, references, and assorted additional items in the following book, sincere thanks go to Jean Wellington, Michael Braunlin, Heather Maloney-Noyes, David Ball, and the entire staff of the Blegen Library at the University of Cincinnati; Israel Finkelstein, David Ussishkin, Nadav Na'aman, Anson F. Rainey, and Norma Franklin of Tel Aviv University; Baruch Halpern of Pennsylvania State University; Neil Asher Silberman of Branford, Connecticut; Ann E. Killebrew of Haifa University; David Armstrong of Austin, Texas; Brian Rose, Barbara Burrell, Holt Parker, Elizabeth Frierson, and Willard Sunderland of the University of Cincinnati; John Larson of the Oriental Institute at the University of Chicago; Edwin Yamauchi and Matthew Gordon of Miami University in Oxford, Ohio; Reuven Amitai-Preiss, Moshe Ma'oz, and Moshe Sharon of Hebrew University, Jerusalem; Gary Oller and David J. White of the University of Akron; Fred Jenkins of the University of Dayton; Michael O. Sugerman of Harvard University; Mark Smith of Saint Joseph's University; Art Clark of the United States Marine Corps; Robert Maldonado of California State University, Fresno; Thomas D. Hall of DePauw University; Carolyn Higginbotham and Harold Kaser of Muskingum College; Carl F. Petry of Northwestern University; Paul Walker of the University of Chicago; Jere L. Bacharach of the University of Washington; Marc Saperstein and Walter Reich of George Washington University; David Maltsberger of North Vancouver, British Columbia; James Weinstein of Cornell University; Susan Heuck Allen of Brown University; Cynthia Edenburg of the Open University of Israel; Gary Beckman of the University of Michigan; Andy Hemmendinger, Bob Burnett, and John Ringstad of GVI; and audiences at the University of Pennsylvania, Emory University, George Washington University, University of Cincinnati, University of Akron, DePauw University, and Muskingum College. For comments on, and criticisms of, rough drafts of various chapters, grateful thanks are due to Edwin Yamauchi. For reading over and commenting on the entire manuscript, I am especially indebted to Jack Meinhardt, Jerry Rutter, and Baruch Halpern. Thanks also go to Ellen Bauerle, Perry Pearson, Hue Huynh, Heather Lengyel, Christina Milton, Michael Kehoe, and Colin Day of the University of Michigan Press and to Wolfgang Amadeus Mozart, without whose music this book could not have been written.

The detailed map of the Jezreel Valley is reproduced from Rogerson 1985

(p. 59), reproduced by kind permission of Andromeda Oxford Limited, www.andromeda.com.uk. © copyright Andromeda 1985; all other maps were created by Robert Hagerty of Raymond Walters College at the University of Cincinnati. Most of the photographs were taken by Zev Radovan of Jerusalem, Israel, and are published with his permission; the narrow view of the Wadi 'Ara/Musmus Pass was taken by Erich Lessing and is published here with his permission. The Shoshenq stele fragment and the possible reconstruction of the original stele are reproduced courtesy of the Oriental Institute of the University of Chicago. The dramatic jacket art was designed by Sara Peled using a photograph of Megiddo by Israel Haramaty and John Martin's painting, *The Great Day of His Wrath*, and is reproduced courtesy of the artist, the photographer, the Tate Gallery of London, and the Tel Aviv University Public Affairs Division. Portions of chapter 1 appeared previously in *Archaeology Odyssey* magazine (Cline 1998, 1999a) and are reproduced here by permission; a portion of the introduction appeared previously in *Biblical Archaeology Review* magazine (Cline 1999b) and is also reproduced here by permission.

The majority of the research and writing for this book was conducted while the author held a Semple Postdoctoral Research Fellowship in the Department of Classics at the University of Cincinnati during the academic year 1998–99. Grateful thanks are due to the members of the department and to the Trustees of the Semple Fund for their generous support.

Contents

Maps

Illustrations

Abbreviations

AUSS	Andrews University Seminary Studies
BA	Biblical Archaeologist
BAR	Biblical Archaeology Review
BASOR	Bulletin of the American Schools of Oriental Research
BibOr	Bibliotheca Orientalis
EHR	English Historical Review
HJAS	Harvard Journal of Asiatic Studies
HSCP	Harvard Studies in Classical Philology
HTR	Harvard Theological Review
HUCA	Hebrew Union College Annual
IEJ	Israel Exploration Journal
JANES	Journal of the Ancient Near Eastern Society of Columbia University
JAOS	Journal of the American Oriental Society
JARCE	Journal of the American Research Center in Egypt
JBL	Journal of Biblical Literature
JEA	Journal of Egyptian Archaeology
JETS	Journal of the Evangelical Theological Society
JNES	Journal of Near Eastern Studies
JPOS	Journal of the Palestine Oriental Society
JSS	Journal of Strategic Studies
JSSEA	Journal of the Society for the Study of Egyptian Antiquities
JTS	Journal of Theological Studies
MIO	Mitteilungen des Instituts für Orientforschung
PEFQ	Palestine Exploration Fund Quarterly
PEFQS	Palestine Exploration Fund, Quarterly Statement
VT	Vetus Testamentum
WTJ	Westminster Theological Journal
ZAW	Zeitschrift für Alttestamentliche Wissenschaft
ZDPV	Zeitschrift des Deutschen Palästina-Vereins

Introduction: The Battles of Armageddon

> Looking down on the broad plain of Esdraelon stretched out from our feet, it is impossible not to remember that this is the greatest battlefield of the world, from the days of Joshua and the defeat of the mighty host of Sisera, till, almost in our own days, Napoleon the Great fought the battle of Mount Tabor; and here also is the ancient Megiddo, where the last great battle of Armageddon is to be fought.
>
> —Lieutenant H.H. Kitchener, 1878

PEACE IS RARE in Israel. Nowhere is this more apparent than in the Jezreel Valley. For four thousand years, this region has suffered almost constant warfare. Indeed, one may seriously ask if there has ever been a time when the rulers of the area, whether local or foreign, were not at war. The turbulent history of all Israel, and Judah, Canaan, and Palestine, is reflected in microcosm in this blood-soaked little valley, for virtually every major invader of Israel has had to fight a battle in the Jezreel Valley. At least thirty-four bloody conflicts have already been fought at the ancient site of Megiddo and in adjacent areas of the Jezreel Valley, with the fateful battle of Armageddon possibly still to come. Egyptians, Canaanites, Israelites, Midianites, Amalekites, Philistines, Hasmonaeans, Greeks, Romans, Byzantines, Muslims, Crusaders, Mamlukes, Mongols, Palestinians, French, Ottomans, British, Australians, Germans, Arabs, and Israelis have all fought and died here.

The Jezreel Valley is a place of firsts: here Thutmose III fought the first battle known in recorded history anywhere in the world; here Gideon conducted the first known night campaign; here the Mongols lost their first major battle ever during their sweep across Asia and the Middle East. It is also a place of endings: here Saul fought his last heroic battle; here Josiah met his doom; here Armageddon is expected to take place. The names of the warring generals and leaders who have fought in this small valley reverberate throughout history: they include Thutmose III, Deborah and Barak, Sisera, Gideon, Saul and Jonathan, Shishak, Jehu, Joram, Jezebel, Josiah, Antiochus, Ptolemy, Vespasian, Saladin, Napoleon, and Allenby, to name but a few of the most famous.

The names of those who have died in battle in the Jezreel Valley also strike a familiar chord: they include many of the leaders named already and others, such as Labayu, ruler of Bronze Age Shechem; the Canaanite general Sisera; Saul, first king of Israel; Jonathan, son of Saul and heir to the throne of Israel; Joram, king of Israel; Jezebel, wife of Ahab and queen mother of Israel; Ahaziah, king of Judah; Josiah, king of Judah; the Mongol general Kitbuqa; and a great many others.

Warfare in the Jezreel Valley has always been a combination of open-air fighting and hit-and-run guerrilla tactics. This unholy mixture is a result of the geography of the land. The horses and chariots of the Canaanites and Israelites have given way to the tanks and airplanes of the Israel Defense Forces, and swords and bows have been replaced by machine guns and hand grenades, but the tactics remain similar. Evidence of history repeating itself abounds, therefore, such as General Allenby's successful emulation in the twentieth century of the tactics used by Pharaoh Thutmose III at Megiddo more than thirty-four hundred years earlier.

Throughout history, Megiddo and the Jezreel Valley have been ground zero for battles that determined the very course of civilization. It is no wonder that the author of Revelation believed that Armageddon, the penultimate battle between good and evil, would also take place in this region. The area of the Jezreel Valley can be compared to the meeting place of two tectonic plates, where the stress and strain frequently result in cataclysmic, earthshaking events of immense magnitude, whose reverberations are felt far away, both geographically and temporally. What is it about this area that prompts such a continuous state of warfare? Only continued study of the military history of the region will yield answers to this question. One thing is, however, already crystal clear. Regarding the battles fought in the confines of the Jezreel Valley over the past four thousand years, one might well paraphrase the immortal words of Sir Winston Churchill: "Never in the field of human conflict have so many fought so often over so little space."

TABLE 1
The Thirty-five Battles Fought or
Still to Come in the Jezreel Valley

Date	Opponents	Location
2350 B.C.	**Pepi I** vs. rebels at "Gazelle's Head"	Jezreel Valley
1479 B.C.	**Thutmose III** vs. Canaanites	Megiddo
1430 B.C.	**Amenhotep II** vs. settlements in the valley	Jezreel Valley
1360–1350 B.C.	**Biridiya** vs. Labayu	Megiddo
1125 B.C.	**Deborah and Barak** vs. Sisera	Taanach/Mount Tabor
1090 B.C.	**Gideon** vs. Midianites/Amalekites	Hill of Moreh/Endor
1016 B.C.	Saul and Jonathan vs. **Philistines**	Mount Gilboa
925 B.C.	**Shoshenq I (Shishak)** vs. Megiddo	Megiddo
841 B.C.	**Jehu** vs. Joram and Ahaziah	Jezreel
609 B.C.	**Necho II** vs. Josiah	Megiddo
218 B.C.	**Antiochus III** vs. Ptolemy IV	Mount Tabor
55 B.C.	**Gabinius** vs. Alexander	Mount Tabor
A.D. 67	**Vespasian** vs. Jewish Rebels	Mount Tabor
A.D. 940	Ikhshidids vs. Abbasids (no victor)	Lejjun
A.D. 946	**Ikhshidids** vs. Hamdanids	Lejjun/Aksal
A.D. 975	**Byzantines** vs. Fatimids	Mount Tabor
A.D. 1113	**Maudud** vs. Crusaders	Mount Tabor
A.D. 1182	**Saladin** vs. Daburiyans	Daburiya
A.D. 1182	**Saladin** vs. Crusaders	Forbelet
A.D. 1183	Saladin vs. Crusaders (no victor)	'Ayn Jalut
A.D. 1187	**Saladin** vs. Crusaders	Mount Tabor, Daburiya, Zarin, and al-Fula
A.D. 1217	Crusaders vs. **Muslims**	Mount Tabor
A.D. 1247	**Ayyubids** vs. Crusaders	Mount Tabor
A.D. 1260	**Mamlukes** vs. Mongols	'Ayn Jalut
A.D. 1263	**Mamlukes** vs. Hospitallers	Mount Tabor
A.D. 1264	**Hospitallers/Templars** vs. Mamlukes	Lejjun
A.D. 1735	**Zahir al-'Umar** vs. Nablus-Saqr alliance	al-Rawdah
A.D. 1771–1773	**Zahir al-'Umar** vs. Lejjun	Lejjun
A.D. 1799	**Napoleon** vs. Ottomans	Mount Tabor
A.D. 1918	**Allenby** vs. Ottomans	Megiddo
A.D. 1948	**Israelis** vs. Arabs	Mishmar Haemek
A.D. 1948	**Israelis** vs. Arabs	Zarin, Megiddo, and Lejjun
A.D. 1967	**Israelis** vs. Arabs	Ramat David airfield
A.D. 1973	**Israelis** vs. Syrians	Ramat David airfield
?	**Good** vs. Evil	Armageddon

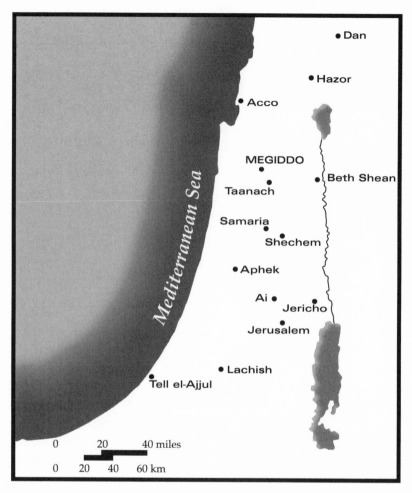

MAP 1. Syria-Palestine in the Bronze and Early Iron Ages (second and early first millennia B.C.)

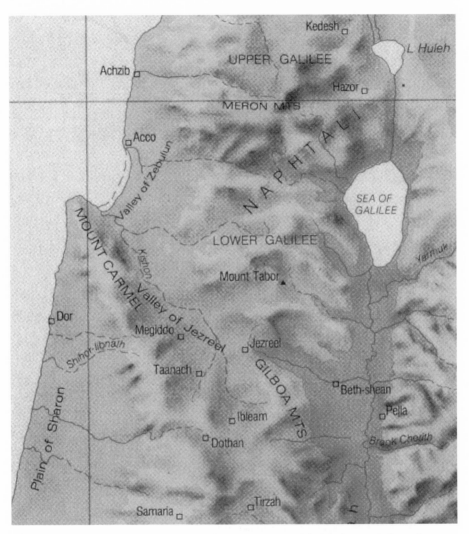

MAP 2. Detailed map of Jezreel Valley. (Reproduced by kind permission of Andromeda Oxford Limited, www.andromeda.co.uk. © copyright Andromeda 1985.)

CHAPTER 1

History Repeats Itself

... the capturing of Megiddo is the capturing of a thousand towns!
Capture ye firmly, firmly!

—Thutmose III, rallying his troops at the battle of Megiddo in 1479 B.C.

HORSES WHINNY SOFTLY, stamping nervously, as their riders mount up in the chill predawn air. The day's mission looms ahead: a dangerous trek straight up the Wadi ʿAra and through the narrow Musmus Pass, followed by a dash across the Plain of Jezreel to engage the enemy controlling ancient Megiddo, a city perched on a hill commanding the main road from Egypt to the Euphrates.

The year is 1479 B.C., and the army marching on Canaanite Megiddo is Egyptian, led by Pharaoh Thutmose III. Or is the year A.D. 1918, near the end of World War I? Are the advancing troops actually Allied forces under the command of General Edmund H.H. Allenby, preparing to attack Ottoman-controlled Megiddo?

The answer, of course, is both. Thutmose III and Allenby both gambled by sending their men through the slender Musmus Pass. Of the three passes leading into the Jezreel Valley near Megiddo, the Musmus Pass is the central one—the most direct route, but also the narrowest and most dangerous. Both men also won decisive victories, catching the enemy unaware and capturing the strategic site of Megiddo.

History had repeated itself after thirty-four hundred years. Was it mere coincidence? Or did Allenby, an avid student of military history, know of Thutmose III's maneuvers in remote antiquity? Most of Allenby's biographers have insisted that he must have known, since his tactics so closely mirrored those of the pharaoh.

The battle fought at Megiddo on 20 September 1918 legitimized the triumphant title "Allenby of Armageddon," which General (later Field Marshal Viscount) Allenby adopted in the days preceding the final Allied offensive against the Turkish army in Palestine. Allenby knew that the name *Armageddon* derives from the Hebrew *Har Megiddo* and means literally "Mount of Megiddo." It is designated in the New Testament as the site where the penultimate world battle between the forces of good and evil will take place.

> They are spirits of demons performing miraculous signs, and they go out to the kings of the whole world, to gather them for the battle on the great day of God Almighty. . . .Then they gathered the kings together to the place that in Hebrew is called Armageddon. (Revelation 16:14–16)[1]

Megiddo is in the Jezreel Valley, also known as the Plain of Esdraelon (*Esdraelon* being the Greek modification of *Jezreel*). The site is located almost exactly halfway between Haifa on the Mediterranean coast to the west and Tiberias on the Sea of Galilee to the east. It is easily the richest archaeological site in Israel, and it is widely regarded as one of the most important sites in the entire Near East. As the current excavators of the site have described, "Megiddo was the Queen of the cities of Canaan/Israel," replete with massive fortification walls, impressive architecture and water installations, lavish palaces and important temples.[2] It is no accident that this was one of the sites on which James Michener based his book *The Source*.

From its advantageous location, Megiddo controlled one of the most important roads in the ancient world, the Via Maris. This was an international military and trade route that ran between Egypt in the south and Syria, Phoenicia, Anatolia, and Mesopotamia in the north and east. Sitting astride this chief north-south trade route, as it came through the Musmus Pass (Wadi ʿAra) and meandered through the Jezreel Valley, Megiddo had great strategic significance, for whoever controlled the city and maintained an army there would dominate this vital international route.

It is no surprise, then, to learn that the area surrounding the ancient site of Megiddo in the Jezreel Valley has seen more fighting and bloodshed over an extended period of time than virtually any other spot on earth—during the past four thousand years, at least thirty-four battles have been fought in this small valley. It was a logical conclusion for the author of the Book of Revelation in the New Testament to believe that the penultimate battle between good and evil would also take place at Megiddo; hence the name *Armageddon* has been given to this battle, which has been the subject of much scholarly and popular debate, especially in recent years.[3]

The Jezreel Valley is shaped approximately like a triangle lying on its side, with its tip touching the Plain of Acco (Acre) at the west and its bottom facing the Jordan River to the east.[4] Its southern edge, walled

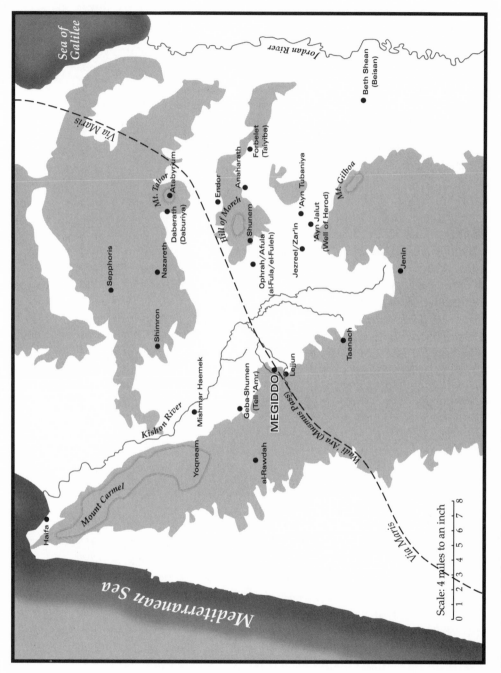

MAP 3. Jezreel Valley and adjacent areas, with relevant ancient and modern sites

Sea of Galilee

Jordan River

Via Maris

Beth Shean
(Beisan)

Forbelet
(Taiyiba)

Mt. Tabor
Atabyrium
Endor
Anaharath

Daberath
(Daburiya)

Hill of Moreh

'Ayn Tubaniya

Mt. Gilboa

Sepphoris

Nazareth

Shunem

'Ayn Jalut
(Well of Herod)

Ophrah/Afula
(al-Fula/el-Fuleh)

Jezreel/Zar'in

Shimron

Jenin

Geba-Shumen
(Tell 'Amr)

Mishmar Haemek

Lejjun

MEGIDDO

Kishon River

Taanach

Yoqneam

al-Rawdah

Mount Carmel

Wadi 'Ara (Musmus) Pass

Haifa

Mediterranean Sea

Via Maris

Scale: 4 miles to an inch

0 1 2 3 4 5 6 7 8

FIG. 1. Jezreel Valley (Zev Radovan, Jerusalem)

FIG. 2. Megiddo and the Jezreel Valley (Zev Radovan, Jerusalem)

off by thousand-foot-high mountains of the Mount Carmel and Gilboa ranges, stretches some twenty miles (thirty-two kilometers) from Mount Carmel to nearly reach the Jordan River. The hills of Nazareth and mountains of Lower Galilee form the northern edge of the Jezreel Valley, again rising nearly one thousand feet above the flat plain of the valley below. This northern side runs for almost fifteen miles (twenty-four kilometers) from Mount Carmel at the west to Mount Tabor at the east. The eastern side of the Jezreel Valley measures a mere seven miles (eleven kilometers) in width from Mount Tabor in the north to Mount Gilboa in the south. However, the eastern end is by no means the narrowest part of the valley; in at least one section, it is as little as three miles (five kilometers) wide.

The floor of the Jezreel Valley is crisscrossed by the perennial Kishon River and its many tributaries. The waters and the poor natural drainage contributed to muddy conditions in the flat plain of the valley for much of the year, except during the driest months of the summer. Indeed, from at least the Byzantine period until recently, and perhaps as early as the Roman period and maybe even back into biblical times, much of the floor of the Jezreel Valley was a swampy mess during the rainy months, contributing to a high incidence of malaria in the area as recently as the 1920s.[5] With better management of the Kishon River and with the draining of the swamps in recent times, conditions have dramatically improved, but this was not the case throughout much of recorded history in the valley.

Entrance into the Jezreel Valley from the north and the south is possible only by a number of narrow mountain passes. Most of these passages are minor; those that are best known along the southern edge include, from easternmost to westernmost, the pass leading from the Dothan Valley and emerging by the ancient site of Taanach; the Wadi ʿAra (Musmus Pass), which disgorges its travelers into the plain by the site of Megiddo; the smaller Abu Shusheh Pass, which comes out near the modern site of Mishmar Haemek; and the pass that emerges by the ancient site of Yoqneam. Passes into the valley that are most frequently used by travelers coming from the north through the hills of Lower Galilee include one running south from Nazareth and another located just to the east of Mount Tabor, leading to and from the area of the Sea of Galilee. Entrance to the valley can also be made from the east, where the valley is split into three sections by Mount Tabor to the north, Mount Gilboa to the south, and the Hill of Moreh in between. In the break created between the Hill of Moreh and Mount Gilboa, the Harod

Valley takes up where the Jezreel Valley leaves off, continuing east until it reaches Beth Shean (Beisan) and the Jordan River. The western tip of the valley is also an entrance, where the Kishon River connects via a narrow pass to the Plain of Acco (Acre), allowing access to and from the Mediterranean Sea and beyond.

The Jezreel Valley runs nearly across the breadth of Israel, connecting the coastal region with the Jordan Valley, and lies at the juncture of several major trade and military routes. Thus, throughout history, travelers journeying through Israel in virtually any direction—be they merchants, pilgrims, or invading warriors—were forced in almost every instance to cross the valley and to deal with its inhabitants. It is no wonder that nearly every invading force from ca. 2350 B.C. to A.D. 2000 has fought a battle in the Jezreel Valley.

Allenby's battle at Armageddon was part of the much larger Allied campaign fought from 18 to 21 September. However, his victory at Megiddo on 20 September, together with his subsequent triumphs at Nazareth, Afula, Jenin, and Beisan (ancient Beth Shean) on that same day, represented a major victory for the Allied campaign. Perhaps the defining moment of the entire offensive, the battle at Megiddo quickly resulted in "the destruction of the enemy's army, the liberation of Palestine and Syria, and the occupation of Damascus and Aleppo," as Allenby himself wrote on 31 October 1918.[6] It may well have been the turning point of the entire war in the Middle East.

The original military plan to take Palestine was apparently proposed by the British Imperial War Cabinet, using information obtained by the South African General Jan Smuts, who visited Allenby in Egypt and Palestine in February 1918. The plan owed much to Allenby, who wanted the British first to cross the Jordan Valley and demolish the Hejaz Railway near Amman, then to advance into the Jezreel Valley, capture Haifa and Tiberias, and continue marching up the Mediterranean coast to Beirut.[7]

The war cabinet approved the campaign plan late in the spring, giving Allenby the green light. By the end of the summer, he was ready to launch the offensive. Less than a month before the offensive was scheduled to begin, however, Allenby modified the original plan substantially.[8] He quietly assembled his forces near Jaffa, some fifty miles (eighty kilometers) southwest of Megiddo, and prepared to attack.

The offensive commenced with an artillery bombardment at 4:30 A.M. on 19 September 1918. About fifteen minutes later, the invasion began. The assault on Megiddo was spearheaded by the Fourth Cavalry

Division, which was composed of the Tenth, Eleventh, and Twelfth Brigades, supported by artillery and armored-car units. Followed by the Australian Light Horse Brigade, the Fourth Cavalry Division left its camp in the orange groves around Sarona and headed up the Wadi 'Ara toward the Musmus Pass. As darkness fell, the leading unit, the Tenth Brigade, tired after traveling all day, missed the entrance to the pass and continued five miles (eight kilometers) too far to the north before discovering the mistake. The division commander, Major General Barrow, who had already driven up the pass with his staff officer and the brigade's advanced guard, the Second Lancers, came back down the length of the pass around midnight—only to find his troops nowhere in sight. After sorting through the confusion, Barrow demoted the commander of the Tenth Brigade, Brigadier General Howard-Vyse, on the spot and gave the privilege of being first through the Musmus Pass to the Twelfth Brigade. They made it through without incident, as did the Eleventh Brigade and, soon thereafter, the truant Tenth Brigade.

By early the next morning, 20 September, all the forces of the Fourth Cavalry Division had breached the Musmus Pass and were ready to enter the southern tier of the Jezreel Valley by Megiddo. At dawn, however, the Allied troops spotted a contingent of Turkish troops—the Thirteenth Depot Regiment based at Nazareth—awaiting them on the plain directly ahead. The previous afternoon, the entire Turkish battalion had been ordered to march to the Musmus Pass and defend it against the approaching Allied troops, but only a small advance guard had reached the plain by the morning of 20 September—even though the Turks had nearly eighteen hours to cover the short journey of fifteen miles (twenty-six kilometers) from Nazareth.

The Allied Second Lancers, usually attached to the Tenth Brigade but now reassigned to the Twelfth Brigade after the confusion of the previous evening, had been at the forefront of the march all through the night. In the early morning light, they charged the Turkish troops and easily overwhelmed them. Only one Allied soldier was wounded in the melee. The Turks, however, did not fare quite so well. The Lancers killed 46 Turkish soldiers and took another 470 prisoner. This turned out to be the only significant fighting in the 1918 battle at Megiddo.

Meanwhile, additional Allied troops were making their way toward the western Jezreel Valley, a few miles north and west of Megiddo. The Fifth Cavalry Division—consisting of the Thirteenth, Fourteenth, and Fifteenth Brigades and artillery and armored-car units—broke camp

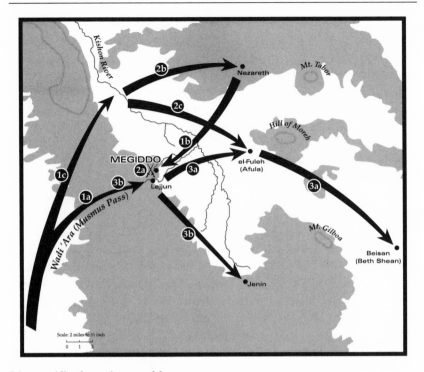

MAP 4. Allenby at Armageddon

1a. The Fourth Cavalry Division marches up the Wadi 'Ara (Musmus Pass),
1b. while the Turkish Thirteenth Depot Regiment advances from Nazareth to
    Megiddo,
1c. and the Fifth Cavalry Division marches up the Abu Shusheh Pass.
2a. The Second Lancers overwhelm the Turkish troops by Megiddo,
2b. while the Thirteenth Brigade heads to Nazareth,
2c. and the Fourteenth Brigade marches to el-Fuleh (Afula) and is joined
    later by the Fifteenth Brigade.
3a. The Fourth Cavalry Division continues to el-Fuleh (Afula) and then to
    Beisan (Beth Shean).
3b. The Third Australian Light Horse Brigade comes through the Musmus
    Pass, reaches Lejjun, and then continues on to occupy Jenin.

early on 19 September and headed toward the Abu Shusheh Pass,
which runs parallel to the Musmus Pass. The division halted briefly at
the village of Liktera (modern Hadera), where the Fifteenth Brigade
and the division's artillery were left so that they could make the rough
journey during daylight hours on the following day. The rest of the division entered the Abu Shusheh Pass early in the evening and reached
the Jezreel Valley, near what is now the settlement of Mishmar

Haemek, a couple of hours past midnight on 20 September.[9]

From here, the Fifth Cavalry's Thirteenth and Fourteenth Brigades both turned east, then headed for separate targets. The Thirteenth Brigade ventured north toward Nazareth, where the enemy headquarters was located; it reached Nazareth by early morning, to the complete surprise of the German commander, Liman von Sanders, who reportedly fled in his pajamas, narrowly escaping capture. The Fourteenth Brigade marched south to el-Fuleh (modern Afula) and took the city with little effort. They were joined there by the Fifteenth Brigade later that same day.

Following the brief but decisive battle at Megiddo, the entire Fourth Cavalry Division continued past the ancient mound to el-Fuleh (Afula), reaching the town at 8:00 A.M.—half an hour after the city had been occupied by the Fifth Cavalry—and then proceeded on to Beisan (Beth Shean), which they reached and captured in the late afternoon of that same day, 20 September. Following hard on the heels of the Fourth Division through the Musmus Pass, the Australian Mounted Division reached Lejjun, the Arab village located next to Megiddo, by noon on 20 September; the Third Australian Light Horse Brigade occupied Jenin that afternoon.

Thus, by the evening of 20 September, barely thirty-six hours after the beginning of the campaign, Allenby's troops had achieved their goal. They had routed the entire Seventh and Eighth Turkish Armies and secured control of Palestine. The Fourth Cavalry alone had astonishingly covered approximately eighty miles (128 kilometers) in less than a day and a half, losing only twenty-six horses in the process. Such a victory exceeded even Allenby's wildest dreams, for it became reality faster than even he could have hoped. On the morning of the attack, he wrote to his wife, "I am beginning to think that we may make a very great success"; only five days later, he wrote to her, "I, myself, am almost aghast at the extent of the victory."[10]

The strategy for the Megiddo campaign, as ultimately approved by the British Imperial War Cabinet, is usually identified as uniquely Allenby's, although Allenby himself later frequently said that it was actually Louis Bols, then his chief of staff and later commander in chief of the British forces in Palestine, who suggested the plan for the decisive battle at Megiddo.[11] According to several of his biographers, Allenby felt that the original plan, submitted by General Smuts and approved by the British Imperial War Cabinet in February 1918, was too limited and unambitious. Captain Cyril Falls, who compiled an official history of World War I based on documents in British archives, later wrote a volume on Allenby's final offensive, noting that the original plan "was a sound scheme enough, but not a bold one," and that "it would not have led to the destruction of the Turkish armies." Falls continues:

> He [Allenby] thought about it for another three weeks before, on returning from a morning ride, he astonished the corps commanders by an emendation of the most drastic kind. . . . [I]t was the role of the cavalry which was most thoroughly transformed. It was to march on El Afule, 25 miles northeast of Tul Karm, and thence enter the Plain of Esdraelon at Lajjun (Megiddo). Dropping forces to close the Turkish retreat northward and northwestward, it was to descend to the Jordan Valley at Beisan. . . . This was quite another plan, daring, grandiose. If anyone asks whether it was the commander-in-chief's own scheme, let him be answered by another question. What staff officer would put up such a plan, involving the certainty that the cavalry would run away from its transport and have to live on the country, a country which, as has been pointed out, was thought to be more barren than was in fact the case? . . . It had indeed little relation to the first plan, any more than to the one, frankly pedestrian, put forward by General Smuts after a visit to Allenby and actually approved by the War Office in the Spring.[12]

How did Allenby come up with this idea? His biographers record the fact that he was a student of military history who read voraciously about ancient Egypt and Syria-Palestine both prior to and during his 1918 campaign. One biographer, Colonel (later Sir General) Archibald Percival Wavell, who wrote a number of books on Near Eastern battles, including Allenby's campaign, observes that Allenby consulted books on the ancient Near East, accounts of the Crusades, and Herodotus's histories—and even carried some of this material to the front with him.[13] Wavell states further:

> Certainly no commander ever gave more careful study to the history and topography of the theatre in which he was operating than did General Allenby. Two books he consulted almost daily, the Bible and George Adam Smith's *Historical Geography of the Holy Land.*[14]

Some thirty-four hundred years before Allenby, Thutmose III had also waged war at Megiddo, in a campaign that is succinctly described in George Adam Smith's volume.

> The earliest historical battle of Megiddo was fought in 1479 B.C. between an army of Thothmes III of Egypt, that had come over from Sharon by

the middle of the three passes into Esdraelon and the forces of certain Syrian states allied against Egypt. The geographical details of the Egyptian preparation for this campaign and advance north from Gaza are of the utmost interest in their close correspondence to all subsequent advances of armies from Sharon to battle in Esdraelon. . . .[15]

Thutmose III was perhaps the greatest of the Egyptian pharaohs, at least in terms of military conquests. He succeeded his father on the throne of Egypt in 1490 B.C., when he was only ten years old. Since he was so young, his stepmother, Hatshepsut, ruled in his stead, first as coregent, then as "pharaoh" in her own right.[16] It took Thutmose III many years to regain exclusive possession of the throne from Hatshepsut. Once he did, he made up for lost time: the years of his sole rule are marked by tremendous building activity and numerous military campaigns. In all, he fought a total of seventeen campaigns in Syria-Palestine over a span of only twenty years.

The first campaign, which culminated in the capture of Megiddo, was the most important and is the most fully recorded. The tale of Thutmose III's attack on Megiddo in 1479 B.C. is thus by now very well known and has been retold many times in recent years. The battle is the first in history for which we have any kind of detailed record anywhere in the world.[17] However, it is really only since the decipherment of Egyptian hieroglyphs, by Champollion in 1823, that the strategy involved in this battle has been revealed to the modern world.

Thutmose III's Megiddo campaign is recorded in the most detail in the copy of his Annals that is inscribed on the walls of the Temple of Amon at Karnak in Egypt. This was transcribed from the daily journal that the king's scribe, Tjaneni, kept during the actual campaign. The journal, originally written on a parchment scroll and deposited in the temple, was written as a series of terse, factual entries, which were later converted into the literary and picturesque prose ultimately inscribed on the wall of the temple. Such seems to have been the pattern for most of the yearly entries inscribed on these walls, although those for the later campaigns are less "chatty" than those for the earlier ones. The information contained in these Annals is supplemented by three additional inscriptions that mention various aspects of the Megiddo campaign, recorded on stelae found at Armant, Gebel Barkae, and Karnak in Egypt.[18]

Thutmose III finally gained the throne of Egypt upon the disappearance (and probable death) of his stepmother, Hatshepsut. At this time, the Canaanite rulers of Syria and Palestine were vassals of the powerful Egyptian Empire to the southwest and paid regular tribute to their Egyptian overlords. Perhaps anticipating a weakness in Egypt on account of the pharaoh's succession, the king of Kadesh, a city on the Orontes River in Syria, led a revolt by the Canaanite kings against the young Egyptian pharaoh. The rebel Canaanite army assembled in the Jezreel Valley, at the city of Megiddo. Numbered among them were rulers and men from countries as far away as Mesopotamia (modern Iraq and Iran), northern Syria, and southern Anatolia (modern Turkey). It is not known precisely how large this rebel army was, although it has been estimated at between ten thousand and fifteen thousand men, including both chariotry and infantry.[19]

In answer, Thutmose III assembled his army at Sile, a fortress in the eastern Delta on the border of Egypt, and then quickly marched as far as Gaza, a distance of 144 miles (240 kilometers), in only ten days. Thutmose III's forced march covered an amazing amount of distance in a very short period of time, especially given the numbers of men, horses, and equipment involved: the Egyptian army is estimated to have numbered between ten thousand and twenty thousand men. Thutmose III's army then continued marching north for another ten days, arriving at Yehem (Yemma), a town on the southern slopes of the Carmel mountain range, probably on 6 May 1479 B.C. The distance from Gaza to Yehem is only about eighty miles (128 kilometers), roughly half the distance from Sile to Gaza, and yet it apparently took the army the same amount of time to cover this lesser distance. This may indicate that the pharaoh devoted some time to subduing rebellious cities, such as Joppa (modern Jaffa) and Gezer, while en route.[20]

Thutmose III's army apparently rested for a few days at Yehem while scouting operations continued. On 11 May, a council of war was held to decide the best route for the advance on Megiddo. The Annals record Thutmose III's opening speech.

> Year 23, 1st month of the third season, day 16—as far as the town of Yehem. . . . [His majesty] ordered a conference . . . speaking as follows: "That [wretched] enemy of Kadesh has come and has entered into Megiddo. He is [there] at this moment. He has gathered to him the princes of [every] foreign country [which had been loyal] to Egypt, as well as (those) as far as Naharin and M[itanni], them of Hurru, them of Kode, their horses, their armies, [and their people], for he says—so it is reported—'I shall wait [here[in Megiddo [to fight against his majesty].' Will you tell me [what is in your heart]?"[21]

It seems that there were three possibilities for how to proceed from Yehem to the Jezreel Valley: a curving northern route that emptied into the plain near what is now Mishmar Haemek, some miles north and west of Megiddo; a curving southern route through the Valley of Dothan that emerged in the plain by the town of Taanach, some miles south and east of Megiddo; and a straight central route up the ʿAruna or Wadi ʿAra Pass (the northeastern end of modern Nahal Iron, also known as the Musmus Pass) that let out onto the plain near the city of Megiddo itself.

The question was whether to take the central pass leading directly to Megiddo or one of the alternate passes to the north and to the south. As we have seen, the central pass was the most direct route, but it was also the narrowest and thus the most susceptible to a Canaanite ambush. The council urged Thutmose III to take either the northern or the southern route; their words are recorded on the walls at Karnak.

> What is it like to go [on] this [road] which becomes (so) narrow? It is [reported] that the foe is there, waiting on [the outside, while they are] becoming (more) numerous. Will not horse (have to) go after [horse, and the army] and the people similarly? Will the vanguard of us be fighting while the [rear guard] is waiting here in ʿAruna, unable to fight? Now two (other) roads are here. One of the roads—behold, it is [to the east of] us, so that it comes out at Taanach. The other—behold, it is to the north side of Djefti, and we will come out to the north of Megiddo. Let our victorious lord proceed on the one of [them] which is [satisfactory] to his heart, (but) do not make us go on the difficult road![22]

Thutmose III, however, stoutly rejected their advice. Assuming that the Canaanite leaders would think like his war council and thus expect the Egyptian army to traverse either the northern or the southern pass (or both of them), he decided to do the unexpected and take his army through the perilous central (Musmus) pass. As the inscription at Karnak records, Thutmose III replied to his council: "I . . . shall proceed upon this ʿAruna road!"

The next day was devoted to preparations. On 13 May, the army marched to ʿAruna, where it spent the night. Early in the morning on 14 May, the march to Megiddo began in earnest. The pharaoh himself was at the head of the army, which, according to estimates, stretched nearly fourteen miles (twenty-two kilometers) long. The Musmus Pass is so narrow (only thirty feet wide at one point) that the Egyptian army probably needed at least twelve hours to reach the Jezreel Valley at the

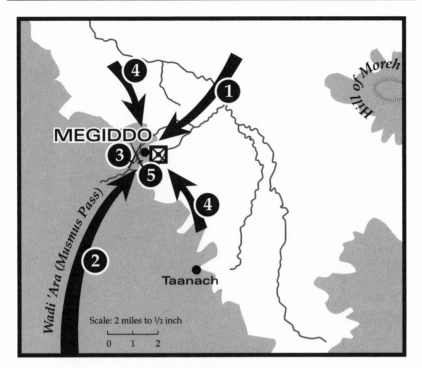

MAP 5. Thutmose III and the Canaanites

1. Canaanite forces gather at Megiddo.
2. Thutmose III marches Egyptian army through Wadi ʿAra (Musmus Pass).
3. Small Canaanite force left to defend Megiddo is caught off guard by Egyptian attack.
4. Canaanite forces stationed to north and south of Megiddo hasten to join battle, but Egyptians are victorious.
5. Surviving Canaanites are besieged inside city of Megiddo before finally surrendering to Thutmose III.

other end. Still, the passage seems to have been fairly uneventful, although one minor skirmish may have taken place at the mouth of the pass. Camping by the Qina Brook where the Musmus Pass opened into the Jezreel Valley behind Megiddo, Thutmose III allowed his forces to close up and rested his men for the night.[23]

As it turned out, Thutmose III was right. The rebel Canaanite army had not expected the Egyptians to come through the central pass and had concentrated their forces at the northern and southern passes, with only a small reserve of men guarding the Musmus Pass. In the early hours of 15 May, the Egyptians attacked, taking the rebels by surprise

FIG. 3. Narrow view of the Wadi ʿAra/Musmus Pass (Erich Lessing, Vienna)

and routing them. The precise details of the battle itself are somewhat unclear, but it seems that Thutmose III first crossed the Qina Brook and spread his men out to the east and west. He then sent one wing of his army, including chariots, charging out and around to the northwest of Megiddo, while he sent another wing charging out and around to the southeast of the city. Thutmose III himself seems to have stationed himself in the center with the rest of his forces, commanding from his golden chariot.[24] The Canaanite forces, attacked from both sides and threatened with encirclement by the Egyptian forces, broke and fled in panic. Thutmose III's account at Thebes concisely records the attack and ensuing results.

> Then [his] majesty issued forth [at the head of] his [army]. . . . [He had not met] a single [enemy. Their] southern wing was in Taanach, [while their] northern wing was on the south side [of the Qina Valley]. . . . His majesty set forth in a chariot of fine gold, adorned with his accou-

FIG. 4. Modern view of the Wadi ʿAra/Musmus Pass (Zev Radovan, Jerusalem)

trements of combat. . . . The southern wing of his majesty's army was at a
hill south of [the] Qina [brook], and the northern wing was to the northwest of Megiddo, while his majesty was in their center. . . . Thereupon his
majesty prevailed over them at the head of his army. Then they saw his
majesty prevailing over them, and they fled headlong [to] Megiddo with
faces of fear. They abandoned their horses and their chariots of gold and
silver. . . .[25]

Unfortunately for Thutmose III, however, his army stopped to pil-
lage and loot the Canaanite army camps, which included the tent of the
king of Kadesh. This allowed the inhabitants of Megiddo ample time to
close the city gates, haul the fleeing soldiers over the walls on ropes
made of twisted clothes, and deny the Egyptians a complete victory that
day. The Egyptians promptly besieged the city, digging a moat around
it and building a girdle wall of wood.[26] But according to the Jebel
Barkal stele, it took fully seven more months before the city fell, during
which time the king of Kadesh managed to escape. The booty finally
captured by the Egyptians more than made up for the long wait—as
Thutmose III recorded at Karnak.

[List of the booty which his majesty's army carried off from the town of] Megiddo: 340 living prisoners and 83 hands; 2,041 horses, 191 foals, 6 stallions, and . . . colts; 1 chariot worked with gold, with a body of gold, belonging to that enemy, [1] fine chariot worked with gold belonging to the Prince of [Megiddo] . . . , and 892 chariots of his wretched army— total: 924; 1 fine bronze coat of mail belonging to that enemy, [1] fine bronze coat of mail belonging to the Prince of Meg[iddo, and] 200 *[leather]* coats of mail belonging to his wretched army; 502 bows; and 7 poles of *meru*-wood, worked with silver, of the tent of that enemy.[27]

It is not completely clear which city at Megiddo (i.e., which of the twenty settlements layered one on top of the other at the site) is the one that was besieged and finally captured by Thutmose III and his forces in 1479 B.C. Most likely, he conquered the city labeled Stratum IX by the Chicago excavators; Stratum VIII, which follows, is generally thought to be the phase of rebuilding dating to immediately after the siege.[28]

After conquering a number of additional cities in the Jezreel Valley, such as Shimon/Shimron, Taanach, Geba-Shumen, Ophel, Shunem, and Yoqneam,[29] Thutmose III and his men finally returned to their homes in Egypt in mid-October, thus concluding the first of their seventeen campaigns in Syria-Palestine, which took place almost every year for the next two decades of his reign. The Megiddo campaign may well have been the most significant, for it immediately reestablished Egyptian authority in the area and showed the Canaanites that their overlords were there to stay; indeed, the Egyptian governor of Canaan may have subsequently been settled deliberately at Megiddo. The Egyptian presence in the southern Levant would remain firm for the next two hundred years.

However, there are still a few remaining mysteries surrounding Thutmose III's conquest of Megiddo. As has been pointed out by previous scholars, no remains of a destruction of Megiddo at this time have been uncovered in any of the excavations. Did the inhabitants finally open the city gates and surrender, thereby avoiding destruction of their city? There also is no evidence for the existence of a Late Bronze Age city wall at Megiddo. How could Thutmose lay siege to an unfortified city for seven months? Three possible solutions have been suggested.[30]

1. Perhaps the earlier, massive Middle Bronze Age fortifications built around Megiddo continued to function in the Late Bronze Age, so that there was no need for a new, Late Bronze Age system of walls.

FIG. 5. Megiddo (Zev Radovan, Jerusalem)

2. Perhaps Megiddo was unfortified. If so, the Egyptian army would not have had to storm any walls but would still have had to attack the city and its defenders.
3. The siege may have lasted only one month, rather than seven. Thutmose III's records may indicate that during the time between the start of the siege and the army's eventual return to Egypt, he and his men also advanced into Lebanon, captured three other cities, and marched all the way back to Egypt. This might suggest that the period of seven months covered a monthlong siege at Megiddo and all of the other activities as well, rather than simply a siege of Megiddo in and of itself.

Further excavations, including those presently being conducted by Tel Aviv University and Pennsylvania State University, may ultimately solve these dilemmas and shed further light on Thutmose III's campaign against Megiddo in 1479 B.C.

The similarities between Allenby's and Thutmose III's invasions of Megiddo, particularly their daring decisions to strike through the Musmus Pass, have led many to conclude that history did not simply repeat itself—it consciously copied itself. As early as 1920, Egyptologist Harold Nelson made the connection, observing that both Allenby and Thutmose III defeated "an enemy advancing from the north toward Egypt." Nelson emphasized the "striking parallels" between "the strategy of the earliest and of the latest victorious commanders of campaigns in central Palestine."[31] The two battles have been linked in print ever since.

But did Allenby really know about Thutmose III's campaign when he put his own battle plan into action? Nelson's book on Thutmose III's battle at Megiddo, which stood as the definitive description and discussion of this campaign for some decades, is usually cited as having been published in 1913, and that is the date given on the title page of the volume, in which case it would have been available to Allenby in 1918. However, Nelson himself notes in the preface that the volume did not actually appear until 1920, because he was "confined behind the Turkish lines in Syria during the whole of the war."[32] It therefore would not have been available to Allenby, even in manuscript form, until well after the ending of the war.

Allenby, as we know, regularly consulted George Adam Smith's *Historical Geography of the Holy Land*. But there are problems in citing this volume as the source of Allenby's strategy. Although Smith's book was originally published in 1894, its first two editions contained no discussion of Thutmose III's campaigns. In 1896, a fourth edition appeared, containing more notes and a new preface but still no mention of Thutmose III's campaign in Canaan. Subsequent editions were published almost yearly, but no substantial changes were made to the text for more than three decades. The edition published in 1919—after Allenby's successful campaign at Megiddo—mentions battles fought at or near Megiddo by Deborah, Barak, and Sisera; Gideon and the Midianites; Saul and the Philistines; Jehu, Joram, and Ahaziah; and Josiah and Pharaoh Necho, as well as conflicts between Saladin and the Crusaders and between Napoleon and the Turks. But there is no reference to Thutmose III's battle at Megiddo.[33]

Smith substantially revised his text in 1931 for the twenty-fifth edition. This edition includes for the first time the description of Thutmose III's campaign to Megiddo that biographers have often cited as the source of Allenby's battle plan. What probably threw biographers off were a couple of sentences in the preface to the twenty-fifth edition.

> In this edition I have traced the successive stages of General Allenby's campaign of 1917–18. . . . I have been much encouraged by the gener-

ous tributes from Field-Marshal Viscount Allenby and many of his officers in Palestine to the real usefulness of my volume in framing the strategy and tactics of their campaign.[34]

However much Allenby may have profited from reading earlier versions of *Historical Geography of the Holy Land*, he could not have read Smith's description of Thutmose III's Megiddo campaign—for it was not written until 1931, fully thirteen years after Allenby hatched his plan to march through the Musmus Pass.

But the story does not end there. By the time of Allenby's 1918 campaign in Megiddo, British archaeologist Sir William Flinders Petrie had published his multivolume *History of Egypt;* the work's first edition appeared in 1896, and subsequent revised editions were published in 1898 and 1904. The second volume of this massive work contained a complete translation of Thutmose III's Annals, including the record of his Megiddo campaign. A similar magnum opus, entitled *Ancient Records of Egypt,* by University of Chicago archaeologist James Henry Breasted (later director of the Oriental Institute at that university and instigator of the Chicago excavations at Megiddo from 1925–39), appeared in 1906; the second volume of the series includes Breasted's own translation of and commentary on Thutmose III's Annals at Karnak, including the entries on the pharaoh's campaign against the Canaanite alliance at Megiddo.

Thus, accounts of Thutmose III's invasion of Canaan were available in 1918. But did Allenby read them prior to his own invasion of Palestine? At the very least, Allenby, who was stationed in Cairo in 1917, must have known about Petrie and Breasted, who were among the world's foremost Egyptologists. It is also possible that Allenby's imagination was spurred by general accounts of Near Eastern campaigns, such as an early review of George Adam Smith's *Historical Geography of the Holy Land* written by Coutts Trotter in 1894 for the *Geographical Journal*—a periodical that we know Allenby read, for Gardner reports:

> Allenby himself studied Palestine with the diligence of a student working for a doctorate, as much as of a General about to conquer the land. Papers which had appeared in *The Geographical Journal* were requested from his wife in London.[35]

Although Trotter does not mention Thutmose III or his campaign to Megiddo in his review of Smith's book, he writes:

> Across the Maritime Plain, and by easy roads into the great plain of Esdraelon, lay the beaten track of Egyptian armies going north to Tyre

and Sidon and Asia Minor, or eastwards by the valley of Jezreel to the Jordan and Damascus; the route also of Syrian, Babylonian, and Persian invaders. Later on, across Esdraelon came the Greek settlers of the Decapolis confederacy, the Romans, and, a thousand years after, the Crusaders.[36]

Would not Allenby, an astute student of military history, have considered emulating battle tactics that had proven successful so often over thousands of years?[37]

Allenby also knew quite a bit about the military history of the Jezreel Valley. H.L. Eason, an ophthalmic surgeon who met Allenby in Egypt in 1917, remembers that even prior to the Palestine campaign, the general was "convinced that in the unchanging East history would repeat itself," and Eason recalls that "from the beginning [Allenby] said that the decisive battle of the campaign would be fought at the Pass of Megiddo."[38] However, if Allenby had known of Thutmose III's campaign at Megiddo, would not he or his biographers have mentioned the fact? One scholar went so far as to wonder whether "it was Col. Lawrence [Lawrence of Arabia], with his knowledge of ancient history, who first made the suggestion which prompted Allenby's move."[39] But again, while this is an intriguing suggestion, surely Lawrence himself, or one of Lawrence's biographers would have mentioned this fact.

It is also important to note that Allenby did not exactly follow Thutmose III's strategy. Though the pharaoh only utilized the central Musmus pass, Allenby actually sent troops through two of the possible passes. The Fourth Cavalry Division followed the Musmus Pass to Megiddo, but Allenby's Fifth Cavalry Division negotiated the smaller Abu Shusheh Pass just to the north, en route to Nazareth and Afula. Fortunately for Allenby, the Turks did not cover the Abu Shusheh Pass, and a deadly ambush was avoided.

During the 1996 excavation season at Megiddo, the current Lord Allenby visited the site and said that if his great-uncle had known of Thutmose III's battle at Megiddo and had altered the British Imperial War Cabinet's proposed campaign accordingly, he would have said so in letters to his wife. No biographer with access to the Allenby archives has ever mentioned seeing such a discussion in the letters of Allenby. Serendipitously, however, there is a definitive answer to be found, but it is not in the Allenby archives. Instead, it comes from an unexpected source—an entry dated 10 November 1919 in University of Chicago archaeologist James Breasted's personal journal.

The entry in Breasted's journal recounts a conversation that took place between himself and General Allenby when they were all in Cairo after the war. The Allenbys had invited Breasted, among others, to a dinner. At the dinner, Breasted spoke at length with Allenby; the conversation is published in Charles Breasted's biography of his father.

> When the Allenbys arrived from England, they invited me to a dinner at the Residency [in Cairo]. It was very pleasant, not a bit stiff or formal, despite the numerous important official personages present. . . . After dinner, Allenby to my great surprise led me to a chair apart from the company, and seating himself, began to take up a remark I had made. . . . He continued to talk to me for the rest of the evening, without interruption or addressing a single word to his other guests. . . . Only a few months ago Allenby dealt the final annihilating blow to the leading oriental Empire [Turkey], which had ruled the Near East for about six centuries. . . . The quiet, matter-of-fact way in which he spoke of the momentous events wherein he played so great a part, his directness and unquestionable sincerity, made a profound impression on me, the more so because the simplicity of his manner at first quite veiled the greatness of the man. . . . I cannot now recall what shifted our conversation at this point to the battle of Megiddo, but Allenby evidently took pleasure in talking of it.

> [Allenby:] "When they gave me a peerage, they wanted me to add 'Armageddon' to the title, but I refused to do that. It was much too sensational, and would have given endless opportunity to all the cranks in Christendom. So I merely took Megiddo."

> J.H.B.: "Probably only the Orientalists know that it is identical with Armageddon, and the public will never discover the identity."

> "Quite true," he [Allenby] answered, "and if such titles are to be used at all, Megiddo has had its appropriateness. . . . You know, I went straight through the Pass of Megiddo, and at the crest I sent the infantry through to make a hole for the cavalry. They found a few battalions of Turks in possession of the height, killed thirty or forty of them, and captured all the rest. The cavalry got through the hole, and went forward with orders not to do any fighting, but to ride across the Plain of Megiddo and get astride of every road leading north, along which the enemy could retreat. . . . Curious, wasn't it, that we should have had exactly old Thutmose's experience in meeting an outpost of the enemy and disposing of them at the top of the Pass leading to Megiddo! You see, I had been reading your book [Ancient Records of Egypt] and [George] Adam Smith [Historical Geography of the Holy Land] and I knew what had taken place there."

J.H.B.: "Unfortunately we have too few in America who know the Near East or realize the obligation of the civilized world to keep order there."[40]

Since we know that the edition of George Adam Smith's book available to Allenby in 1918 did not contain a discussion of Thutmose III's battle at Megiddo, it must have been from Breasted's volume that Allenby learned the details of Thutmose III's tactics at Megiddo. Of course, Allenby may have read Petrie's book as well. If so, he graciously refrained from commenting on it while conversing with Breasted.

Thus, this matter is now settled once and for all. We know that to the list cited by his biographers, there is yet to be added one more book that Allenby read that positively affected his performance and tactics during the Great War. Before his 1918 march on Megiddo, Allenby had studied the second volume of James Henry Breasted's *Ancient Records of Egypt;* he knew that Thutmose III had gambled by following a dangerous attack route to capture the enemy unaware. Allenby deliberately borrowed Thutmose III's strategy and, in an uncanny redramatization of a historical circumstance, took the Turks by storm.

George Santayana reportedly once said that those who cannot remember the past are condemned to repeat it, but it is also true that those who *do* remember the past are *able* to repeat it, if they should so desire. In Allenby's case, his study of the past battles fought at Megiddo and in the Jezreel Valley resulted in "one of the most quickly decisive campaigns and the most completely decisive battles in all history."[41]

CHAPTER 2

On the Outskirts of Egypt

Say to the king, my lord and my Sun: Message of Biridiya, the ruler of Magidda, the loyal servant of the king. I prostrate myself at the feet of the king, my lord and my Sun, 7 times and 7 times. I herewith give what the king, my lord, requested: 30 oxen. . . . [. . . And in]deed, [the . . .] . . . of the [l]and are at peace, but I am at war.

—Amarna Letter EA 242, sent to Pharaoh Amenhotep III ca. 1360–1350 B.C.

IF NOT FOR THE AUTOBIOGRAPHY of an Egyptian army officer named Weni, the first battle probably fought in the Jezreel Valley would be lost in the mists of history.[1] Weni lived during the Old Kingdom's Sixth Dynasty ca. 2350 B.C. and served the first three pharaohs of the Sixth Dynasty—Teti, Pepi I, and Merenre. His was the first of several battles fought in the Jezreel Valley by Egyptians who considered the region to be Egyptian territory or on its periphery. These include the battle fought at Megiddo by Thutmose III ca. 1479 B.C. (discussed in chap. 1), a campaign by the Pharaoh Amenhotep II ca. 1430 B.C., and Egyptian involvement in a local quarrel between two Canaanite vassals, Labayu, the ruler of Shechem, and Biridiya, the ruler of Megiddo, ca. 1360 B.C.

Weni's autobiography is inscribed on a large slab of limestone at his tomb (or possibly cenotaph) at Abydos. He rose from obscurity to lead five military campaigns during the time of Pepi I in the twenty-fourth century B.C.[2] The last of these campaigns, perhaps fought ca. 2350 B.C., represents the first known Egyptian invasion of Palestine. The relevant portion of the inscription reads:

This army returned in safety,
  After it had hacked up the land of the [Sand]-Dwellers.
This army returned in safety,
  After it had crushed the land of the Sand-Dwellers.
This army returned in safety,
  After it had thrown down its enclosures.
This army returned in safety,
  After it had cut down its fig trees and its vines.
This army returned in safety,

After it had cast fire into all its dwellings.
This army returned in safety,
   After it had killed troops in it by many 10-thousands.
This army returned in safety,
   [After it had taken troops] in it, a great multitude as
   living captives. . . .

When it was said that rebels because of some affair were among these foreigners at the Nose of the Gazelle's Head, I crossed over in transports with these troops. I made a landing at the rear of the heights of the mountain range on the north of the land of the Sand-Dwellers. While a full half of this army was (still) on the road, I arrived, I caught them all, and every rebel among them was slain.[3]

Just who were these "Sand-Dwellers" that Weni attacked? Where was their land located? And what and where was the "Nose of the Gazelle's Head"? Most historians agree that the "land of the Sand-Dwellers" is the ancient Egyptian name for the lands to the east of Egypt and that the "Nose of the Gazelle's Head" is probably a reference to the Carmel mountain range in Israel, whose "nose" juts out into the Mediterranean Sea.[4] However, these basic questions represent only the tip of the iceberg in terms of dealing with Weni's problematic autobiography.

Since these few lines provide the only available evidence for this campaign, the details are obviously vague and can be interpreted in several ways. Clearly, Weni and at least half of his men sailed to the region that had risen in rebellion, disembarking behind the "Nose of the Gazelle's Head," that is, the Carmel headlands. He then marched inland, possibly through the Plain of Acco and into the Jezreel Valley, attacked the rebels, and killed them all.[5] His inscription says only: "While a full half of this army was (still) on the road, I arrived, I caught them all, and every rebel among them was slain." This can be interpreted in two different ways. Weni could mean that his entire force had been sent via troopships and that the battle had been won so quickly that fully 50 percent of his army was still marching in from the coast when the rebels were caught and killed. Alternatively, he could mean that only half of his men had come by sea, while the other half had been sent overland from Egypt, in which case those traveling by ship arrived first and had already defeated the rebels by the time those traveling by land got to the area.[6]

Returning in triumph to Egypt, Weni was later promoted and in due course served with distinction as governor of Upper Egypt under

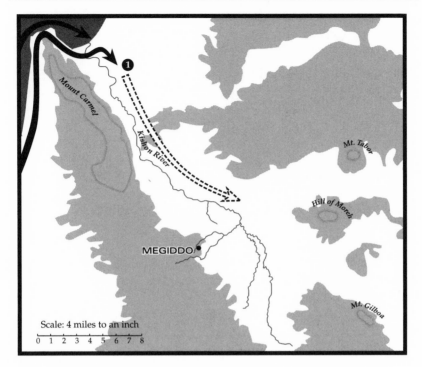

MAP 6. Pepi I and the "Nose of the Gazelle's Head"
1. Pepi I invades the Jezreel Valley (proposed route).

Merenre, successor to Pepi I. His successful military expedition to the
"Nose of the Gazelle's Head" may have been the first recorded battle in
the Jezreel Valley, but it was only the initial entry in a long list of battles
to come.

The city of Stratum XVI at Megiddo, dating to the Early Bronze Age,
came to an end ca. 2350 B.C. The succeeding city of Stratum XV has
radical changes in its architecture, which may indicate that it was now
occupied by new people or at least that it was under the control of a
new ruler.[7] It is therefore tempting to attribute the destruction of the
city of Stratum XVI and the new innovations seen in the city of Stratum
XV at Megiddo to Pepi I's campaign in the Jezreel Valley ca. 2350 B.C.
and to possible subsequent control of the area by the Egyptians, but
such a hypothesis cannot be proved at the present time and must
remain only a suggestion.

The next known Egyptian campaign to the Jezreel Valley was that of
Thutmose III in 1479 B.C., which has already been discussed in detail

in chapter 1. As I noted there, Thutmose III campaigned seventeen times in Syria-Palestine during the course of his reign and brought the area firmly under the control of Egypt. Canaan remained an Egyptian vassal for the next two centuries and was regarded as part of Egyptian territory, at least by the Egyptians.[8] Therefore, the battles fought in Canaan and the Jezreel Valley by the Egyptian pharaohs during the remainder of the Late Bronze Age (ca. 1400–1200 B.C.) were regarded not so much as invasions of enemy territory but as campaigns in their own peripheral lands.

Thus, a century after Thutmose III's famous battle at Megiddo, Pharaoh Amenhotep II conducted at least two, and more probably three, forays into Syria-Palestine. Of these, the last took place ca. 1430 B.C. and was aimed primarily at the Jezreel Valley and adjacent regions. The campaign seems to have been somewhat out of the ordinary, not least insofar as it took place during the month of November, a very unusual time for the Egyptians to be campaigning, because it was so late in the year.[9]

The impetus for the campaign seems to have been a rebellion by the Canaanites living in the area of the Jezreel Valley and possibly Lower Galilee as well. The rebellion was probably a rather local affair, although Mitanni, a political power located in northern Syria and Mesopotamia, might have furnished the unseen hand beneath the unrest.[10] It seems to have been a fairly minor revolt, yet it was still large enough that the Egyptian garrison based at Megiddo was apparently unable to quell the rebellion on its own.

The troubles in the Jezreel Valley during the time of Amenhotep II are reflected in two letters inscribed on clay tablets found at the site of Taanach, located approximately five miles (eight kilometers) southeast of Megiddo in the Jezreel Valley. A total of thirteen such letters were found at the site, part of the fifteenth century B.C. archives of the prince of Taanach, a man named Talwishar (previously read as "Rewassa" or "Riashar"). The letters are written in Akkadian, the *lingua franca* of the day for diplomatic correspondence in Egypt and the Near East.

In letter 6, which seems to be the earlier of the two, the prince of Taanach is accused of disloyalty to the Egyptians, of not paying homage, of not supplying soldiers for the local Egyptian garrison, and of neither sending a representative nor coming himself while Amenhotep was temporarily visiting the city of Gaza.[11] In letter 5, Amen-

Fig. 6. Taanach region (Zev Radovan, Jerusalem)

hotep demands that the prince of Taanach send soldiers, supplies, and horses to Megiddo.

> To Talwishar, thus (speaks) Amenhotep: May the Storm god guard your life! Send your brothers (colleagues) with their chariots; and send your quota of horses and the tribute and all the *ashiru* troops who are with you, send them tomorrow to Megiddo.[12]

There are problems with the interpretation of these letters, of course. There always are in such cases, for in studying ancient texts, nothing is ever as simple as it seems. In this instance, the primary question cuts right to the chase: exactly who is the Amenhotep writing these letters? Is the author actually Pharaoh Amenhotep II, or is it a local Egyptian administrator with the same name who was posted in Canaan at approximately the same time—perhaps the man named Amenhotep who later became governor of Nubia during the following reign of Thutmose IV? And even if they were written by Pharaoh Amenhotep II, as most scholars think, were they written before or after he became pharaoh? It seems most likely, to follow Occam's razor (the principle that the simplest solution is probably correct), that the letters were indeed written by Amenhotep II and were sent after he had succeeded to the throne of Egypt and become pharaoh. For one thing, although the name *Amenhotep* appears in the letters without royal titles, the tone in the letters is quite regal. More precisely, it may be suggested that these letters were written about the time of Amenhotep II's military campaign to the Jezreel Valley ca. 1430 B.C.[13]

Our information about this campaign comes primarily from two sources, which partially duplicate each other. One is very damaged—an inscription found to the south of the Eighth Pylon at Karnak in Egypt. The other, more detailed and therefore more important, is an inscribed stele containing the Annals of Amenhotep II, which was found at Memphis in Egypt—where it had been reused as the ceiling of the burial chamber in a tomb built for a prince of the Twenty-second Dynasty ca. 875 B.C.[14]

The Annals report that Amenhotep II and his forces apparently followed the Via Maris from Egypt to Syria-Palestine. They marched first to Aphek and thence to Yehem, where they halted, just as had Thutmose III half a century before him. Several side expeditions were then sent against small towns in the Sharon Valley, to the south of the Jezreel Valley.

> Year 9, 3rd month of the first season, day 25. His majesty proceeded to Retenu on his second victorious campaign, against the town of Aphek. . . . His majesty went forth by chariot, adorned with weapons of warfare, against the town of Yehem. Now his majesty captured the settlements of Mepesen, together with the settlements of Khettjen, two towns on the west of Socho. . . . His majesty went forth by chariot at dawn, against the town of Iteren, as well as Migdol-yen. . . . He carried off their princes: 34; *merui:* 57; living Asiatics: 231; hands: 372; horses: 54; chariots: 54; in addition to all the weapons of warfare, every able-bodied man of Retenu, their children, their wives, and all their property. After his majesty saw the very abundant plunder, they were made into living prisoners, and two ditches were made around all of them. Behold, they were filled with fire, and his majesty kept watch over it until daybreak, while his battle-axe was in his right hand, alone, without a single one with him, while the army was far from him, far from hearing the cry of Pharaoh.[15]

However, the main thrust of the campaign was made against the town of Anaharath several days later. The location of Anaharath is debated, but the city is considered to be the same as that mentioned in

Joshua 19:19 ("Anaharath of Issachar"). It is most likely to be identified either with Tell el-Mukharkhash in the Jezreel Valley, some five miles (eight kilometers) southeast of Mount Tabor, or with Tell al-Ajjul in Lower Galilee, just north of the Jezreel Valley, in an area leading from Mount Tabor to the Jordan River.[16] Either way, it is clear that Amenhotep II and his forces marched through the Wadi 'Ara, again just as had Thutmose III before him, en route to the Jezreel Valley and possibly just beyond.

> Now after daybreak of a second day, his majesty went forth by chariot at dawn, adorned with the equipment of Montu. The day of the Feast of the Royal Coronation of his majesty: Anaharath was plundered. List of the booty of his majesty alone within this day: living *maryanu:* 17; children of princes: 6; living Asiatics: 68; hands: 123; teams: 7; chariots of silver and gold: 7; in addition to all their weapons of warfare; bulls: 443; cows: 370; and all (kinds of) cattle, without their limit. Then the army presented very abundant booty, without its limit.[17]

Anaharath was captured only six days after Amenhotep II's forces were at Aphek. It is therefore very likely that the local Canaanites did not put up much resistance as the Egyptian army marched through the Sharon and Jezreel Valleys on their way to Anaharath, since so little time elapsed. The inhabitants of Anaharath presumably did not put up much of a fight either, but we cannot be certain of this, because the Annals do not provide any details about the battle except to say that the Egyptians won and that Anaharath was plundered.

The battle at Anaharath was the northernmost point of Amenhotep II's campaign, for the Annals indicate that the army then turned and marched back to the vicinity of Megiddo.[18] Here the army camped, but there was no need for a battle to be fought. The Egyptian garrison that had been stationed at Megiddo since the days of Thutmose III seems to have had things under control by this time.

Instead, a certain Prince Qaqa, ruler of a town named Geba-Shumen, along with his wife, children, and retainers, was brought to Megiddo. There he was admonished by the pharaoh and removed from office. "His majesty reached the vicinity of Megiddo. The Prince of Geba-Shumen, whose name was Qaqa, was brought, his wife, his children, and all his retainers as well. Another prince was appointed in his place."[19] Geba-Shumen was probably located at what is now Tell 'Amr, some four miles (six and a half kilometers) northwest of Megiddo, on the road leading out of the Jezreel Valley toward Acre (Acco) and the

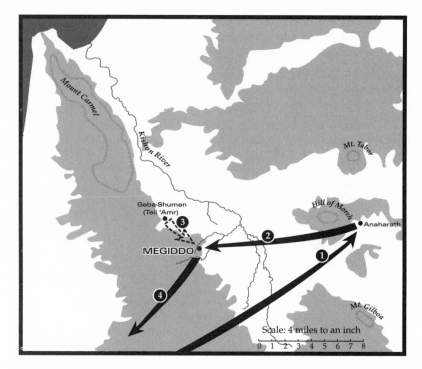

MAP 7. Amenhotep II and the Jezreel Valley
1. Egyptian forces march on Anaharath.
2. Egyptian forces march to Megiddo.
3. Prince Qaqa is brought to Megiddo.
4. Amenhotep II and his men return to Egypt.

Mediterranean coast. It is thought to be identical with the town later known during the Roman period as "Gaba of the Cavalry."[20] It is unclear exactly why Prince Qaqa was removed from office, but presumably it was for being disloyal or some similar offense. It is interesting to note that in the two letters found at Taanach mentioned earlier in this chapter, the prince of Taanach was admonished by Amenhotep II for what were probably the exact same sort of loyalty issues for which Qaqa, the ruler of Geba-Shumen, was replaced.

From Megiddo, Amenhotep II and his army proceeded back to Egypt without incident. They probably retraced their steps through the Wadi 'Ara back to Aphek and thence to Memphis, rather than marching west through the Jezreel Valley to the coast and then proceeding south as some scholars have suggested.[21] If they had marched west to the coast, they would have passed directly by Geba-Shumen, and there would have been no need to summon Prince Qaqa to Megiddo earlier.

From the available sources, it is clear that the Egyptians were in control of the Jezreel Valley during the reign of Amenhotep II, and Megiddo seems to have been a center for Egyptian administration in the region. This conclusion is further confirmed by a document dating to about the twentieth year of Amenhotep II's reign. Known as Papyrus Hermitage 1116A and written about a decade after Amenhotep II's campaign to the Jezreel Valley, it is a list of envoys to Egypt sent from various towns and localities in Syria-Palestine, to whom grain and beer were presented by the Egyptians. Included among the names are representatives from both Megiddo and Taanach.[22] Thus, Egyptian control over the Jezreel Valley apparently continued through the reign of Amenhotep II, in part because of the battle that he fought at Anaharath ca. 1430 B.C.

Because of the Egyptian control of Syria-Palestine during the fourteenth through the twelfth centuries B.C., the Egyptian pharaoh served as overlord to the numerous and squabbling rulers of the various Canaanite city-states. Thus, it was a matter of some concern to Amenhotep II's descendant, ruling as Pharaoh Amenhotep III nearly a century later, when one of his Canaanite vassals, Labayu, ruler of Shechem, a city some twenty-five miles (forty kilometers) to the south of Megiddo, near modern Nablus, engaged in a very serious attempt at empire building during the mid–fourteenth century B.C. Labayu and his two sons desired to add to their holdings the wealthy cities and towns of the Jezreel Valley, especially Megiddo.[23]

The details of Labayu's attempt at empire building are known from ten letters sent to Pharaoh Amenhotep III and his son and successor, Akhenaten, most likely during the years 1360–1350 B.C. They were found by an Egyptian peasant woman in 1887 as part of a cache of correspondence known collectively as the Amarna Letters, at Akhenaten's short-lived capital city of Akhetaten, located halfway between modern Cairo and Luxor in Egypt.[24] Of the ten relevant letters (EA 234, 242–48, 250, 365), seven were sent by Biridiya, the besieged ruler of Megiddo (EA 242–47, 365). Also in the Amarna archives are three letters sent from Shechem by Labayu, but they are concerned with protestations of his innocence in various activities other than his invasions of the Jezreel Valley. All of these letters were written in Akkadian, the diplomatic *lingua franca* of the Late Bronze Age in the ancient Near East. Thus, Megiddo is referred to as "Magidda" in these documents.

We do not yet have the replies to any of these letters, and therefore we currently only know the story from the perspective of the Canaanite participants—but it is possible that the Egyptian responses will be found during the ongoing excavations by Tel Aviv University and Pennsylvania State University now underway at the site of Megiddo.

According to the extant letters, Biridiya wrote an initial letter to Pharaoh Amenhotep III to let him know that a problem existed, saying in conclusion: "[. . . And in]deed, [the . . .] . . . of the [l]and are at peace, but I am at war" (Amarna Letter EA 242).[25] Biridiya quickly followed this with a second letter to Pharaoh Amenhotep III containing more details.

> I have obeyed the orders of the king, my lord and my Sun, and I am indeed guard[ing] Magidda, the city of the king, my lord, day and night. By day I guard (it) [f]rom the fields with chariots, and by n[ight] on the wall[s of] the king, my lord. And as the warring of the 'A[pi]ru in the land is seve[re], may the king, my lord, take cognizance of his land. (Amarna Letter EA 243)

Although no specific names have yet been given, Biridiya singles out the Hapiru, a much-debated group of outlaws and other people on the fringes of society, who were at this time causing trouble not only in the Jezreel Valley but also in other areas of Syria-Palestine and the Near East.[26]

With his next letter, Biridiya finally names Labayu, ruler of Shechem, as the man causing him the most problems.

> May the king, my lord, know that since the return (to Egypt) of the archers, Labayu has waged war against me. We are thus unable to do the plucking (harvesting), and we are unable to go out of the city gate because of Labayu. When he learned that archers were not co[ming o]ut, he immediately [de]termined to take Magidda. May the king save his city lest Labayu seize it. Look, the city is consumed by pestilence. . . . So may the king give a garrison of 100 men to guard his city lest Labayu seize it. Look, Labayu has no other purpose. He seeks simply the seizure of Magidda. (Amarna Letter EA 244)

Apparently, according to the events described in this letter, when a troop of Egyptian archers had been recalled to Egypt from Megiddo, Labayu seized the opportunity to attack. It is unknown whether the pharaoh then actually sent the requested garrison of one hundred soldiers to help Biridiya guard against the attacks of Labayu, but Biridiya was able to successfully defend Megiddo so that the city did not fall.

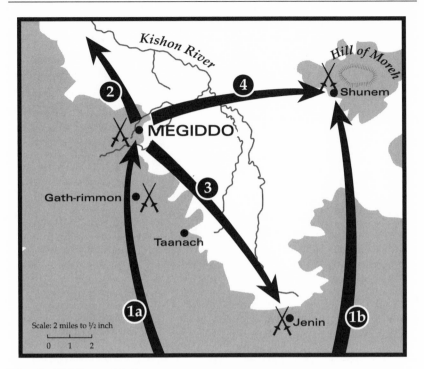

MAP 8. Biridiya and Labayu

1a. Labayu attacks Megiddo unsuccessfully, but occupies Gath-rimmon.

1b. At approximately the same time, Labayu attacks and destroys Shunem.

2. Labayu is captured and taken from Megiddo to Acco (Acre), but pays a ransom and escapes.

3. Biridiya marches to fight Labayu, but Labayu is killed in battle near Gina (probably modern Jenin) before Biridiya arrives.

4. Biridiya sends corvée workers to cultivate the devastated fields of Shunem.

Labayu may have had spies active in nearby cities, such as Beth Shean (Beisan), if a letter recently found at that site is any indication. This letter, sent to Labayu, describes the activities of Tagi, ruler of Gath Carmel, whose men were stationed in Beth Shean. It is usually thought to be an official letter sent between the two rulers, but it may actually be the furtive report of a spy in the employ of Labayu, keeping him up to date.[27] At some point, either before attempting to capture Megiddo or after his attempt failed, and perhaps using intelligence gathered by informers, such as his man in Beth Shean, Labayu also attacked other nearby cities and towns in the Jezreel Valley.

One Amarna Letter (EA 250) records that Labayu destroyed Shunem (Akkadian *Shunama*) in the Jezreel Valley and also attacked and occupied Gath-rimmon (Akkadian *Gittirimmunima*) near Taanach. It is likely that the attack against Gath-rimmon took place while Labayu and his men were on their way to attack Megiddo, since their route from Shechem passed right by this town. The destruction of Shunem probably occurred on a separate raid, however, since it lies in a different direction within the Jezreel Valley. It might be suggested that the raid that destroyed Shunem took place before the attack on Megiddo, so that Biridiya was forewarned and had time to prepare his defense of Megiddo. But it could just as easily have taken place afterward. The relevant Amarna Letters unfortunately do not give any indication of the chronological sequence of these specific events.

Following these attacks, the pharaoh ordered Labayu to be brought to Egypt for questioning. Labayu was quickly captured and was taken from Megiddo to Acco (Acre) to be transported to Egypt. However, once in Acco, Labayu bribed the ruler of the city, a man named Surata, and regained his freedom. A chagrined Biridiya was then forced to explain the situation to the pharaoh.

> It had been Surata that took Labayu from Magidda and said to me, "I will send him to the king by boat." Surata took him, but he sent him from Ḫinnatunu to his home, for it was Surata that had accepted from him his ransom. . . . It was Surata that let Labayu go, and it was Surata that let Baʻl-meḫir go, (both) to their homes. And may the king, my lord, know. (Amarna Letter EA 245)[28]

In the same letter, Biridiya was also forced to confess that Labayu had subsequently been killed in battle, perhaps in an ambush, before he, Biridiya, had arrived on the scene.

> Moreover, I urged my brothers, "If the god of the king, our lord, brings it about that we overcome Labayu, then we must bring him alive to the king, our lord." My mare, however, having been put out of action (having been shot), I took my place behind him and rode with Yashdata. But before my arrival they had struck him [Labayu] down. . . . (Amarna Letter EA 245)

Labayu's death most likely occurred near Gina (probably modern Jenin), just to the south of the Jezreel Valley. This specific location is implied in a threatening statement attributed to his sons: "Wage war against the people of [G]ina for having killed our father. And if you do not wage war, then we will be your enemies" (Amarna Letter EA 250).

At some point, probably soon after Labayu's death, Biridiya sent corvée workers to cultivate the fields belonging to the city of Shunem in the Jezreel Valley, which Labayu had earlier destroyed. Meanwhile, upon the death of Labayu, his two sons, one of whom was ruler of Pella across the Jordan River, decided to continue their father's policy of expansion. Aligning themselves with the Hapiru as Labayu had done previously, the two sons began once again to harass Biridiya of Megiddo and other local Canaanite rulers. These Egyptian vassals lost no time in informing the pharaoh of the new turn of events.

> May the king, my lord, know [t]hat the two sons of the rebel against the kin[g], my [l]ord, the two sons of Laba[y]u, have made their purpose the loss of the land of the kin[g], my lord, over and above the loss that the[ir] father caus[ed]. . . . (Amarna Letter EA 250)

Fortunately, the Jezreel Valley appears to have successfully held out against the expansionist aims and desires of Labayu's two sons and other rapacious men with similar desires, perhaps in part because of troops finally sent by the Egyptian pharaoh to Megiddo.[29]

However, there were numerous other small disturbances in the Jezreel Valley during this same period. Yashdata, the ruler of a town or city near Megiddo, reported in a letter to the pharaoh that the men of Taanach (Akkadian *Tahnaka*) had taken over his holdings and that he had been forced to seek refuge with Biridiya at Megiddo. There are also reports elsewhere in the Amarna Letters that Shum-Adda, the ruler of Shimon (Akkadian *Shamhuna;* biblical *Shimron*) in the northwest part of the Jezreel Valley, and Satatna, the new ruler of nearby Acco, joined forces and attacked a Babylonian caravan traveling through the adjacent area of Hannathan. The Babylonian king, Burna-Buriash II, was quite displeased when this incidence of highway robbery was brought to his attention, and he complained vigorously about it to the Egyptian pharaoh.[30]

All of the various events involving Biridiya and Labayu can be dated to approximately 1360–1350 B.C. According to the most recent calculations, Amenhotep III's rule over Egypt lasted from ca. 1391–1353 B.C. One of Labayu's letters found in the Amarna archive, giving his side of the story in events unrelated to his shenanigans in the Jezreel Valley, has a calendrical notation written on it that indicates that it was probably sent to Egypt in Amenhotep III's thirty-second year. The letter would therefore be from ca. 1360 B.C. and indicates that Labayu was already causing trouble during the last decade of Amenhotep III's reign. Other letters in the Amarna archive indicate that Labayu and, after him, his sons continued to cause trouble for the next seven years or more, early into the reign of Akhenaten.[31]

The exact city at Megiddo that Labayu was trying to capture cannot be pinpointed for certain, but is probably the city of Stratum VIII, as defined by the University of Chicago excavators. The absolute dates for Stratum VIII have been debated for decades, with some scholars arguing that this city came to an end as early as 1380 B.C. and others asserting that it lasted until 1250 B.C. The most recent suggestion, that the city came to an end ca. 1320/1310 B.C., fits well with the proposed dates for Labayu's attempted capture of Megiddo sometime during the decade between 1360 and 1350 B.C. The only other possibility is that Labayu may have been trying to capture the city of Stratum VIIB, if this city had begun as early as ca. 1380 B.C. as some have suggested. Both cities at Megiddo, that of Stratum VIII and that of Stratum VIIB, were quite prosperous, and both would have been tempting targets for Labayu.[32]

It is not surprising that Megiddo and the Jezreel Valley were viewed as desirable acquisitions. Already at this time, Megiddo had achieved international prominence and was known to the rulers of the great powers of the day. Nearly a century after the Amarna Letters were written, Megiddo (referred to as "Makkitta") is named in a now incomplete and broken letter written to the Hittite ruler Hattusili III ca. 1250 B.C. The context and contents of the letter are now unclear, but Megiddo appears to have served as a stopover on the road between the Egyptian and Hittite royal courts, a place where messengers paused on the long journey between Egypt and central Anatolia (modern Turkey).[33]

Egypt continued to be actively involved in Syria-Palestine and the Jezreel Valley through the twelfth century B.C., for as long as Egyptian control of southern Palestine was maintained. The Egyptian pharaoh Seti I may have marched through the Jezreel Valley en route to suppressing a rebellion at Beth Shean (Beisan) ca. 1291 B.C.[34] During the time of Pharaoh Ramses II, ruling at the same time as the aforementioned Hittite king Hattusili III in the thirteenth century B.C., we learn of trouble in the Wadi 'Ara, in the form of roving brigands preying on travelers journeying to or from the Jezreel Valley through this vital pass.

> The narrow valley is dangerous with Bedouin, hidden under the bushes. Some of them are of four or five cubits from their noses to the heel, and fierce of face. Their hearts are not mild, and they do not listen to wheedling. Thou art alone; there is no scribe with thee, no army behind

thee. Thou findest no scout, that he might make thee a way crossing. Thou comest to a decision going forward, although thou knowest not the road. Shuddering seizes thee, the hair of thy head stands up, and thy soul lies in thy hand. Thy path is filled with boulders and pebbles, without a toe hold for passing by, overgrown with reeds, thorns, brambles, and "wolf's paw." The ravine is on one side of thee, and the mountain rises on the other. Thou goest on jolting, with thy chariot on its side, afraid to press thy horse hard. If it should be thrown toward the abyss, thy collar-piece would be left uncovered and thy girth would fall. Thou unfasten the yoke in order to repair the collar-piece in the middle of the narrow valley. Thou art not competent in a way to bind it; thou knowest not how to lash it. . . . Thou startest to trot. The sky is opened. Then thou thinkest that the foe is behind thee. . . .[35]

The University of Chicago excavators believed that the city of Stratum VIIB at Megiddo came to an end in a fiery destruction so severe that piles of debris accumulated up to one meter thick in places. If this indeed occurred, and depending on when it is dated (usually anywhere from ca. 1250 B.C. to ca. 1200 B.C.), it could have been the result of a raid on Megiddo by the roving brigands reported during the time of Ramses II or even the result of an otherwise unrecorded attack on Megiddo by Ramses II himself.[36] It could also have been the result of a destruction by Pharaoh Merneptah, for although it cannot be confirmed, Merneptah may have marched through the Jezreel Valley and captured the city of Megiddo during his famous campaign to Canaan ca. 1207 B.C. This campaign was recorded on a wall perpendicular to the south side of the Karnak temple in Egypt, but it is better known from the victory poem that Merneptah had inscribed on what is now called the "Israel Stele."

> Plundered is Canaan with every evil;
> carried off is Ashkelon;
> seized upon is Gezer;
> Yanoam has been made as that which does not exist;
> Israel is laid waste, his seed is not.[37]

Israel was not laid waste for very long, however, for Deborah, Barak, Gideon, and other Israelite heroes and heroines made their appearance in the twelfth and early eleventh centuries B.C., during the conquest of Canaan. The spotlight then once again shone firmly upon Megiddo and the Jezreel Valley.

CHAPTER 3

The Conquest of Canaan

O God, do not keep silence;
do not hold your peace or be still, O God! . . .
Do to them as you did to Midian,
as to Sisera and Jabin at the Wadi Kishon,
who were destroyed at En-dor,
who became dung for the ground.

—Psalm 83:1, 9–10

THE TWELFTH AND eleventh centuries B.C. were a tumultuous time in Syria-Palestine, as the Israelites attempted to conquer the land of Canaan and establish their own kingdom. The battles fought in the Jezreel Valley during these centuries are a microcosm of the larger struggle for all of Canaan. The battles of Deborah and Barak against the Canaanites, of Gideon against the Midianites and Amalekites, and of Saul and Jonathan against the Philistines are an integral part of the wars fought by the Israelites in trying to establish first a toehold and then a monarchy in the "land of milk and honey." The battles are also a compelling mixture of firsts and lasts, including one of the first campaigns in history successfully led by a woman, the very first recorded night battle, and the last battle of the much beloved King Saul.

We meet up first with Deborah and her battle against Sisera in the Jezreel Valley ca. 1125 B.C. The Song of Deborah in the Book of Judges (5:1–31) is considered to be one of the oldest passages in the Bible. In poetic form, it tells of Deborah and Barak's battle in the Jezreel Valley against Sisera and his allies—an army of Israelites fighting against an army of Canaanites during the second half of the twelfth century B.C. The tale is also told with more detail in a prose account, placed immediately prior to the poetic version in the Book of Judges (4:1–24), but probably written quite some time later than the song. The story itself is one of the most problematic of all those found in the Bible, not least because of the difficulty of locating the specific places mentioned in both the poetic and the prose accounts. This makes it hard not only for scholars to reconstruct the topography and tactics involved in the battle but also for the general public to figure out what really happened. The situation is made even more difficult by the wide variety of available English translations, not all of which are completely faithful to the original Hebrew text.

The actual events that occurred during the conflict are not all that complicated, at least on the surface.[1] Deborah was a prophetess who was based in the hill country of Ephraim, south of the Jezreel Valley. She called on Barak, a general in the Israelite army, to defeat the Canaanite forces of King Jabin of Hazor. Jabin's army was led by his general Sisera and was allied with the forces of other unnamed Canaanite kings. The battle was fought in the Jezreel Valley near the Kishon River, at one of two possible locations—either at "Taanach, by the waters of Megiddo" (Judges 5:19, cited later in this chapter), or on the valley floor somewhere between the Kishon River and Mount Tabor. The lightly armed infantry of the Israelites won a resounding victory over the Canaanite forces, despite the Canaanites' superior numbers and their nine hundred chariots of iron.

This may have been the second phase of the Israelite War of Conquest against the Canaanites, probably begun some decades earlier by Joshua. There is, though, a possibility that Joshua's campaigns may actually have taken place after that of Deborah and Barak. Some of the better-known conquests of Joshua may have also involved sites in the Jezreel Valley, although most of his battles seem to have taken place further to the north, such as the battle of "the waters of Merom" in Galilee (Joshua 11:5), or more to the south, such as at Gibeon, Ai, and perhaps Jericho. Confusingly, while the Bible says that Joshua defeated the kings of Megiddo, Taanach, Shimron, Yoqneam, and other cities in the Jezreel Valley (Joshua 12:20–21), it also says that the Israelites did not drive the Canaanites out of Megiddo, Taanach, and other cities in the Jezreel Valley (Judges 1:27–28). The extent of Joshua's campaigns in the Jezreel Valley and the exact date and effect of such campaigns are therefore still matters of much debate.[2] In contrast, the timing and result of Deborah and Barak's campaign against the Canaanites in the Jezreel Valley are not in question, although some of the internal details are not as clear as they could be.

While the poetic version of Deborah and Barak's battle against Sisera and the Canaanites is concise (Judges 5:1–31), the prose account of this same conflict is much more detailed, with names and locations provided throughout (Judges 4:1–24). However, we are not at all certain whether these details can be trusted. The poetic version seems to be the original, older account of the battle, while the prose account appears to be a later attempt to expand the story, which may have unintentionally introduced some errors in the process. The narrative written by Josephus, the Jewish general who turned author and apologist during the time of Vespasian in the first century A.D., is of little help, for he faithfully follows the prose account without question, albeit with his usual additional elaboration and exaggeration.[3]

Overall, however, despite the differences between the poetic version and the prose account of Deborah and Barak's fight against Sisera, the two narratives seem to complement rather than to contradict each other. Although it is by no means obvious whether we would be better off following the succinct description found in the poem or the expanded version found in the prose, if the two accounts are merged to some extent, the following scenario may be tentatively suggested.[4] The story begins with Jabin, king of Hazor, and his general Sisera.

> The Israelites again did what was evil in the sight of the Lord, after Ehud died. So the Lord sold them into the hand of King Jabin of Canaan, who reigned in Hazor; the commander of his army was Sisera, who dwelt in Harosheth-ha-goiim. Then the Israelites cried out to the Lord for help; for he had nine hundred chariots of iron, and had oppressed the people of Israel cruelly for twenty years. (Judges 4:1–3)

Where exactly was Harosheth-ha-goiim, where Sisera dwelt? We do not know for certain, so it has been located in a bewildering variety of places in both the Jezreel Valley and surrounding regions. One particularly favored suggestion places Harosheth-ha-goiim at the northwestern end of the Plain of Esdraelon, near Mount Carmel, at the entrance to the coastal plain of Haifa and Acco. While this may be correct, a more attractive suggestion, for a variety of reasons, is that Harosheth-ha-goiim is not a specific site but rather a geographical term designating the region of the Jezreel Valley around Megiddo, including Taanach.[5]

At any rate, in response to the Israelites' cries for help against Jabin, the prophetess Deborah summoned the military commander Barak to Ephraim, south of the Jezreel Valley, and proposed a plan of attack against Sisera and the Canaanites.

> At that time Deborah, a prophetess, wife of Lappidoth, was judging Israel. She used to sit under the palm of Deborah between Ramah and Bethel in the hill country of Ephraim; and the Israelites came up to her for judgment. She sent and summoned Barak son of Abinoam from

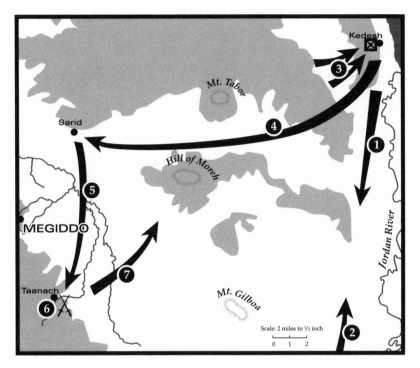

MAP 9. Deborah, Barak, and Sisera (possibility no. 1, following poetic version in Judges 5:1–31)

1. Deborah summons Barak to Ephraim.
2. Deborah and Barak go to Kedesh.
3. Israelites assemble at Kedesh.
4. Barak and Israelites march to Sarid.
5. Israelites move south to meet the Canaanite forces.
6. Battle is fought by the Kishon River near Taanach; Israelites are victorious.
7. Sisera flees northward after the defeat of his forces, only to be killed by Jael.

Kedesh in Naphtali, and said to him, "The Lord, the God of Israel, commands you, 'Go, take position at Mount Tabor, bringing ten thousand from the tribe of Naphtali and the tribe of Zebulun. I will draw out Sisera, the general of Jabin's army, to meet you by the Wadi Kishon with his chariots and his troops; and I will give him into your hand.'" Barak said to her, "If you will go with me, I will go; but if you will not go with me, I will not go." And she said, "I will surely go with you; nevertheless, the road on which you are going will not lead to your glory, for the Lord will sell Sisera into the hand of a woman." Then Deborah got up and went with Barak to Kedesh. Barak summoned Zebulun and Naphtali to Kedesh; and ten thousand warriors went up behind him; and Deborah went up with him. (Judges 4:4–10)

Barak having agreed to Deborah's plan, on the condition that she accompany him, the two of them journeyed back to Kedesh, Barak's hometown, which was to serve as an assembly point for the Israelite forces. A number of problems need to be resolved here. First, it is possible that the ten thousand men accorded to Deborah and Barak in the prose account might be exaggerated or could be a conventional folkloric figure. In addition, while most scholars accept this figure at face value, some have put the figure as high as twenty thousand, on the off chance that the text might be referring to ten thousand men from each of the two tribes, although it clearly states, "and ten thousand warriors went up behind him." Still others have suggested that this might simply be a reference to ten battalions of men, with perhaps only ten men in each battalion. This would mean that Barak had as few as one hundred men at his disposal, which seems perhaps too low a figure to do battle successfully with the Canaanites. The actual number probably lies somewhere between the two extremes of one hundred men and twenty thousand.

The prose account says that only two tribes (Zebulun and Naphtali) sent men. In contrast, the poetic version says that six tribes took part, of which the first five are named as follows:[6]

> Then down to the gates marched the people of the Lord.
> Awake, awake, Deborah!
> Awake, awake, utter a song!
> Arise, Barak, lead away your captives,
> O son of Abinoam.
> Then down marched the remnant of the noble;
> the people of the Lord marched down for him against the mighty.
> From Ephraim they set out into the valley,
> following you, Benjamin, with your kin;
> from Machir [Manasseh] marched down the commanders,
> and from Zebulun those who bear the marshal's staff;
> the chiefs of Issachar came with Deborah,
> and Issachar faithful to Barak;
> into the valley they rushed out at his heels.

(Judges 5:11–15)

The poem then lists four Israelite tribes that did not respond to Deborah's call to arms (Reuben, Gilead [Gad], Dan, and Asher), followed by the same two tribes that the prose account says did respond (Zebulun, repeated for a second time in this poetic version, and Naphtali). This rounds out the group of six tribes listed in the song as participating in the battle.

> Among the clans of Reuben
> there were great searchings of heart.
> Why did you tarry among the sheepfolds,
> to hear the piping for the flocks?
> Among the clans of Reuben
> there were great searchings of heart.
> Gilead [Gad] stayed beyond the Jordan;
> and Dan, why did he abide with the ships?
> Asher sat still at the coast of the sea,
> settling down by his landings.
> Zebulun is a people that scorned death;
> Naphtali too, on the heights of the field.

(Judges 5:15–18)

Why did the tribes of Reuben, Gilead (Gad), Dan, and Asher fail to answer the call to arms issued by Deborah? We will never know for certain, but it is possible that these particular tribes were too involved in economic and commercial activities with the Canaanites to go to war against them. That only ten tribes, rather than twelve, are listed in the Song of Deborah is also a cause for some concern, but there may have been only ten tribes making up the entity known as "Israel" in the twelfth century B.C. It is conceivable that the expansion to the better-known amphictyonic league of the twelve tribes of Israel did not take place until later in the eleventh century B.C.[7] At any rate, it appears that Deborah and Barak were able to assemble between one hundred men and twenty thousand men, primarily from the tribes of Zebulun and Naphtali. There may have been a number of others as well—from the tribes of Ephraim, Benjamin, Machir (Manasseh), and Issachar—who either also fought in the battle or, more likely, were held in reserve in case of need.

Another sticky problem involves the location of Barak's hometown of Kedesh in Naphtali, where Barak and Deborah assembled their men. Where was this place? Like Harosheth-ha-goiim (discussed earlier in this chapter), Kedesh has been located by scholars in a dizzying number of possible places. A favorite early identification located the site of Kedesh some seven miles northwest of Hazor in Upper Galilee, by Lake

Huleh. This seems rather unlikely, because it is too far from the action in the Jezreel Valley, and because Deborah and Barak would probably not have assembled, or been able to assemble, their army so close to the Canaanite capital city of Hazor. Another favored suggestion has identified Kedesh with Tel Qedesh (Tell Abu Qudeis), a small mound located only a few miles north of Taanach in the Jezreel Valley itself. However, this location also seems unlikely, because it is too close to Harosheth-ha-goiim and Sisera's forces, regardless of where Harosheth is to be located in the Jezreel Valley. Once again, Deborah and Barak would probably not have assembled, or been able to assemble, their army so close to Sisera's camp. Of all the suggested possibilities for the location of Kedesh, the most likely is the site of Khirbet Qadis (Horvat Qedesh), located near the Sea of Galilee on the steep slopes of the mountains between the plain of Jezreel and the Jordan River. This site would have been on the southern border of Naphtali and could have served as a perfect assembly point for volunteers arriving from the regions controlled by the tribes of Naphtali and Zebulun, for they would not have had to pass through the Jezreel Valley en route to the meeting place.[8]

The question that next arises is, Where exactly in the Jezreel Valley did the Israelites go once they left Kedesh in Naphtali, before they met the Canaanites in combat? The prose account of the story says that the Israelites marched to Mount Tabor, a position that was then leaked to the Canaanites by Heber the Kenite (husband of Jael), perhaps with the prior knowledge and approval of the Israelite commanders.[9]

> Now Heber the Kenite had separated from the other Kenites, that is, the descendants of Hobab the father-in-law of Moses, and had encamped as far away as Elon-bezaanannim, which is near Kedesh. When Sisera was told that Barak son of Abinoam had gone up to Mount Tabor. . . . (Judges 4:11–12)

However, the poetic version makes no mention of Mount Tabor at all. It simply says, "Then down marched the remnant of the noble; the people of the Lord marched down for him against the mighty" (Judges 5:13). It has been suggested that a problematic Hebrew word in this line, *sayd*, should be identified as the town of Sarid, located near Megiddo. It has also been suggested that the song's verses concerning both the first five participating tribes and the four nonparticipatory tribes (Judges 5:14–17) are a later insertion that has separated the verse concerning Zebulun and Naphtali (Judges 5:18) from its original rightful place earlier in the poem, following verse 13. The original version may therefore have been as follows:

> Then down to Sarid he marched towards the mighty ones.
> The people of YHWH [the Lord] marched down for him with warriors.
> Zebulun is a people that scorned his life to the death.
> Naphtali too, on the heights of the field.[10]

It seems likely, to judge from the prose account as well as the preceding discussion, that the Zebulun and Naphtali tribes had the major role in the following battle, a fact that would have been stressed when the verses were in their original proper order in the song.

If this new translation is correct, it would give us the name of the Israelite camp in the Jezreel Valley, which is otherwise lacking in the poetic version. Unfortunately, proposing that the Israelites marched from Kedesh to Sarid contradicts directly the prose account, which says that the Israelites marched instead to Mount Tabor. Therefore, we cannot reach a definitive conclusion; we can only say that the Israelite forces marched from Kedesh in Naphtali into the Jezreel Valley, either to Mount Tabor (prose account) or to the town of Sarid near Megiddo (revised poetic version). Nadav Na'aman has proposed the novel solution that the author or redactor of the prose account may have changed the location from the town of Sarid to the better-known Mount Tabor for the benefit of the later audience.[11]

Meanwhile, Sisera had assembled the men and nine hundred iron chariots of his Canaanite army at Harosheth-ha-goiim, which we have already said was an area likely to have been located at the southern edge of the Jezreel Valley, and which included both Megiddo and Taanach. Megiddo may, in fact, have served as Sisera's headquarters, although this is no more than an educated guess on the part of some scholars.[12] The Canaanite army seems to have been composed primarily of men from Sisera's forces, who, according to the biblical account, answered to King Jabin of Hazor. It was supplemented with men from the private armies of other unnamed Canaanite kings.

It is by no means certain, though, that Sisera's forces should actually be linked to King Jabin of Hazor. Were they really King Jabin's men, led by his general Sisera? Or were they simply Sisera's men? King Jabin is more usually associated with Joshua's battles in the biblical stories. Moreover, the city of Hazor is said to have been utterly destroyed during Jabin's final battle with and defeat by Joshua. If Joshua's campaigns preceded that of Deborah and Barak by several decades, how could

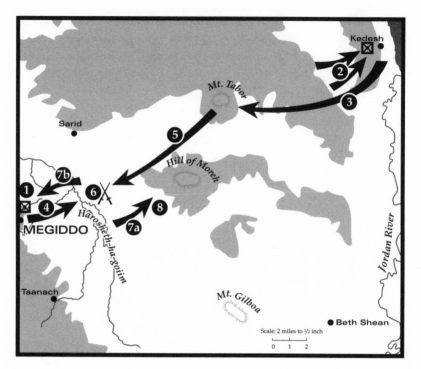

MAP 10. Deborah, Barak, and Sisera (possibility no. 2, following prose account in Judges 4:1–24)

1. Sisera and Canaanite forces are based at Harosheth-ha-goiim.
2. Israelites assemble at Kedesh.
3. Barak and Israelites march to Mount Tabor.
4. Sisera marches his chariots and troops to the Wadi Kishon.
5. Barak and Israelites come down from Mount Tabor and approach the Canaanite forces.
6. Israelites defeat Canaanites in battle.
7a. Sisera flees northward on foot after the defeat of his forces, only to be killed by Jael,
7b. while the surviving Canaanites retreat to Harosheth-ha-goiim, pursued by Barak and Israelites.
8. Barak follows Sisera northward, only to find him already dead at the hands of Jael.

Jabin still have been ruling in Hazor and have an army with nine hundred iron chariots? Two possible explanations come immediately to mind. First, Hazor could have been rebuilt by the time of Deborah. Second, the name Jabin may have been a throne name used by more than one king of Hazor. However, I have already mentioned that Joshua's campaigns might have occurred after Deborah and Barak's, rather than before. In this case, Joshua would simply have destroyed Hazor and put the finishing touches on King Jabin and his forces after they had already been significantly weakened by their earlier loss to Deborah and Barak in the Jezreel Valley. A final suggestion is that Sisera's forces had absolutely nothing to do with Jabin of Hazor and were only erroneously linked by a later unlearned author. Although this explanation seems far less likely, it cannot be excluded.[13] In short, the jury is still out on this issue.

Sisera's nine hundred chariots of iron are themselves a matter of some curiosity, for the number is eerily reminiscent of the 892 Canaanite chariots captured by Thutmose III at Megiddo nearly four centuries earlier. The similarity in numbers can be taken as evidence that it was indeed possible for Sisera to field fully nine hundred chariots and that this is therefore not an exaggerated number. Alternatively, the similarity can be seen as possible evidence that the author or later redactor of the prose account used elements from other, earlier stories to embellish this story; additional parallels can be found between the battle of Thutmose III at Megiddo and the prose account of Deborah and Barak's battle against Sisera in the Jezreel Valley.[14] The poetic version makes no mention of chariots or even of the numbers of men involved on either the Canaanite or the Israelite side.

To continue with the story now, the two opposing armies finally met in battle in the Jezreel Valley. But where in the valley did they meet? The prose account says:

> When Sisera was told that Barak son of Abinoam had gone up to Mount Tabor, Sisera called out all his chariots, nine hundred chariots of iron, and all the troops who were with him, from Harosheth-ha-goiim to the Wadi Kishon. Then Deborah said to Barak, "Up! For this is the day on which the Lord has given Sisera into your hand. The Lord is indeed going out before you." So Barak went down from Mount Tabor with ten thousand warriors following him. (Judges 4:12–14)

If the text is read as indicating that Sisera moved his men and chariots "from Harosheth- ha-goiim to the Wadi Kishon," it would seem that

Sisera neatly and unintentionally followed Deborah's original proposal to lure the Canaanite army into exactly that location, by the Kishon River (Judges 4:7).[15] However, the text may be read a second way, namely, as saying that the troops that Sisera called on were so numerous that their camp stretched "from Harosheth-ha-goiim to the Wadi Kishon." If this is the case, it is unclear where the subsequent battle actually took place, but it must have been somewhere between the Kishon River and either Sarid or Mount Tabor, that is, on the floor of the Jezreel Valley.

The poetic version only complicates matters, for in what are perhaps the most famous lines in the Song of Deborah, it says:

> The kings came, they fought;
> then fought the kings of Canaan,
> at Taanach, by the waters of Megiddo;
> they got no spoils of silver.
> The stars fought from heaven,
> from their courses they fought against Sisera.
> The torrent Kishon swept them away,
> the onrushing torrent, the torrent Kishon.
> March on, my soul, with might!

(Judges 5:19–21)

This passage obviously implies that the battle was fought at Taanach. The "waters of Megiddo" must be a reference to a Kishon River tributary that ran by both the mound of Megiddo and the site of Taanach. Thus, the best we can do at the moment is to say that the two armies met by the Wadi Kishon, either near "Taanach, by the waters of Megiddo" (poetic version) or on the valley floor directly east of Megiddo and the region known as Harosheth-ha-goiim (prose account). Either way, the choice of battleground obviously benefited the Israelites, especially if it started raining just before or during the battle, as the poetic version seems to indicate.

Scholars usually interpret the phrase "the stars fought from heaven" from Judges 5:20 to mean that a fortuitous or providential rainstorm occurred. This not only would have affected the troops themselves during the battle but also would have rendered the Canaanite chariots useless in the muddy clay of the valley floor near the river. Indeed, both chariots and men of the Canaanite army may have been carried away by the rising waters of the Kishon River and perhaps even by a flash flood in the Wadi Kishon itself.[16] The Chinese military strategist Sun-Tzu of the fifth century B.C. warned, "If battle is desired, do not locate near rivers when encountering opponents,"[17] but this advice was of little help to Sisera, living and fighting as he did fully six centuries earlier. Undoubtedly, Deborah and Barak knew of and had perhaps counted on the possibility of such a rainstorm occurring, particularly if the battle were being fought in the wintertime, as many scholars believe.

Fighting during the winter was rather unusual, however, for most of the battles in the Jezreel Valley took place in late spring, summer, or early fall, after the spring rains had ended and before the winter rains had begun. This timing was undoubtedly chosen precisely because of the use of cavalry and/or chariots in the battles, for this was the time when the ground was hardest and could be most easily maneuvered by both men and horses. Precise dates are known for twenty-four battles fought in the Jezreel Valley during the past four thousand years, and twenty of those battles occurred in the eight months between April and November, almost evenly split between spring (six battles), summer (eight battles), and fall (six battles). That only two battles took place during December and only two during January, February, or March is not surprising, for the rainy season in the Jezreel Valley is from December through April.[18] However, that no battles were fought in August is perhaps a bit more surprising, although it may simply have always been too hot to fight in the Jezreel Valley at that time of the year.

The coalition of Canaanite kings mentioned in these lines is reminiscent of the confederation of rebel Canaanite princes faced by Pharaoh Thutmose III in this same Jezreel Valley several centuries earlier and of King Jabin of Hazor's confederation of lesser Canaanite kings faced by Joshua either immediately preceding or following Deborah and Barak's battle. There is a slim possibility that these are not three separate Canaanite coalitions but one and the same alliance, used again and again by the various biblical authors, but this seems a remote and perhaps overly sensitive suggestion.[19]

Meanwhile, according to the prose account (since the poetic version gives no further details of the battle itself), the victorious Israelites chased the Canaanites back to their original camp at Harosheth-ha-goiim and annihilated them.

> And the Lord threw Sisera and all his chariots and all his army into a panic before Barak; Sisera got down from his chariot and fled away on foot, while Barak pursued the chariots and the army to Harosheth-ha-goiim. All the army of Sisera fell by the edge of the sword; no one was left. (Judges 4:15–16)

Barak then went in pursuit of Sisera, who had escaped on foot, but Barak found him already dead at the hand of Jael, wife of Heber the Kenite, the same man who may have revealed to the Canaanites the location of the Israelite army on Mount Tabor. Here we run into some interesting problems between the poetic version and the prose account of the story.

The poetic version, thought by many to be the older of the two (as I mentioned earlier in this chapter), does not describe how Sisera fled from the battlefield, abandoning his men and ending up at the tent of Jael. This is left to the prose account, which fills in the missing gap by reporting, "Now Sisera had fled away on foot to the tent of Jael wife of Heber the Kenite; for there was peace between King Jabin of Hazor and the clan of Heber the Kenite" (Judges 4:17). Instead, the song simply picks up with Jael offering Sisera refreshments. She then takes up a peg (or nail) and, coming up from behind and hitting him on the head with it, manages to kill him.

> Of women, Jael is most blessed,
> the woman of the Kenite community;
> Of the women of the tent she is blessed.
> Water he asked;
> milk she provided;
> in a lordly crater she proffered ghee.
> She sent her hand to the peg,
> her right hand to the workers' smiter.
> She smote Sisera;
> she smashed his head;
> she splintered, she broke through his gullet [interior of the mouth
>   or throat].
> At her feet, he kneeled, fell, stretched out.
> At her feet, he kneeled, he fell.
> Where he kneeled, there he fell, slain.

(Judges 5:24–27)[20]

As Baruch Halpern has pointed out, there is much poetic repetition in these lines. We are probably to understand that Jael offered Sisera at most only one type of beverage, namely, goat's milk (ghee), in response to his request for water, but it is also possible that we should not be reading too many specifics into these poetic couplets and that these lines should simply be understood as a generic statement that Sisera asked for and received a drink of some kind. Similarly, the "peg" and the "workers' smiter" probably refer to one instrument only, the peg (or nail) with which Jael struck and killed Sisera.[21]

The author or redactor of the later prose account misunderstands these nuances and so changes the story somewhat.

> Jael came out to meet Sisera, and said to him, "Turn aside, my lord, turn aside to me; have no fear." So he turned aside to her into the tent, and she covered him with a rug. Then he said to her, "Please give me a little water to drink; for I am thirsty." So she opened a skin of milk and gave him a drink and covered him. He said to her, "Stand at the entrance of the tent, and if anyone comes and asks you, 'Is anyone here?' say, 'No.'" But Jael wife of Heber took a tent peg, and took a hammer in her hand, and went softly to him and drove the peg into his temple, until it went down into the ground—he was lying fast asleep from weariness—and he died. Then, as Barak came in pursuit of Sisera, Jael went out to meet him, and said to him, "Come, and I will show you the man whom you are seeking." So he went into her tent; and there was Sisera lying dead, with the tent peg in his temple. (Judges 4:18–23)

The differences between the poetic version and the prose account concerning Jael's method of killing Sisera are probably the result of a misunderstanding of the original poem's repetitive nature by the author or later redactor of the prose account. For instance, there was probably only a single peg (or nail) involved in the murder, rather than both a hammer and a tent peg as per the prose account. The use of two items rather than one demands all sorts of problematic additions to the original story, including the need for Sisera to be lying down rather than standing up and for him to be asleep rather than awake. Other potential problems found in the prose account include the apparently extensive marching back and forth on the part of first Barak and then Deborah (from Kedesh to Ephraim and back to Kedesh, before finally marching to the Jezreel Valley), the precise direction in which Sisera fled from the battlefield, and the location of Elon-bezaanannim, where the prose account says the tent of Heber and Jael was situated. These problems have been explained in a variety of ways. The simplest and most convincing suggestion is that either the author or the later redactor of the prose account was unfamiliar with the geography of the Jezreel Valley and surrounding regions.[22]

Following Sisera's death at the hands of Jael, the poetic version ends with an image of Sisera's mother waiting in vain for her son to return from the battlefield (Judges 5:28–30), a cursing of the enemies and a blessing of the friends of the Lord, and a final declaration that there was then peace in the land for the next forty years (Judges 5:31), during which period the Israelites were able to consolidate and expand their territory.[23] The prose account elaborates a bit, saying that the destruction of King Jabin of Canaan followed soon after the Canaanite defeat in the Jezreel Valley. "So on that day God subdued King Jabin of Canaan before the Israelites. Then the hand of the Israelites bore harder and harder on King Jabin of Canaan, until they destroyed King Jabin of Canaan (Judges 4:24)." Thus ended a major phase of warfare between the Canaanites and the Israelites, either concluding or anticipating Joshua's campaigns against the same foe. However, as always, the peace was only temporary.

Concerning the archaeological side of the story, much has been written by scholars trying to decide which strata or levels at the sites of Taanach and Megiddo should be associated with Deborah and Barak's battle against Sisera. The excavators of Taanach believed that the entire city had been destroyed ca. 1125 B.C., with a lengthy gap in occupation following the catastrophe, and so they promptly linked this destruction to the Canaanite defeat.[24] However, neither the poetic version nor the prose account says anything about Taanach being destroyed either during or after the battle, so it is a leap of faith to assert that the destruction found by the excavators at Taanach was a direct result of the battle. Other archaeologists and historians argue that the entire affair must have taken place during a time when Megiddo was basically abandoned and uninhabited, otherwise the Song of Deborah would have mentioned Megiddo itself rather than simply the "waters of Megiddo." Thus, extended debates have focused on whether the period is better represented by the hiatus between the cities of Megiddo Strata VIIA and VIB or by the hiatus between the cities of Megiddo Strata VIA and VB. But if Megiddo were indeed Sisera's headquarters as some have argued, not only would the city have been occupied at the time of the conflict, but a destruction of the city at the conclusion of the battle might be expected. The violent and fiery end of the prosperous city of Stratum VIIA at Megiddo is now dated to ca. 1140–1130 B.C., which puts it at approximately the same time as Deborah and Barak's battle against Sisera, give or take a few years.[25]

Thus, it is possible to suggest a correlation between this observed destruction at Megiddo and the battle fought by Deborah, Barak, and Sisera in the area, but it is not highly recommended. For one thing, if Joshua's campaign(s) in the Jezreel Valley were conducted a decade or two prior to that of Deborah and Barak, and if he defeated the kings of Megiddo, Taanach, Shimron, Yoqneam, and other cities in the Jezreel Valley as one biblical account says (Joshua 12:20–21), then the destruction of the city of Stratum VIIA at Megiddo ca. 1140–1130 B.C. would fit the timing of Joshua's campaign(s) as well as, if not better than, Deborah and Barak's battle against Sisera. For another, if Megiddo were indeed Sisera's headquarters, more probably would have been made of this fact in the texts. Moreover, Taanach, Mount Tabor, and even Harosheth-ha-goiim were probably as well known as was Megiddo in terms of familiarity to any potential audience. There was thus no need to mention Megiddo, but this in no way implies that the site was necessarily abandoned at the time of Deborah and Barak's nearby battle.

Following their defeat at the hands of Deborah and the Israelites, the Canaanite grip on the Jezreel Valley was weakened to some extent. While the Israelites were able to claim land and settle in the valley, wandering nomadic tribes from the desert were also able to enter the Jezreel Valley and lay waste to its riches and resources.[26] Among these were the Midianites and the Amalekites, according to Judges 6:33–35: "Then all the Midianites and the Amalekites and the people of the east came together, and crossing the Jordan they encamped in the Valley of Jezreel." The Israelites turned for help to Gideon, a local man reportedly born and raised in the town of Ophrah (probably modern Afula).[27] The ensuing campaign to evict the nomadic camelborne raiders from the Jezreel Valley is rightfully famous in the annals of both biblical and military history, not only because Gideon's initial attack against the Midianites and Amalekites is the first night battle in history for which we have a detailed account, but also because of the very unusual way in which he chose the men who were to accompany him into this battle.[28]

The trouble first began some seven years before Gideon and his army appeared on the scene. According to the account in Judges 6, the nomadic invaders were waging a war aimed at destroying the resources of the Israelites. Each spring, as the harvest was nearly ready to be gathered, the camelborne raiders would arrive en masse and destroy the crops, leaving the Israelites with little or nothing to eat.

> For whenever the Israelites put in seed, the Midianites and the Amalekites and the people of the east would come up against them. They would encamp against them and destroy the produce of the land, as far as the neighborhood of Gaza, and leave no sustenance in Israel, and no sheep or ox or donkey. For they and their livestock would come up, and

> they would even bring their tents, as thick as locusts; neither they nor their camels could be counted; so they wasted the land as they came in. Thus Israel was greatly impoverished because of Midian. . . . (Judges 6:3–6)

Interestingly, the Spartans pursued similar tactics against the Athenians nearly seven hundred years later in Greece, raiding and burning the ripening harvest in the fields outside of Athens every spring during the opening years of the Peloponnesian War ca. 431 B.C.[29]

The Israelites in the Jezreel Valley decided to put an end to the Midianite and Amalekite incursions. Led by Gideon, a member of the Abiezer clan from the tribe of Manasseh, the preparations for an all-out war began. The Midianites and their allies were camped below the Hill of Moreh, near Endor, just to the south of Mount Tabor (Judges 7:1). The biblical account says that they numbered 135,000 (Judges 8:10). This figure seems quite large and may be somewhat exaggerated, although Josephus's later account gives an even larger number of 138,000 men.[30] Gideon and his men originally numbered thirty-two thousand, drafted from the tribes of Asher, Zebulun, Naphtali, and Manasseh (Judges 6:35, 7:3). They gathered near the Well of Harod, on a hilltop overlooking the enemy camp (Judges 7:1, 7:8).[31] The well, probably in the same region as, if not actually identical to, the later 'Ayn Jalut, or "Spring of Goliath", was located just to the northwest of Mount Gilboa and directly south of the Hill of Moreh.

An initial sortie by the Israelites, led by Gideon's brothers, resulted in a skirmish fought on the slopes of Mount Tabor, to the north of the Midianite camp (Judges 8:18–19). Possibly designed as a maneuver to stop the nomadic enemy from advancing farther into the valley, as well as to keep them occupied and in one place while Gideon gathered his troops and prepared his attack, the expedition succeeded in buying time for the Israelites and allowed them to gather undetected, but it cost the lives of Gideon's brothers.[32]

Gideon, meanwhile, was busy weeding out the cowards, those "fearful and trembling," from his army. Fully twenty-two thousand of the thirty-two thousand Israelites gathered at the Well of Harod fit this description and were sent home (Judges 7:3). This left ten thousand men, a number also given in Josephus's account.[33] Gideon then proceeded to choose three hundred men from the remaining ten thousand. It should perhaps not be too surprising that he wanted so few men, since he was not planning to attack the Midianites in open-field,

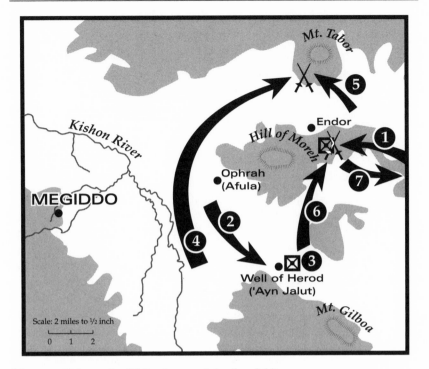

MAP 11. Gideon, the Midianites, and the Amalekites
1. Midianites and Amalekites migrate into Jezreel Valley.
2. Gideon goes to Well of Harod (possibly 'Ayn Jalut) from Ophrah (Afula).
3. Gideon's men gather and are whittled down to the final three hundred.
4. Gideon's brothers carry out an initial sortie on Mount Tabor.
5. Midianites clash with and kill Gideon's brothers.
6. Gideon and Israelites attack Midianite/Amalekite camp.
7. Midianites and Amalekites flee, pursued by Gideon and Israelites.

face-to-face, daylight combat but rather had in mind a surprise attack
under cover of darkness, which called for fewer, braver men whom he
could trust implicitly. In an open battle fought under the searing sun of
the Jezreel Valley, the Israelites would have been vastly outnumbered
by the Midianite and Amalekite nomadic army even if Gideon had not
dismissed any of the men who initially reported for duty (32,000
Israelites versus 135,000 Midianites and Amalekites, according to the
biblical account). Moreover, the nomads were mounted on camelback
and would have wreaked havoc among the Israelites, who were primarily on foot. Gideon's tactics could negate both the nomads' camel

mounts and their superior numbers. Finally, even if Gideon's surprise attack should fail, virtually all of the original thirty-two thousand Israelite troop members (less only the three hundred men chosen by Gideon) would still be available to confront the Midianites and Amalekites, should such a defense prove necessary.[34]

The manner in which Gideon chose his vaunted three hundred men for the attack was highly original, to say the least. Moreover, it is the subject of some controversy, for there are problems with the biblical text as it is usually translated. The New Revised Standard Version of the Bible presents this passage as follows:

> Then the Lord said to Gideon, "The troops are still too many; take them down to the water and I will sift them out for you there. When I say, 'This one shall go with you,' he shall go with you; and when I say, 'This one shall not go with you,' he shall not go." So he brought the troops down to the water; and the Lord said to Gideon, "All those who lap the water with their tongues, as a dog laps, you shall put to one side; all those who kneel down to drink, putting their hands to their mouths, you shall put to the other side." The number of those that lapped was three hundred; but all the rest of the troops knelt down to drink water. Then the Lord said to Gideon, "With the three hundred that lapped I will deliver you, and give the Midianites into your hand. Let all the others go to their homes." (Judges 7:4–7)

In the original Hebrew text, however, there is an additional, slightly contradictory phrase added to the next-to-last sentence of the preceding quotation: "And the number of them that lapped, putting their hand to their mouth, were three hundred men: but all the rest of the people bowed down upon their knees to drink water" (Judges 7:6). It has been suggested that the phrase "putting their hand to their mouth" is misplaced here, perhaps the result of a copyist error, and that the phrase should in fact have gone at the end of the sentence, for only those who had knelt down would need to bring the water to their mouth via a cupped hand, as described in the sentence immediately preceding this contradictory one.[35]

Be that as it may, the question still remains as to why Gideon chose the 300 men who lapped the water, rather than the 9,700 men who knelt to drink. Most military experts suggest that Gideon was testing his men in a variety of ways. First, those soldiers who were reluctant to throw themselves on the ground to drink might be also reluctant to face the discomfort that the upcoming campaign would demand. Second, those who lay down on the ground to drink showed their military experience, for they would present to the enemy a reduced target, one harder to hit with an arrow or spear than a man kneeling to drink. Finally, if one accepts the Hebrew text at face value, those warriors who both lay face down and then brought the water to their mouth via a single cupped hand would have been able to keep their weapons in their free hand and their eyes focused on the enemy while they drank their fill.[36]

That Gideon chose only three hundred men is also not as surprising as it might at first appear. Numerous battles throughout history have been fought in which one side deliberately used only three hundred soldiers. The most famous of these would be the battle of Leonidas and his band of three hundred Spartans, who made a dramatic stand in Greece against the Persians at the pass of Thermopylae in 480 B.C. In 327/326 B.C., Alexander the Great chose three hundred men from his army to attack thirty thousand enemy soldiers ensconced in a camp high in the mountains in India, and the Byzantine emperor Nicephorus II Phokas chose three hundred men from his army of eighty thousand soldiers to conduct a night attack against the city of Antioch in A.D. 968. As has been pointed out by previous scholars, three hundred to four hundred men is the maximum number of men that can be effectively guided by a single leader, and three hundred men can be easily divided into three companies of one hundred men each. The three companies can then be readily distributed so as to form a center unit with two flanking wings.[37]

Thus, Gideon reduced his troops to the maximum number allowed by his daring plan, which took into account the terrain to be crossed at night, the abilities of his men, the number of the enemy, and the need for both silence and speed. He himself then went on a reconnaissance mission, accompanied only by his servant Purah, to study the layout of the enemy camp, the timing of the guard changes, and the morale of the enemy soldiers (Judges 7:9–15). Having ascertained that the morale of the enemy was low, and having determined the frequency with which the guards were changed, Gideon returned to his camp and divided his men into three companies, with one hundred men in each company. Each man was given a trumpet and a torch with its lit end hidden inside a jar, presumably in addition to his usual weapons of sword or spear.[38] They attacked sometime around midnight, just after a changing of the guards, with devastating results.

> After he divided the three hundred men into three companies, and put trumpets into the hands of all of them, and empty jars, with torches inside the jars, he said to them, "Look at me, and do the same; when I

come to the outskirts of the camp, do as I do. When I blow the trumpet,
I and all who are with me, then you also blow the trumpets around the
whole camp, and shout, 'For the Lord and for Gideon.'" So Gideon and
the hundred who were with him came to the outskirts of the camp at the
beginning of the middle watch, when they had just set the watch; and
they blew the trumpets and smashed the jars that were in their hands. So
the three companies blew the trumpets and broke the jars, holding in
their left hands the torches, and in their right hands the trumpets to
blow; and they cried, "A sword for the Lord and for Gideon!" Every man
stood in his place all around the camp, and all the men in camp ran; they
cried out and fled. When they blew the three hundred trumpets, the
Lord set every man's sword against his fellow and against all the army;
and the army fled as far as Beth-shittah toward Zererah, as far as the border of Abel-meholah, by Tabbath. And the men of Israel were called out
from Naphtali and from Asher and from all Manasseh, and they pursued
after the Midianites. (Judges 7:16–23)

By the time dawn broke, the Midianite and Amalekite army had also
been broken. Gideon's trumpet blasts and sudden blazing lights had
quickly created panic, alarm, and confusion. The noise no doubt also
caused the camels and herd animals of the Midianites and Amalekites
to stampede as well, adding to the turmoil and chaos. Thus, Gideon's
small force of three hundred men, with the three companies each presumably attacking from a different direction, was easily able to terrorize
the much larger enemy force.[39] Fully 120,000 Midianite and Amalekite
soldiers were reportedly killed in the melee (Judges 8:10), although
this number should undoubtedly be taken with the proverbial grain of
salt. Many were apparently slain by their own comrades in the confusion and darkness.

The remaining fifteen thousand enemy troop members fled headlong to the east, in the only direction left open to them, chased by additional Israelite forces from Asher, Naphtali, and all Manasseh (Judges
7:23–24).[40] Pursuing the Midianites and Amalekites across the Jordan
River, Gideon called on reinforcements from the men of Ephraim, who
captured and killed Oreb and Zeeb, the two Midianite army generals,
and brought their heads to Gideon (Judges 7:25). Gideon himself, with
his men, proceeded to attack the remaining enemy troops and captured and put to death the two Midianite kings, Zebah and Zalmunna
(Judges 8:10–21), which provided at least some small measure of
revenge for his brothers who had been killed on Mount Tabor in the
early stages of the campaign.

Gideon's surprise attack on the Midianites and Amalekites was an unqualified success, in part because his strategy was so unorthodox. His masterful tactics—pitting a small, highly maneuverable force against a much larger enemy and utilizing the terrain, darkness, surprise, sudden noise, light, and confusion—are still studied and cited by military scholars today, more than three thousand years after his brilliant plan was first used so effectively. In fact, nineteenth-century Prussian military strategist Carl von Clausewitz, whose works are also still studied by army tacticians today, highly approved of such tactics, writing, "the regular surprise attack (by night . . .) is the best way to get the most out of a very small army."[41]

Thereafter declining to be appointed king, Gideon lived on to a ripe old age (Judges 8:22–23, 32), having successfully vanquished the Midianite/Amalekite threat and brought peace to the Jezreel Valley: "So Midian was subdued before the Israelites, and they lifted up their heads no more. And the land had rest forty years in the days of Gideon" (Judges 8:28). Again, however, the peace was to be only temporary.

As time marched on, the Israelites completed their takeover of Canaan and began their efforts to form a kingdom of their own in the land. Near the end of the eleventh century B.C., they turned to Saul and anointed him the first king of the Israelite monarchy. This was to become the United Monarchy, made famous by Saul's successors David and then Solomon. All was not tranquil in the land, however, for there were still bitter enemies contesting the Israelites' claim to this area. These enemies were the Philistines, against whom Saul spent most of his reign fighting. Indeed, after years of warfare, Saul and three of his sons fought their last great battle and met their deaths ca. 1016 B.C. at Mount Gilboa in the Jezreel Valley, defeated at last by their vindictive enemies.[42]

The battle between Saul and the Philistines in the Jezreel Valley was crucial to the Philistine goal of encircling and capturing the heartland of Saul's kingdom. They already held Beth Shean (Beisan) to the east of the Jezreel Valley, as well as the coastal plain to the west of the valley. If they won at Mount Gilboa, they could cut Saul's kingdom into two parts and separate the Israelites in Galilee and the Jezreel Valley from the rest of the tribes. Saul therefore had no choice but to fight the Philistines for control of the Jezreel Valley. He well knew what would be the result if he lost, while if he won, not only would he relieve the threat to his kingdom, but his army would also probably be able to advance on Philistine-controlled Beth Shean.[43]

The story is told only in I Samuel 28–31, II Samuel 1, and I Chronicles 10 of the Hebrew Bible. There are, as yet, no contemporary extrabiblical sources available to confirm these accounts, just as there are none for the battles of either Deborah or Gideon. However, in Saul's case, his story was repeated, with some embellishment, approximately a thousand years later by Josephus, in his volume entitled *The Antiquities of the Jews.*[44] Meanwhile, the account in I Samuel concisely records the troop movements and machinations that occurred before the beginning of the actual conflict.

> In those days the Philistines gathered their forces for war, to fight against Israel. . . . The Philistines assembled, and came and encamped at Shunem. Saul gathered all Israel, and they encamped at Gilboa. . . . When Saul saw the army of the Philistines, he was afraid, and his heart trembled greatly. When Saul inquired of the Lord, the Lord did not answer him, not by dreams, or by Urim, or by prophets. Then Saul said to his servants, "Seek out for me a woman who is a medium, that I may go to her and inquire of her." His servants said to him, "There is a medium at Endor." So Saul disguised himself and put on other clothes and went there, he and two men with him. . . . Now the Philistines gathered all their forces at Aphek, while the Israelites were encamped by the fountain that is in Jezreel. As the lords of the Philistines were passing on by hundreds and by thousands, and David and his men were passing on in the rear with Achish, the commanders of the Philistines said, "What are these Hebrews doing here?" Achish said to the commanders of the Philistines, "Is not this David, the servant of King Saul of Israel, who has been with me now for days and years? Since he deserted to me I have found no fault in him to this day." But the commanders of the Philistines were angry with him; and the commanders of the Philistines said to him, "Send the man back, so that he may return to the place that you have assigned to him; he shall not go down with us to battle, or else he may become an adversary to us in the battle." . . . So David set out with his men early in the morning, to return to the land of the Philistines. But the Philistines went up to Jezreel. (I Samuel 28–29)

The account given in the biblical text does not make complete sense, for it seems to be out of chronological order.[45] It is not logical for the Philistines to encamp at Shunem in the Jezreel Valley (I Samuel 28:4); then to gather all their forces at Aphek, quite some distance to the south of the valley (I Samuel 29:1); then to dismiss David and his men (I Samuel 29:2–11); and only then to go back up to Jezreel (I Samuel 29:11) and finally fight at Mount Gilboa (I Samuel 31:1). Similarly, it makes little sense for the Israelites to encamp at Gilboa (I Samuel 28:4) and have Saul venture past the Philistines at Shunem to see the witch in Endor near Mount Tabor (I Samuel 28:6–25); then to move camp to "the fountain that is in Jezreel" (I Samuel 29:1);[46] and only then to retrace their steps to fight at Mount Gilboa (I Samuel 31:1).

It would be more logical if the Philistines first gathered their forces at Aphek, during which time David and his men would have been dismissed; then marched to Shunem in the Jezreel Valley; and finally prepared for battle while encamped at Jezreel (presumably the spring rather than the city, although the latter is not out of the question). The Israelites, in their turn, would have first camped at the spring of Ein Jezreel, during which time Saul could have visited the witch at Endor well before the arrival of the Philistines, and then moved back toward Mount Gilboa when the Philistine forces advanced to Shunem and thence to Jezreel. Such a revised scenario keeps the pairings presented in the biblical story together, while making better chronological and geographical sense: that is, first the Philistines gather at Aphek and dismiss David while the Israelites gather at Ein Jezreel and Saul visits the witch at Endor; next the Philistines march to Shunem while the Israelites retreat to Mount Gilboa; later the Philistines advance to Jezreel while the Israelites presumably maintain their position at Mount Gilboa.

The biblical account of the fighting itself is brief, only a few sentences.

> Now the Philistines fought against Israel; and the men of Israel fled before the Philistines, and many fell on Mount Gilboa. The Philistines overtook Saul and his sons; and the Philistines killed Jonathan and Abinadab and Malchishua, the sons of Saul. The battle pressed hard upon Saul; the archers found him, and he was badly wounded by them. . . . So Saul and his three sons and his armor-bearer and all his men died together on the same day. When the men of Israel who were on the other side of the valley and those beyond the Jordan saw that the men of Israel had fled and that Saul and his sons were dead, they forsook their towns and fled; and the Philistines came and occupied them. (I Samuel 31:1–3, 6–7; cf. I Chronicles 10:1–3, 6–7)

No record of the total number killed or wounded on either side is given in the biblical account, apart from a laconic note that many in the Israelite army fell and died (II Samuel 1:4). Much later, Josephus

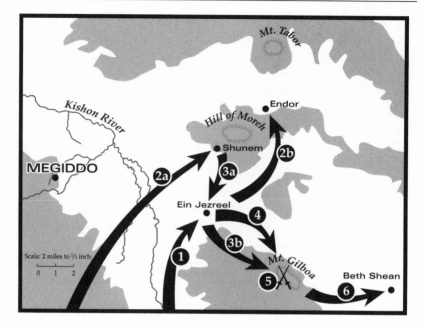

MAP 12. Saul, Jonathan, and the Philistines
1. Israelites gather at Ein Jezreel.
2a. Philistines march to Shunem,
2b. while Saul visits witch of Endor.
3a. Philistines move to Jezreel,
3b. while Israelites move to Mount Gilboa.
4. Philistines advance to Mount Gilboa.
5. Israelites are defeated in battle; Saul and Jonathan are killed.
6. Philistines march to Beth Shean and hang Saul and Jonathan on city wall.

(*Antiquities of the Jews* 6.368–7.6) claimed that many of the Philistines were killed and that many ten thousands of the Israelites were cut off (and presumably killed), but his figures are unsupported and probably exaggerated.[47]

Although the battle was clearly fought in the vicinity of Mount Gilboa—that is where many of the Israelites were reportedly killed (I Samuel 31:1)—the precise location and the exact details of the battle are not at all clear. Most scholars assume that the Philistines took advantage of the broad valley floor at the foot of Mount Gilboa to use their chariots to good advantage against the Israelites, who were quickly decimated and forced to retreat up the western slope of the mountain, where they were further annihilated.[48] However, the biblical

FIG. 7. Endor (Zev Radovan, Jerusalem)

text actually only says, "the Philistines fought against Israel; and the men of Israel fled before the Philistines, and many fell on Mount Gilboa" (I Samuel 31:1). There is no mention anywhere of where the initial encounter took place; it is only said to have ended on Mount Gilboa.

Moreover, there is no mention of the specific tactics used by either side, except for the mention of Philistine archers who badly wounded Saul (I Samuel 31:3). The single reference to the use of Philistine chariots and horsemen is given when a young Amalekite survivor reporting to David after the battle says, "I happened to be on Mount Gilboa; and there was Saul leaning upon his spear, while the chariots and the horsemen drew close to him" (II Samuel 1:6). None of the accounts mentions Israelite chariotry or horsemen. This is not surprising, though, for in all of the battles fought by Saul, Jonathan, and David against the Philistines before the battle at Mount Gilboa (cf. I Samuel 13–27), neither chariots nor cavalry are ever mentioned as part of the Israelite forces. There is no reason to assume that the Israelite army that was assembled at Gilboa under Saul was equipped any differently. For that

FIG. 8. Ein Jezreel, near the site of Jezreel (Zev Radovan, Jerusalem)

matter, the biblical text does not mention any Israelite chariotry among the forces of Deborah and Barak fighting against Sisera (Judges 4–5), nor are any Israelite chariotry listed among Gideon's forces fighting the Midianites and Amalekites (Judges 7). It appears that Yigael Yadin was correct in concluding that chariots were not extensively used by the Israelite army until the time of David.[49] They were certainly in use by the time of Solomon, David's son, however, for he had "fourteen hundred chariots and twelve thousand horses, which he stationed in the chariot cities and with the king in Jerusalem" (I Kings 10:26; cf. I Kings 9:15, I Kings 4:26, and II Chronicles 9:25).

If the Israelites were indeed already at Gilboa when the Philistines were at Shunem (as I postulated earlier in this discussion) and then maintained their position when the Philistines advanced to Jezreel, it actually seems unlikely that the battle would have been fought on the open plain at the foot of Mount Gilboa as many have previously suggested. If the lords of the Philistine army did indeed number in the hundreds and thousands (I Samuel 29:2), and if they did indeed possess chariots (II Samuel 1:6), it would make more sense for the chari-

FIG. 9. Mount Gilboa (Zev Radovan, Jerusalem)

otless Israelites to prepare for battle in a hilly area that would render absolute numbers less important and enemy chariotry as useless as possible. The western slopes of Mount Gilboa presented just such an opportunity, and the Israelites more than likely took advantage of it.[50] Thus, it seems likely that the Israelite forces were initially stationed in a defensive position on the western slopes of Mount Gilboa (rather than retreating up the mountain after being routed in the valley as most previous scholars have postulated) and that the entire battle was deliberately fought there. It would not have been the first time—nor would it be the last—that a major battle was fought on the slopes of a mountain in the Jezreel Valley. However, if such was the Israelites' plan, it unfortunately came to naught, for they lost the battle anyway, and Saul and three of his sons were killed.

Clausewitz pointed out much later, in his magisterial book of military strategy entitled *On War:*

> mountainous terrain is of no help to the defender; on the contrary . . . it favors the attacker. . . . [I]n the case of a major battle, the advantages will

all be on the side of the attacker. . . . Military history shows clearly how unsuited mountains are for decisive defensive battles.[51]

Saul's defeat proves Clausewitz's assessment to be correct, for Saul's stationing himself and his men on the slopes of Mount Gilboa, if that was indeed his plan, did not prevent the Israelites from being overrun by the Philistines.

Toward the end of the battle, after the Philistines had killed three of Saul's sons—Jonathan, Abinadab, and Malchishua—Saul took his own life rather than risk being captured or killed by the Philistines. According to one version of the story, Saul asked his armor-bearer to kill him, but the armor-bearer was unwilling, so Saul took his own sword and fell on it, thus committing a heroic suicide at his own hands.[52]

> The battle pressed hard upon Saul; the archers found him, and he was badly wounded by them. Then Saul said to his armor-bearer, "Draw your sword and thrust me through with it, so that these uncircumcised may not come and thrust me through, and make sport of me." But his armor-bearer was unwilling; for he was terrified. So Saul took his own sword and fell upon it. When his armor-bearer saw that Saul was dead, he also fell upon his sword and died with him. (I Samuel 31:3–5 and I Chronicles 10:3–5)

A slightly different version of Saul's demise is presented in II Samuel 1. Here it is reported that Saul did not personally kill himself but instead prevailed on a young Amalekite soldier to ensure his demise.

> After the death of Saul, when David had returned from defeating the Amalekites, David remained two days in Ziklag. On the third day, a man came from Saul's camp, with his clothes torn and dirt upon his head. When he came to David, he fell to the ground and did obeisance. David said to him, "Where do you come from?" He said to him, "I have escaped from the camp of Israel." David said to him, "How did things go? Tell me." He answered, "The army fled from the battle, but also many of the army fell and died; and Saul and his son Jonathan also died." Then David asked the young man who was reporting to him, "How do you know that Saul and his son Jonathan died?" The young man reporting to him said, "I happened to be on Mount Gilboa; and there was Saul leaning upon his spear, while the chariots and the horsemen drew close to him. When he looked behind him, he saw me, and called to me. I answered, 'Here sir.' And he said to me, 'Who are you?' I answered him, 'I am an Amalekite.' He said to me, 'Come, stand over me and kill me; for convulsions have seized me, and yet my life still lingers.' So I stood over him, and killed him, for I knew that he could not live after he had fallen. I took the

crown that was on his head and the armlet that was on his arm, and I have brought them here to my lord." (II Samuel 1:1–10; see also Josephus *Antiquities of the Jews* 6.368–73)

No explanation is given for the conflicting accounts, which have occasioned quite a bit of debate in the scholarly literature.[53] It is most likely that the Amalekite of II Samuel 1 represents a rhetorical device used by the author of II Samuel so that the last moments of Saul's life and his heroic death in battle could be told to an audience—in this case, to David in his camp at Ziklag—and thus confirm to some degree the account given in I Samuel 31. Even so, it is a bit surprising that the biblical text does not have more internal agreement concerning the exact details of Saul's death.

Following the battle, the Philistines cut off Saul's head and those of his three sons, including Jonathan. The bodies of Saul and his sons were stripped of armor and clothing and taken by the Philistines to Beth Shean (Beisan). There, the armor was placed in the Temple of Astarte, and the bodies were hung on the city wall, so they would be exposed to the elements and seen by all.

> The next day, when the Philistines came to strip the dead, they found Saul and his three sons fallen on Mount Gilboa. They cut off his head, stripped off his armor, and sent messengers throughout the land of the Philistines to carry the good news to the houses of their idols and to the people. They put his armor in the temple of Astarte; and they fastened his body to the wall of Beth-shan. But when the inhabitants of Jabesh-gilead heard what the Philistines had done to Saul, all the valiant men set out, traveled all night long, and took the body of Saul and the bodies of his sons from the wall of Beth-shan. They came to Jabesh and burned them there. Then they took their bones and buried them under the tamarisk tree in Jabesh, and fasted seven days. (I Samuel 31:8–13; cf. I Chronicles 10:7–12; Josephus *Antiquities of the Jews* 6.374–77)

There is no doubt that the bodies would have remained hanging from the wall at Beth Shean, rotting in the sun for an indefinite period of time, if the men of Jabesh-gilead had not rescued the bodies in a daring nighttime raid and given them a decent burial in their own city.[54] It is not clear what was done with the decapitated heads of Saul and his sons, although it is quite likely that they were sent around the land of the Philistines along with the messages of victory (I Samuel 31:9). It is not mentioned whether the men of Jabesh-gilead rescued the severed heads at the time they retrieved the mutilated bodies of Saul and his sons, and it seems rather unlikely that their body parts were successfully reunited before burial.

Thus ended Saul's career, in a futile attempt to battle once again the Philistine nemesis against which he had spent much of his career fighting. The victorious Philistines gained control of the entire Jezreel Valley and cut Saul's kingdom into two parts, just as they had planned. Saul's realm never fully recovered. Following Saul's death, the northern half of his kingdom was given over to Ishbaal, one of Saul's remaining sons, while David had himself proclaimed king over Judah, the southern part of the kingdom (II Samuel 2:1–4, 8).[55]

King David himself may well have subsequently campaigned in the Jezreel Valley, incorporating it into his fledgling kingdom ca. 1000 B.C. But no textual records left anywhere, even in the Bible, document his specific battles or conquests at any sites within the Jezreel Valley. It is not even completely clear which of the many destructions at Megiddo might be attributable to David's forces, although the destruction of Stratum VIA could be the result of a campaign by David. Local tradition does hold that a young David, long before he became king, fought and defeated the Philistine warrior Goliath at the place called ʿAyn Jalut (the "Spring of Goliath"), a few miles from Megiddo, but this is probably an erroneous story best relegated to the realm of folklore, since this famous event more likely took place near Jerusalem, far to the south of the Jezreel Valley.[56] Thus, at the moment, even if David did campaign in the Jezreel Valley, the details are currently lost in the mists of history.

CHAPTER 4

Kingdoms under Siege

In the territory of Jezreel the dogs shall eat the flesh of Jezebel; the
corpse of Jezebel shall be like dung on the field in the territory of
Jezreel, so that no one can say, This is Jezebel.

—II Kings 9:36–37

ON 31 OCTOBER 1925, during the first few days of the University of
Chicago's inaugural excavation season, a large piece of limestone was
brought down from the top of the mound of Megiddo by a workman
helping to construct the dig house for the excavators. The house, complete with a tennis court courtesy of money donated by the Rocke-
fellers, was to be situated at the base of the mound. It is still standing
there today, but has long since been converted into the present-day
museum, gift shop, and restaurant. The block of stone had been recovered from a dump of discarded earth and debris near the eastern edge
of the mound, where it had been thrown by Schumacher's workmen
during the previous set of excavations twenty years earlier.[1]

It just so happened that one of the Egyptian foremen working for
the Chicago team serendipitously noticed that the limestone block had
faint traces of hieroglyphs inscribed on it and called attention to this
fact. James Henry Breasted, by then director of the Oriental Institute at
the University of Chicago, came to visit the site a few weeks later and
identified the royal cartouche on the block as that of Pharaoh
Shoshenq I, the Libyan mercenary who founded the Twenty-second
Dynasty of Egypt and ruled ca. 945–923 B.C.[2] The fragment came from
an inscribed victory monument that would originally have stood more
than ten feet high but that had been broken up and reused after
Shoshenq's death. If comparisons with other Egyptian victory stelae are
correct, there would have been a scene of Shoshenq I worshiping the
god Amon at the top of the Megiddo stele, with an inscription recording the king's victories covering the entire lower part of the monument.[3]

The fragment that was found that October day in 1925 is from the
upper right-hand part of the carved scene on the monument. The two

cartouches present on the fragment read simply, "Hedj-kheper-Re, Bright is the form of (the sun-god) Re, Amun's beloved, Shoshenq (I)."[4] This type of victory monument was usually erected by an Egyptian pharaoh in a foreign land, particularly at cities that they had conquered and subsequently occupied.[5] Similar victory stelae had been erected centuries earlier in nearby Beth Shean by the pharaohs Seti I and Ramses II, following their successful campaigns in Syria-Palestine.

Had Shoshenq I indeed fought a battle and captured Megiddo ca. 925 B.C., as the inscribed fragment found at the site seemed to indicate? He certainly had, as the pharaoh himself attested in another, much larger inscription carved on the wall of the so-called Bubasite Portal at the Temple of Amon at Karnak in Egypt. James Breasted had in fact already published a discussion of this inscription in volume 4 of his monumental *Ancient Records of Egypt*, which may explain the ease with which he identified Shoshenq's royal cartouche on the Megiddo fragment.[6]

According to Shoshenq's inscribed account at Karnak, not only Megiddo but also Taanach, Shunem, and other cities in the Jezreel Valley, along with a large number of additional towns in Israel and the Negev, fell victim one after the other to the victorious Egyptian army. His campaign in Syria-Palestine should probably be seen as an attempt to recapture the earlier glory days of Egyptian dominance when

FIG. 10. Fragment of Shoshenq I's stele at Megiddo (Fisher 1929, fig. 7B. Courtesy of the Oriental Institute of The University of Chicago.)

FIG. 11. Reconstruction of Shoshenq I's stele at Megiddo (Fisher 1929, fig. 9. Courtesy of the Oriental Institute of The University of Chicago.)

Canaan was regarded as peripheral territory belonging to the Egyptian Empire. Moreover, if Shoshenq I is the same person as the Egyptian pharaoh Shishak mentioned in I Kings and II Chronicles in the Bible, as is probably the case, he also fought in Judah with twelve hundred chariots and sixty thousand cavalry during this same campaign, besieging Jerusalem and carrying away a great ransom.

> In the fifth year of King Rehoboam, King Shishak of Egypt came up against Jerusalem; he took away the treasures of the house of the Lord

and the treasures of the king's house; he took everything. He also took
away all the shields of gold that Solomon had made. (I Kings 14:25–26;
cf. II Chronicles 12:2–9)

The cities named in the Egyptian and the biblical accounts are
almost completely different (only the city of Aijalon may be the same in
both lists).[7] This is undoubtedly because the biblical record is primarily
concerned with events in Judah, while the Egyptian account empha-
sizes the major military events that took place in Israel and the Negev,
since Judah offered only minimal resistance. It is highly unlikely that
these are records of two different campaigns. Thus, the battle fought by
Shoshenq I (Shishak) at Megiddo was part of a larger Egyptian campaign in Israel, Judah, and the Negev following the end of the United
Monarchy that had been established by David and Solomon during the
previous century.[8]

The Jezreel Valley was clearly within the kingdom maintained by
Solomon, David's son and successor. The cities of the valley were split
among three of the kingdom's administrative districts. Megiddo served
as the seat of the Fifth District, with a man named Baana, son of Ahilud,
serving as the district governor and living in the city itself (I Kings
4:7–12).[9] Solomon does not seem to have fought a battle within the
Jezreel Valley during his reign, but the Bible records that he fortified
Megiddo and possibly turned it into one of his "chariot cities."

> This is the account of the forced labor that King Solomon conscripted to
> build the house of the Lord and his own house, the Millo and the wall of
> Jerusalem, Hazor, Megiddo, Gezer . . . , as well as all of Solomon's storage
> cities, the cities for his chariots, the cities for his cavalry, and whatever
> Solomon desired to build, in Jerusalem, in Lebanon, and in all the land
> of his dominion. (I Kings 9:15–19)

Precisely why Solomon fortified Megiddo, Gezer, and Hazor is not
clear, but it probably had to do with the rise to prominence of
Shoshenq I in Egypt. Solomon was indeed wise to have feared the
pharaoh's growing power, as Shoshenq's campaign into Syria-Palestine
after Solomon's death shows.

The actual analysis of Shoshenq's long, inscribed account at Karnak
has proven surprisingly difficult over the years.[10] The text, written on
the wall of the Temple of Amon, consists primarily of the names of the
captured cities and towns in Syria-Palestine, written in ten rows. The
Egyptologists who first copied down the inscription believed that all of

the names were to be read from right to left, and they numbered them accordingly (nos. 1–39), reading the first three rows as follows:

> (Row I, starting at the right-hand side): (1–9) The Nine Bows, (10) Introduction, (11) Gaza, (12) Makkedah, (13) Rubuti;

> (Row II, starting at the right-hand side): (14) Taanach, (15) Shunem, (16) Beth Shean, (17) Rehob, (18) Hapharaim, (19) Adoraim, (20) [Lost], (21) Shaud[y], (22) Mahanaim, (23) Gibeon, (24) Beth-horon, (25) Kiriathaim?, (26) Aijalon;

> (Row III, starting at the right-hand side): (27) Megiddo, (28) Adar, (29) Yadhamelek, (30) [Heb]el?, (31) Honim, (32) Aruna, (33) Borim, (34) Gathpadalla, (35) Yehem, (36) Betharuma, (37) Kekry, (38) Socoh, (39) Bethtappuah.

If the names are read in this order, they do not make geographical sense and do not look like a proper itinerary of a military campaign. For example, Shunem and Taanach, both sites in the Jezreel Valley, should be written next to Megiddo, but instead they are separated from Megiddo by eleven other names, none of which are located in the Jezreel Valley. A breakthrough may have been made by Benjamin Mazar, who suggested that the rows of this list were not meant to be read each from right to left, but rather should be read boustrophedon, that is, reading from right to left on row I, then dropping directly down to row II and reading from left to right, then dropping directly down to row III and reading from right to left, and so on, in a movement like that of an ox plowing a field, which is the image from which the term *boustrophedon* is derived.[11] Thus, the names in rows I–III should actually be read in the following order, starting at the right-hand side of the first row:

$\Leftarrow$13, 12, 11, 10, 9, 8, 7, 6, 5, 4, 3, 2, 1$\Leftarrow$
⇓
$\Rightarrow$26, 25, 24, 23, 22, 21, 20, 19, 18, 17, 16, 15, 14$\Rightarrow$
⇓
39, 38, 37, 36, 35, 34, 33, 32, 31, 30, 29, 28, 27$\Leftarrow$

Shishak's order of conquest would therefore proceed from (16) Beth Shean to (15) Shunem to (14) Taanach to (27) Megiddo to (28) Adar and on through the Jezreel Valley until passing through (32) Aruna, which makes a great deal of sense from geographical, topographical, and military points of view.

A similar suggestion, perhaps more acceptable to the Egyptologists who have pointed out that the Egyptians did not usually write in the boustrophedon manner, is that the second row of names may have simply been miscopied and placed in reverse order, either by the modern Egyptologists responsible for recording the inscription or by the ancient Egyptian scribes/artists inscribing the names on the wall of the temple.[12] If this is the case, we need to renumber the names in row II so that Aijalon is number 14 and Taanach is number 26. Then the names in rows I–III can simply be read from 1–39 in order, reading each line from right to left. This results in the same reading as does reading *boustrophedon,* with Shunem and Taanach immediately preceding Megiddo in the list.

Thus, whether the text should be read *boustrophedon* as Mazar has suggested or the second row of names was simply miscopied and must be read in reverse order, Shoshenq I's primary campaign force appears to have set out from Gaza for Judah and the Shephelah; then to have moved on to Transjordan and up the Jordan Valley to Beth Shean (Beisan); then to have turned west and marched through the Jezreel Valley, capturing Shunem, Taanach, and Megiddo in that order, followed by other smaller sites in the valley; and then to have turned south again through the Wadi ʿAra and the Musmus Pass, cut down across the Plain of Sharon, and headed back to Egypt. A secondary campaign force may have left the main body camped at Megiddo and fought in the area of the Negev before rejoining the rest of the army.[13]

It is also possible that Shoshenq I did not just send a single huge army that followed a set route of conquest but may have instead sent out several different smaller forces of soldiers, each with a different objective, such as the Jezreel Valley or the Negev. If so, the main force, led by Shoshenq I himself, probably attacked and subdued Judah and then proceeded north and made their headquarters at Megiddo, staying there for quite some time while sending out smaller contingents in various directions to fight in nearby areas.[14]

Whichever scenario is preferred, it is clear from his inscription on the temple wall at Karnak in Egypt that Shoshenq I claimed to have captured Megiddo. Although the details of the battle are not given, the fragment from Shoshenq's victory monument found at Megiddo by the Chicago excavators indicates that Shoshenq's claim at Karnak was not an idle boast. Why the campaign itself was conducted in the first place is not completely clear, although it seems likely that Shoshenq I had long wanted to invade Judah and Israel, perhaps to return Egypt to its previous days of glory as I have already suggested, and that he simply

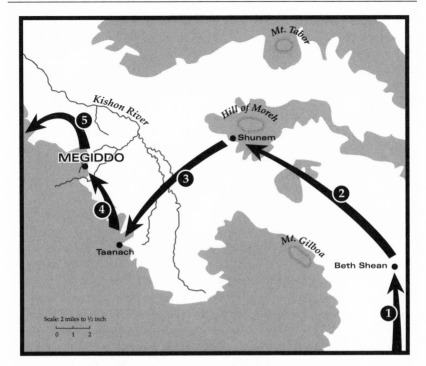

MAP 13. Shoshenq I (Shishak) in the Jezreel Valley
1. Egyptian forces move up Jordan Valley,
2. then march to Shunem,
3. continue to Taanach,
4. then to Megiddo,
5. and finally head west through the Jezreel Valley and south back to Egypt.

postponed putting an army into the field until after Solomon died.[15] A fragment of a stele from Karnak suggests that there may have been a rebellion in Syria-Palestine that provided Shoshenq I with an excuse to attack.

> Now, My Majesty found that [. . . they] were killing [. . .] army-leaders. His Majesty was upset about them. . . . [His Majesty went forth,] his chariotry accompanying him without (the enemy's) knowing it. His Majesty made great slaughter among them, . . . at the edge of the Bitter Lakes.[16]

Thus, to judge from the inscribed fragment found accidentally by the Chicago excavators at Megiddo in 1925, from Shoshenq's own inscription at Karnak, and from the biblical account given in I Kings

and II Chronicles, the city that Solomon fortified at Megiddo was captured by the pharaoh Shoshenq I (Shishak) five years into the reign of
Solomon's successor Rehoboam, as part of a successful Egyptian campaign to Syria-Palestine ca. 925 B.C. That Shoshenq I did not completely destroy Megiddo when he captured the city is shown by the very
fact that he erected the victory monument, something that the Egyptians generally only did in cities that they subsequently occupied.[17] It is
generally thought that the city at Megiddo labeled Stratum VA–IVB by
the Chicago excavators is the city fortified by Solomon and captured by
Shoshenq I. Only a few buildings in this level were destroyed by fire,
including building 10 and parts of palace 6000; the majority remained
standing and unscathed. Shoshenq I's capture of Megiddo was therefore probably swift and may even have been accomplished without the
need for a siege or protracted tactical maneuvers.[18]

Once Shoshenq I's campaign in Syria-Palestine ended, any Egyptian
army units or political personnel left behind as an occupying force do
not seem to have stayed long, even in crucial cities, such as Megiddo.
Shoshenq I apparently died soon after this victorious campaign, perhaps within the year or immediately thereafter, and the long Egyptian
involvement in Syria-Palestine effectively came to an end then.[19]

In part because of Shoshenq I's campaign to Syria-Palestine, any
hope that the kingdoms of Israel and Judah would be reunited and
the United Monarchy reestablished was shattered forever. Although
their histories continued to be irrevocably intertwined, the two kingdoms remained separate entities until Israel was conquered by the
Assyrians in 721 B.C. and Judah by the Babylonians in 586 B.C. The
Jezreel Valley, particularly the cities of Megiddo and Jezreel, figured
prominently in the kingdom of Israel during these centuries.
Megiddo was rebuilt and greatly enhanced, most likely by the Israelite
kings Omri and Ahab (Omri's son), who were probably responsible
for digging the famous water tunnel and constructing the so-called
stables of Stratum IVA. Jezreel became an auxiliary residence for
these kings and grew in importance, becoming second only to the
state capital at Samaria.

At the city of Jezreel (modern Zarin), Jehu staged his infamous coup
ca. 841 B.C., in which Joram, king of Israel, and his mother, Jezebel,
widow of King Ahab, met an untimely end. This fulfilled a prophecy
made years earlier, which had laid a curse on the House of Ahab for
having caused the death of an innocent man. Some seventy additional
descendants of Ahab were also slain during Jehu's coup, as was

Ahaziah, the newly anointed king of Judah, who had the misfortune of being at Jezreel when the vengeful Jehu arrived, as well as some forty-two of Ahaziah's relatives, who were on their way to visit him at Jezreel. Mortally wounded, Ahaziah managed to flee as far as Megiddo, only to die there.[20]

The curse laid on Ahab and his descendants stemmed from the death of Naboth, a prominent member of a wealthy Jezreelite family. According to the well-known story told in I Kings, Ahab, king of Israel, desired the vineyard that Naboth possessed outside the city of Jezreel, but Naboth refused to give it up. Queen Jezebel, wife of Ahab, proceeded to have Naboth falsely accused of blasphemy, put on trial, and then stoned to death outside the city. She and Ahab then simply seized the vineyard that Ahab had so greatly desired (I Kings 21).[21] Josephus records the subsequent events.

> God had great indignation at it, and sent Elijah the prophet to the field of Naboth, to speak to Ahab, and to say to him, that he had slain the true owner of that field unjustly. And as soon as he came to him, and the king had said that he might do with him what he pleased, . . . Elijah said, that in that very place in which the dead body of Naboth was eaten by dogs both his own blood and that of his wife's should be shed, and that all his family should perish, because he had been so insolently wicked, and had slain a citizen unjustly, and contrary to the laws of his country. Hereupon Ahab began to be sorry for the things he had done, and to repent of them; and he put on sackcloth, and went barefoot and would not touch any food; he also confessed his sins, and endeavored thus to appease God. But God said to the prophet, that while Ahab was living he would put off the punishment of his family, because he repented of those insolent crimes he had been guilty of, but that still he would fulfill his threatening under Ahab's son; which message the prophet delivered to the king. (Josephus *Antiquities of the Jews* 8.355–62)[22]

Some years later, during the summer of 841 B.C., after Ahab had died and Joram had come to the throne of Israel, Joram led the army of Israel against King Hazael of Aram (a kingdom located in modern Syria). At the battle at Ramoth-gilead, across the Jordan River from the Jezreel Valley, Joram was wounded, perhaps by an Aramean arrow, and apparently severely enough that he was taken from the battlefield and brought to Jezreel to recover in relative peace. Ahaziah, king of Judah and himself a relative of Joram, came to Jezreel to visit Joram during his convalescence (II Kings 9:14–16; II Chronicles 22:5–7; Josephus *Antiquities of the Jews* 9.105–13).[23]

Jehu, a commander in King Joram's army, took advantage of the king's absence to stage a coup and have himself declared king. Jehu may actually have been more than a mere army commander, for he is described in Assyrian records as being a member of the House of Omri, established by Joram's grandfather. He thus may have been a relative of Joram and the royal family.[24] Jehu rode quickly to Jezreel before the news of the coup became generally known, but he was identified by the guards at the gate long before he arrived at the city. Joram and Ahaziah therefore had time to mount their chariots and proceed outside the city, where they met Jehu and their fate in Naboth's vineyard.

> When Joram saw Jehu, he said, "Is it peace, Jehu?" He [Jehu] answered, "What peace can there be, so long as the many whoredoms and sorceries of your mother Jezebel continue?" Then Joram reined about and fled, saying to Ahaziah, "Treason, Ahaziah!" Jehu drew his bow with all his strength, and shot Joram between the shoulders, so that the arrow pierced his heart; and he sank in his chariot. Jehu said to his aide Bidkar, "Lift him out, and throw him on the plot of ground belonging to Naboth the Jezreelite; for remember, when you and I rode side by side behind his father Ahab how the Lord uttered this oracle against him: 'For the blood of Naboth and for the blood of his children that I saw yesterday, says the Lord, I swear I will repay you on this very plot of ground.' Now therefore lift him out and throw him on the plot of ground, in accordance with the word of the Lord." (II Kings 9:22–26; cf. Josephus *Antiquities of the Jews* 9.114–21)

According to the account in II Kings, upon seeing Joram cut down in cold blood, Ahaziah tried to flee in the direction of Beth-haggan, toward modern Jenin. According to this account, either Jehu himself or Jehu's men pursued Ahaziah and shot him also, by the town of Ibleam, but were unable to physically capture him; Ahaziah changed direction and made it as far as Megiddo, but he died there, most likely having bled almost to death during the wild chariot ride; his body was subsequently taken to Jerusalem and buried there in a tomb with his ancestors (II Kings 9:27–28; cf. Josephus *Antiquities of the Jews* 9.114–21).[25]

The account in II Chronicles tells a slightly different story concerning Ahaziah's demise, beginning with the claim that he had in fact been allied with Joram against King Hazael of Aram and had been present at the battle at Ramoth-gilead when Joram was wounded. This account states that following the murder of Joram in Naboth's vineyard, Ahaziah made good his escape from Jezreel, unscathed by Jehu, but was subsequently captured while hiding in Samaria. According to this

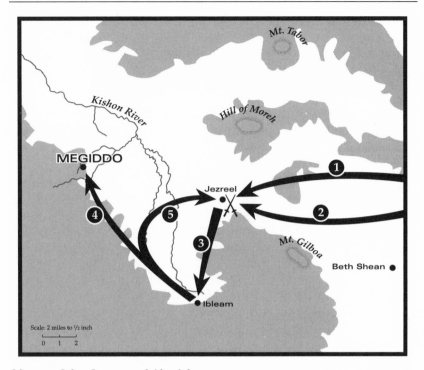

MAP 14. Jehu, Joram, and Ahaziah
1. Joram goes to Jezreel from Ramoth-gilead to recuperate; Ahaziah follows.
2. Jehu rides to Jezreel from Ramoth-gilead.
3. Joram is killed at Jezreel; Ahaziah flees but is mortally wounded near Ibleam.
4. Ahaziah reaches Megiddo, where he dies.
5. Jehu returns to Jezreel and kills Jezebel.

account, he was then brought to Jehu and put to death. No mention is here made of Ahaziah being wounded while in his chariot, of him dying at Megiddo, or of his body subsequently being taken to Jerusalem for burial (II Chronicles 22:5–9). However, the Chronicler either mistakenly or deliberately transfers virtually all of these different or missing details to the subsequent story concerning the death of Josiah, king of Judah, at Megiddo in 609 B.C. (discussed later in this chapter).

Following the murders of Joram and Ahaziah, Jehu turned his attention to Jezebel, widow of Ahab, mother of Joram, daughter of the Phoenician king Ethbaal of Sidon, and, at that time, queen mother in Israel. She was not only blamed for orchestrating the unjust death of

Naboth for the sake of his vineyard but also accused of worshiping foreign gods, such as Baal. Entering the city of Jezreel, Jehu saw Jezebel waiting for him. She was looking out of a second-story window, having painted her eyes and adorned her head. The account in II Kings relates:

> He looked up to the window and said, "Who is on my side? Who?" Two or three eunuchs looked down at him. He said, "Throw her down!" So they threw her down; some of her blood spattered the wall and on the horses, which trampled on her. Then he went in and ate and drank; he said, "See to that cursed woman and bury her; for she is a king's daughter." But when they went to bury her, they found no more of her than the skull and the feet and the palms of her hands. When they came back and told him, he said, "This is the word of the Lord, which he spoke by his servant Elijah the Tishbite, 'In the territory of Jezreel the dogs shall eat the flesh of Jezebel; the corpse of Jezebel shall be like dung on the field in the territory of Jezreel, so that no one can say, This is Jezebel.'" (II Kings 9:32–37; cf. Josephus *Antiquities of the Jews* 9.122–24)

Thus, the curse on the House of Ahab was brought to fruition by Jehu with the murders of Joram and Jezebel, the subsequent slaying of all Ahab's relatives in Jezreel, and the beheading of an additional seventy sons of Ahab living in Samaria, whose severed heads Jehu ordered sent to him and had stacked in two piles outside the city gates of Jezreel. Ahaziah seems to have been an unfortunate, although perhaps not so innocent, bystander who was caught up and killed in this coup. As I already mentioned, some forty-two of Ahaziah's relatives, en route to Jezreel to visit Ahaziah, were also unfortunate enough to run into Jehu and were slain as well (II Kings 10:1–14; II Chronicles 22:8; cf. Josephus *Antiquities of the Jews* 9.125–31).[26] Jehu then apparently proceeded to Samaria, where he put to death "all who were left to Ahab . . . until he had wiped them out" (II Kings 10:17).

Recent archaeological discoveries may shed additional light on the story of Jehu's rebellion and on the death of Joram and Ahaziah. Three fragments of an Old Aramaic inscription discovered at Tel Dan in 1993 and 1994 have been attributed to a stele of King Hazael of Aram. Hazael had usurped the throne of Aram only a short time before Jehu's revolt, between 845 and 842 B.C., and was the very same king against whom Joram (and perhaps Ahaziah as well) was fighting when he received the wound that caused him to retreat to Jezreel.[27] If the restoration and translation of the inscription on this stele are correct, Hazael claims that he, not Jehu, killed Joram and Ahaziah.

And Hadad went in front of me, [and] I departed from the seven [...] of my kingdom/kings, and I slew [might]y . . . kin[gs], who harnessed tho[usands . . . of cha]riots and thousands [of] chariot horses. [I killed Jo]ram . . . son of A[hab], king of Israel, and [I] killed [Ahaz]iahu son of [Joram, kin]g of the House of David. And I set [their towns into ruins and turned] their land into [desolation . . .].[28]

As the excavators of the stele themselves have pointed out, there is a serious contradiction between the inscription found at Tel Dan, in which Hazael claims credit for killing Joram and Ahaziah, and the biblical account found in II Kings 9, which blames Jehu for these murders. However, a verse in I Kings might help resolve the contradiction, for it implies that the two men were probably working together.

Then the Lord said to him [Elijah], "Go, return on your way to the wilderness of Damascus; when you arrive, you shall anoint Hazael as king over Aram. Also you shall anoint Jehu son of Nimshi as king over Israel. . . . Whoever escapes from the sword of Hazael, Jehu shall kill." (I Kings 19:15–17)[29]

Although the exact relationship of Jehu and his rebellion to the invasion of Hazael and his Aramaic forces is unclear (in large part because the details of the Aramaic invasion are currently lost to scholars and historians), it has recently been suggested that Jehu could not have staged his revolt without the implicit consent of his Aramean opponent in the battle at Ramoth-gilead, that is, Hazael himself. Otherwise, Jehu could not have safely left the battle and driven his chariot to Jezreel to kill Joram and Ahaziah. In short, Jehu's coup may have been underwritten or supported by Hazael to a large extent. It therefore also seems a distinct possibility that Jehu's subsequent rule over Israel may have been as a vassal of or at least in alliance with King Hazael of Aram. Perhaps it is best to assign joint credit, or pin joint blame, on both Jehu and Hazael for the murders of Joram and Ahaziah. Jehu may well have committed the murders himself, but if so, Hazael apparently saw Jehu as his agent or vassal acting on his behalf and therefore subsequently took the credit on his own stele.[30]

On a related note, a fiery destruction recorded at the site of Jezreel by the modern excavators and assigned by them to Jehu's coup might instead be from its subsequent capture and conquest by Hazael. It has recently been suggested that the destructions noted at a whole series of sites in the Jezreel Valley, including Megiddo, Taanach, and Yoqneam, in addition to Jezreel, might be assigned to Hazael's victorious campaign against the Israelites. At least one of the current excavators of Megiddo agrees that this is a distinct possibility, but the hypothesis remains to be fully explored.[31]

Upon taking the throne of Israel, Jehu probably not only had to deal with Hazael of Aram but was also immediately faced with an invasion by the dreaded Neo-Assyrians, led by King Shalmaneser III. This was already Shalmaneser's fifth campaign to the West from his homelands in Mesopotamia, and it is dated to 841 B.C., which means that Jehu's reign got off to a rocky start, probably in the same year that he usurped the throne of Israel. The campaign is recorded on the so-called Black Obelisk, an inscribed limestone stele that stood about six and a half feet high and was discovered by Austen Henry Layard at Nimrud (on the Tigris River in modern Iraq) in 1846.[32] On one of the panels of the Black Obelisk, Jehu is shown prostrating himself with his forehead to the ground in front of Shalmaneser. The accompanying inscription reads: "Tribute of Iaua [Jehu], son of Omri. Silver, gold, a golden bowl, a golden beaker, golden goblets, pitchers of gold, tin, staves for the hand of the king, [and] javelins, I [Shalmaneser] received from him." There is no mention in the Bible of Jehu paying tribute to Shalmaneser, but three additional Assyrian inscriptions also refer to "Jehu, son of Omri," and imply that Jehu and his descendants became loyal vassals following the Assyrian campaign of 841 B.C.[33]

The Neo-Assyrian army swept through Israel again in 733–732 B.C., this time under the command of Tiglath-Pileser III, known as "Pul" in the Bible (II Kings 15:19–20, 29–30). His army stormed southward from the Beqa' Valley in Lebanon, conquering Upper Galilee, Hazor, Kedesh, Yiron, and Merom in short order. Ramoth-gilead and the "land beyond Jordan" fell to Tiglath-Pileser III next, followed by "Galilee of the nations" as Isaiah describes it (Isaiah 9:1), which has been identified as the Jezreel Valley by some scholars.[34]

At least one battle (probably more) was undoubtedly fought in the Jezreel Valley during Tiglath-Pileser III's campaign. The town of Dabara (biblical *Daberath*/later *Daburiya*) just west of Mount Tabor and the town of Samhuna (biblical *Shimon/Shimron*) near the northwestern edge of the Jezreel Valley may be mentioned in Tiglath-Pileser III's combined account of his campaign and list of exiles deported from the area in 733–732 B.C.: "[I razed to the gr]ou[nd xx cities] of the 16 districts of the land of Bit [Humri (that is, the Land of Omri, i.e. Israel) . . . xx captives of the city of Da]bara . . . 650 captives of the city of Sa[mhuna . . .]." It is unlikely that these cities would have capitulated and their inhabitants been deported without a fight, but further details are unfortunately not available in this account, and no additional records documenting these events have yet come to light.[35]

Neo-Assyrian armies marched past Megiddo at least twice more during the reign of Sargon II, in 721–720 B.C. and 713–712 B.C., during campaigns aimed further south, against Samaria and Ashdod, respectively. It is not clear if any battles were fought in the Jezreel Valley during either of these campaigns. Half a century later, during Esarhaddon's second and successful attempt to invade Egypt in 671 B.C., the Neo-Assyrian army once again probably marched past Megiddo at a time when the Jezreel Valley was a "contested periphery" (see chap. 5), but again it is not clear if any battles were fought in the Jezreel Valley during this campaign.[36]

With the fall of Samaria to Sargon II in 722–721 B.C., the kingdom of Israel ceased to exist and the land was completely annexed by Assyria. The city of Megiddo, perhaps flush with new immigrants courtesy of the Assyrian practice of moving captive populations around the empire, eventually became the capital of the Assyrian province of Magiddu and remained in this position for more than a century. The province of Magiddu included not only the Jezreel Valley but also the Beth Shean Valley and probably at least Lower Galilee as well. As the capital of this province, the city of Megiddo is mentioned several times in Neo-Assyrian records, and the name of one governor of Megiddo, a certain Itti-Adad-aninu, is specifically recorded for the year 679 B.C.[37]

The end of the Omride-period occupation of Megiddo, assigned to Stratum IVA by the excavators, is marked by some evidence for destruction in the so-called governor's quarters (building 338) and elsewhere on the site, which probably occurred during Tiglath-Pileser III's invasion of 733–732 B.C. The following city of Stratum III has a completely new layout, with buildings strongly reminiscent of Assyrian architectural styles. Almost certainly we are looking at the Assyrian provincial capital in this level at Megiddo.[38]

Megiddo and the Jezreel Valley remained firmly under Assyrian domination, as part of the far-flung Neo-Assyrian Empire, until the coming of the Babylonians at the beginning of the sixth century B.C. But events did not remain peaceful in the area under the Assyrians. The death of Josiah, king of Judah and the last effective royal descendant of the House of David, at the hands of Pharaoh Necho II of Egypt at Megiddo in 609 B.C. was like a stone thrown into a pond, for it had a larger ripple effect with enormous repercussions. Jehu's assassination of Joram and Ahaziah may have been a catastrophic blow for both Israel and Judah, but Necho's regicide of Josiah was literally a disaster of biblical proportions for the entire Western world. Moreover, the manner of Josiah's death remains an unsolved murder mystery for the ages.

Josiah had come to the throne of Judah in 639 B.C. as a smooth-cheeked eight-year-old boy. Midway through his reign, he instituted a series of far-reaching reforms when a scroll of laws (probably a copy of Deuteronomy) was "found" in the Temple in Jerusalem.[39] Realizing that the people of Judah had strayed, Josiah implemented sweeping religious and political reforms, which included expanding Judah's territory to the north and annexing Samaria and the Jezreel Valley. Hailed by later writers as a "second David," not least because he was the legitimate descendant of the House of David, Josiah set Judah on a road aimed to bring his people back to the greatness of the days of the United Monarchy three centuries earlier.

Unfortunately, when Josiah died at the hands of Pharaoh Necho II of Egypt, his dreams for a Judean renaissance were buried with him. For many scholars and students of religion and history, therefore, the meeting of Josiah and Necho II at Megiddo in 609 B.C. is the most significant of all the events that have occurred in the Jezreel Valley during the past four thousand years, because of the importance of Josiah's ongoing reforms and the immediate halt that his death brought to them.

On the surface, reconstructing the events at Megiddo that led to Josiah's death in 609 B.C. would seem to be relatively straightforward, for the accounts include not only II Kings 23:29–30 and II Chronicles 35:20–25 within the Bible itself but also 1 Esdras 25–32 of the Apocrypha and a recounting by Josephus (*Antiquities of the Jews* 10.74). However, precisely these varying accounts have caused the problem, for, like eyewitnesses at a crime scene, each tells a different version of what occurred. Moreover, various modern translations of the Bible have contributed to the confusion, for each presents a slightly different picture of the events.[40]

If we reconstruct the events by combining all of the available sources, the story proceeds as follows: In the late spring or early summer of the year 609 B.C., Pharaoh Necho II of Egypt and his army were hastening to the aid of their ally Assyria, preparing to fight against their common foe Babylonia. The battle was to be fought at Carchemish in northern Syria, and Necho's army had to traverse the length of Syria-Palestine to get there. Necho asked permission from Josiah, king of

Judah, to march through his lands en route to northern Syria and the upcoming battle with the Babylonians. Rather than granting permission to the Egyptian king, Josiah and his army instead marched to the Jezreel Valley and waited for the Egyptian army to emerge from the Musmus Pass (Wadi ʿAra). Why they did this is not entirely clear, although it is possible that Josiah was either under pressure from the Babylonians to do so or wanted to defend his newly annexed territory.

When the Egyptians gathered in the Jezreel Valley near Megiddo after traversing the narrow and dangerous mountain pass (just as Thutmose III's soldiers had done nearly a thousand years before), they found the Judean army waiting. Josiah climbed into his chariot and rode up and down his front lines while in disguise, encouraging the men. He sounded the attack and prepared to watch his forces annihilate the Egyptian invaders. Just as the battle got underway, however, an Egyptian archer let fly with an arrow and struck Josiah, mortally wounding him. Either dead or dying, Josiah was transferred to a second chariot and spirited south to Jerusalem, where he was buried, along with his dreams for a rejuvenated Judah.

The grieving Judeans set Jehoahaz, son of Josiah, on the throne, while Necho and his Egyptian army proceeded north to link up with the Assyrians and fight a great battle at Carchemish against the Babylonians, only to be soundly defeated. While returning to Egypt, Necho summoned Jehoahaz to meet him at Riblah in Syria, then removed him from the Judean throne and set up another son of Josiah, Jehoiakim, to rule Judah instead. Jehoahaz was taken to Egypt, where he later died, while Jehoiakim and the Judeans were left to face Nebuchadnezzar and the marauding Babylonians just a few years later.

There are grave problems with the preceding hypothetical reconstruction. The major stumbling block is simply this: although it is quite possible that there was indeed a battle at Megiddo—perhaps even a surprise attack by Josiah on Necho's army—and that Josiah was killed during the course of that battle, there is also a good possibility that there was no battle fought at Megiddo at all in 609 B.C. Since, however, according to all accounts, Josiah clearly met his fate at Megiddo at that time, the one-hundred-thousand-dollar question is, Did Josiah die while fighting against the Egyptians at Megiddo, or was he murdered there by Necho II? Was he killed during the heat of battle, or was he treacherously assassinated on the orders of the Egyptian pharaoh? The case hinges on the different accounts given in the Bible, the Apocrypha, and Josephus, as well as on the different translations found in

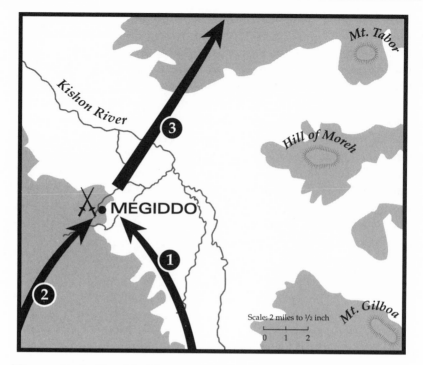

MAP 15. Necho II and Josiah
1. Josiah and his men advance from Jerusalem.
2. Necho II and his men march from Egypt via the Wadi ʿAra (Musmus Pass).
3. Necho kills Josiah and continues marching to Carchemish.

various modern editions of the Bible.[41] It is a mystery worthy of Hercule Poirot and his "little grey cells," as Agatha Christie would have said.

Virtually all authorities accept the minimalistic account found in II Kings at face value, although some suggest that it might be an addition or appendix added by a later writer.[42] Most modern editions of the Bible translate this verse as follows:

> In his days Pharaoh Neco king of Egypt went up to the king of Assyria to the river Euphrates. King Josiah went to meet him; and Pharaoh Neco slew him at Megiddo, when he saw him. His servants carried him dead in a chariot from Megiddo, brought him to Jerusalem, and buried him in his own tomb. (II Kings 23:29–30)

The original Hebrew text states that Necho "went up against the king of Assyria," rather than "went up to the king of Assyria." This would mean

that Necho was on his way to fight against the Assyrians rather than to
ally with them against the Babylonians. This is an obvious historical
error, since it is known from other sources that the Egyptians and the
Assyrians were allies in fighting against the Babylonians at the battle of
Carchemish in 609 B.C. Modern scholars have long tried to explain this
error in the Hebrew text, which was perhaps deliberate on the part of
the redactor of this section.[43] In the meantime, almost all modern
translations have long since "corrected" the text to read that Necho
"went up to the king of Assyria" rather than the original "went up
against the king of Assyria."

Some versions of the Bible translate the sentence concerning the
meeting of Necho and Josiah rather differently, contributing even
more to the confusion. The *New Student Bible* (New International Version) translates this verse as follows:

> While Josiah was king, Pharaoh Neco king of Egypt went up to the
> Euphrates River to help the king of Assyria. King Josiah marched out to
> meet him in battle, but Neco faced him and killed him at Megiddo.
> Josiah's servants brought his body in a chariot from Megiddo to
> Jerusalem and buried him in his own tomb.

The original Hebrew text of II Kings 23:29–30 makes no mention of
any battle, stating only that Necho slew Josiah "when he saw him." The
translators of the New International Version have incorrectly added
words that were not present in the original Hebrew text and have
thereby substantially changed the meaning of what II Kings says transpired at Megiddo in 609 B.C. The same improper translation occurs in
other editions of the Bible as well.[44]

One does not have to go very far to see how this mistranslation
occurred, for the translators of the New International Version simply
and erroneously extrapolated from the longer account found later in II
Chronicles.

> After all this, when Josiah had set the temple in order, King Neco of
> Egypt went up to fight at Carchemish on the Euphrates and Josiah went
> out against him. But Neco sent envoys to him, saying, "What have I to do
> with you, king of Judah? I am not coming against you today, but against
> the house with which I am at war; and God has commanded me to hurry.
> Cease opposing God, who is with me, so that he will not destroy you." But
> Josiah would not turn away from him, but disguised himself in order to
> fight with him. He did not listen to the words of Neco from the mouth of
> God, but joined battle in the plain of Megiddo. The archers shot King

Josiah; and the king said to his servants, "Take me away, for I am badly wounded." So his servants took him out of the chariot and carried him in his second chariot and brought him to Jerusalem. There he died, and was buried in the tombs of his ancestors. All Judah and Jerusalem mourned for Josiah. Jeremiah also uttered a lament for Josiah, and all the singing men and singing women have spoken of Josiah in their laments to this day. They made these a custom in Israel; they are recorded in the Laments. (II Chronicles 35:20–25)

Where did the Chronicler get this longer and more detailed version of the story of Josiah's death at the hands of Pharaoh Necho II of Egypt? While it is possible that the Chronicler made use of some details available in the Book of Jeremiah (which mentions Carchemish, for instance), he may have had access to yet another set of documents that provided him with additional details. It seems unlikely, however, that the Chronicler was using an expanded version of Deuteronomy that is now lost or even a copy of the Midrash, as some have suggested. More likely as a potential source are the so-called Babylonian Chronicles, a set of cuneiform texts from Mesopotamia that document, among other things, events that occurred during the reign of the Babylonian king Nabopolassar. However, while these Babylonian Chronicles, which are now in the British Museum, mention that an Egyptian army came to the aid of the Assyrians in 609 B.C., only to be defeated, there is neither mention in them of either Josiah or Judah nor even any indication that anything untoward happened during Necho's march to Carchemish. Overall, it cannot be proved that the Chronicler had access to other sources of information, either biblical or extrabiblical, but it also cannot be disproved.[45]

One group of scholars firmly believes in the validity of the Chronicler's account and argues that Josiah attempted a surprise attack on Necho's army after the Egyptian soldiers had emerged from the Musmus Pass. This would have finally put into play a military stratagem that the Canaanites failed to use when facing Thutmose III's Egyptian army in the same region a thousand years earlier and that the Ottomans also failed to use when facing General Allenby's Allied forces at Megiddo some twenty-five hundred years later. However, it has been observed that Josiah would have been better off ambushing the Egyptians while they were marching through the Musmus Pass, rather than waiting until they had emerged onto the Plain of Jezreel.[46]

There would be no inherent reason to doubt the Chronicler's version of events, at least at face value, if it were not for the fact that it can be readily shown that the Chronicler embellished and/or otherwise exaggerated other stories found elsewhere in his narrative. In fact, several of the details within the Chronicler's Josiah narrative are strangely reminiscent of details found in stories concerning episodes that had occurred several centuries earlier. In particular, the entire series of events starting from the wounding of Josiah by an enemy arrow, including his journey by chariot to die elsewhere, and ending with his burial in Jerusalem bears a distressingly similar resemblance to the earlier stories of both King Ahab of Israel and King Ahaziah of Judah from the ninth century B.C., as related in I and II Kings. In the case of King Ahab, he is said to have been shot and wounded by an enemy archer while disguised and to have asked his men to remove him from the battlefield at Ramoth-gilead (I Kings 22:34; II Chronicles 18:28–34). In the case of King Ahaziah, he was mortally wounded by an arrow shot by Jehu's men but managed to make it via chariot to Megiddo before dying; he was then taken to Jerusalem for burial (II Kings 9:21–28). Both of these events occurred at least two hundred years prior to the battle between Josiah and Necho II. Rather than eerie coincidence, the similarities are probably the result of the Chronicler's use of details from these earlier stories to help in embellishing the story of Josiah's death at Megiddo in 609 B.C.[47]

Thus, like skeptical detectives, a second group of scholars do not believe the Chronicler's account. Indeed, it is possible that he simply elaborated on the events at Megiddo himself, much as he did with other stories elsewhere in his narrative. Simply by taking features from earlier episodes in Israelite and Judean history, the Chronicler could have augmented the details of this crucial meeting at Megiddo in 609 B.C. He could have added that Josiah survived until reaching Jerusalem, a critical point if the events at Megiddo were to be correlated with a prophecy made earlier by the prophetess Huldah, which had predicted that Josiah would die in peace and be buried with his ancestors in Jerusalem (II Kings 22:15–20).[48]

The account given in 1 Esdras of the Apocrypha is of little help in solving the mystery, for it was probably a later elaboration based on the account given in II Chronicles.[49] The text reads:

> After all these acts of Josiah, it happened that Pharaoh, king of Egypt, went to make war at Carchemish on the Euphrates, and Josiah went out against him. And the king of Egypt sent word to him saying, "What have we to do with each other, king of Judea? I was not sent against you by the Lord God, for my war is at the Euphrates. And now the Lord is with me!

> The Lord is with me, urging me on! Stand aside, and do not oppose the Lord." But Josiah did not turn back to his chariot, but tried to fight with him, and did not heed the words of Jeremiah the prophet from the mouth of the Lord. He joined battle with him in the plain of Megiddo, and the commanders came down against King Josiah. And the king said to his servants, "Take me away from the battle, for I am very weak." And immediately his servants took him out of the line of battle. And he got into his second chariot; and after he was brought back to Jerusalem he died, and was buried in the tomb of his fathers. And in all Judea they mourned for Josiah. Jeremiah the prophet lamented for Josiah, and the principal men, with the women, have made lamentation for him to this day; it was ordained that this should always be done throughout the whole nation of Israel. (1 Esdras 25–32)

This account does not even say that Josiah was mortally wounded at Megiddo; it says only that he was "weak." It was only when he got back to Jerusalem that he died and was subsequently buried, thus even more concretely fulfilling the earlier prophecy made by Huldah (II Kings 22:15–20).

The account found in Josephus, written during the Roman period nearly seven hundred years after Josiah and Necho met at Megiddo, is similar to that found in II Chronicles and 1 Esdras but adds some significant details.

> Now Neco, king of Egypt, raised an army, and marched to the river Euphrates, in order to fight with the Medes and Babylonians, who had overthrown the dominion of the Assyrians, for he had a desire to reign over Asia. Now when he was come to the city Mendes [Megiddo], which belonged to the kingdom of Josiah, he brought an army to hinder him from passing through his own country, in his expedition against the Medes. Now Neco sent a herald to Josiah, and told him that he did not make this expedition against him, but was making haste to Euphrates; and desired that he would not provoke him to fight against him, because he obstructed his march to the place whither he had resolved to go. But Josiah did not admit of this advice of Neco, but put himself into a posture to hinder him from his intended march. I suppose it was fate that pushed him on this conduct, that it might take an occasion against him; for as he was setting his army in array, and rode about in his chariot, from one wing of his army to another, one of the Egyptians shot an arrow at him, and put an end to his eagerness of fighting; for being sorely wounded, he commanded a retreat to be sounded for his army, and returned to Jerusalem, and died of that wound; and was magnificently buried in the sepulcher of his fathers, when he had lived thirty-nine years, and of them

had reigned thirty-one. But all the people mourned greatly for him, lamenting and grieving on his account many days; and Jeremiah the prophet composed an elegy to lament him. (Josephus *Antiquities of the Jews* 10.74–77)[50]

Josephus, a former army general, tells us that Josiah was riding around in his chariot, visiting the wings of his army to urge on his men, when he was mortally wounded by the Egyptian arrow. For this and other, similar reasons, some scholars have suggested that Josephus, too, had access to additional documents, such as letters perhaps exchanged between the rulers involved. However, Josephus's account was probably also based on the account given in II Chronicles, perhaps supplemented by information from the Book of Jeremiah and by Josephus's vision of what he himself would have done in Josiah's place immediately preceding the battle.[51]

The only other ancient source that might shed additional light on this mystery at Megiddo is the Greek historian Herodotus, who says simply:

Necos then ceased from making the canal and engaged rather in warlike preparation; some of his ships of war were built on the northern sea, and some in the Arabian Gulf, by the Red Sea coast: the landing-engines [winches] of these are still to be seen. He used these ships at need, and with his land army met and defeated the Syrians at Magdolus, taking the great Syrian city of Cadytis after the battle. He sent to Branchidae of Miletus and dedicated there to Apollo the garments in which he won these victories. Presently he died after a reign of sixteen years, and his son Psammis reigned in his stead. (Herodotus *Histories* 2.159.1–3)[52]

Previous scholars commonly suggested that Herodotus's city of "Magdolus," where "Necos" fought the "Syrians," was in fact the city of Megiddo, where Necho fought Josiah. However, "Magdolus" is now more usually identified as the city of Migdol, a fortress on the border of Egypt, which Necho may have captured at some other time, and it likely has nothing to do with either Megiddo or Josiah.[53] Thus, we may probably omit Herodotus's testimony from our deliberations.

The three points on which all of the accounts are in agreement is that Josiah did indeed "meet his maker" at Megiddo, that the perpetrator of this evil deed was the Egyptian pharaoh Necho II, and that this event occurred in 609 B.C. It is unclear, however, if even these basic details are actually correct, for there is absolutely no extrabiblical evidence available to support this fundamental set of beliefs. Even the

Egyptian records, usually so quick to record a victory against a foreign opponent, are silent on the topic of Necho's "battle" against Josiah at Megiddo. The closest one gets to supporting documentation is the evidence for the date of this event, provided circumstantially by the Babylonian Chronicles. These indicate that Jehoiakim had succeeded to the throne of Judah by at least 604/603 B.C., when tribute was first paid to the Babylonian ruler Nebuchadnezzar.[54] Thus, Josiah's reign must have ended sometime prior to this date, but the fact that he died, or at least was mortally wounded, at Megiddo must be taken literally as a matter of faith.

Perhaps a battle between Necho II and Josiah did take place at Megiddo in 609 B.C., and perhaps Josiah was killed during the fighting, as told in the accounts given by II Chronicles, 1 Esdras, and Josephus. We have still to ask why Josiah decided to attack the Egyptian army in the first place, rather than allowing them to march through his territory, and why he chose the Jezreel Valley as the place to attack the Egyptian army. On the one hand, it is readily understandable why the Jezreel Valley was perfectly suited for Josiah's defensive stand, particularly if he knew that Necho's army would be coming through the Musmus Pass.[55] Attacking the Egyptian army as it came out of the mountain pass near Megiddo would have been an obvious strategy for an undermanned and outnumbered Judean army. In that case, one can only wonder at the possible outcome of the battle if Josiah had not been mortally wounded at the outset. On the other hand, Necho's army may not have marched through Judah at all; it may have sailed as far north as Acco (Acre) to save both time and stamina and only then disembarked to march the rest of the way to Carchemish on foot.[56] If so, Megiddo in the Jezreel Valley would have been the closest rendezvous point for Josiah marching north from Jerusalem and Necho marching inland from Acco (Acre). It is still not clear why Josiah would have felt obliged to attack the Egyptian army, rather than allowing them to pass through his territory unmolested, but Babylonian pressure to do so or a desire to defend newly acquired territory are two possible suggestions (as mentioned earlier).

If, contrary to the claims of II Chronicles, I Esdras, and Josephus, there was no battle fought at Megiddo in 609 B.C. and Josiah's death was not the result of an arrow shot by an Egyptian archer during the opening phase of the conflict, how did Josiah come to die at Megiddo as II Kings reports? Necho II had only ascended the Egyptian throne upon the death of his father, Psammetichus I, one year earlier, in 610

B.C. He may have decided to take advantage of his campaign to northern Syria to stop en route and demand that Josiah swear allegiance to him, as befitting the new pharaoh, and thus to renew the bonds between Judah and Egypt. Having arranged for Josiah to meet him at Megiddo, Necho then treacherously double-crossed Josiah and murdered him. This would fit the brusque description given by II Kings, which simply records that Necho killed Josiah "when he saw him." But why would Necho have killed Josiah? In all likelihood, while Josiah's religious reforms may have frightened Necho to some extent, it would have been Josiah's attempts to acquire territory and expand Judah's northern borders by annexing Samaria and the Jezreel Valley that antagonized Necho and drove him to commit regicide.[57]

But if there was no battle fought between Josiah and Necho at Megiddo, and only a meeting set up so that Josiah could swear his allegiance to the new pharaoh, one may legitimately ask why such a meeting would have been held at Megiddo rather than in Jerusalem or even Memphis (Cairo), complete with all pomp and circumstance. Perhaps Necho was trying to avoid allowing Josiah any show at ritual or at displaying his power, which would have been the case if the meeting were held in Jerusalem. But Necho undoubtedly could have insisted that Josiah come to Egypt for the allegiance ceremony, where Necho would certainly have held the upper hand. It is quite possible that Megiddo and the Jezreel Valley represented a relatively neutral middle ground in which to meet and would have been fairly convenient, particularly if the pharaoh was in the area anyway, en route to Carchemish.

At the time, the Assyrian city of Megiddo, of Stratum III according to the University of Chicago excavators, had given way to the city of Stratum II at the site. It is, however, unclear whether the city of Stratum II was in Egyptian hands in 609 B.C. or was already in Josiah's hands as a result of his recent expansion and annexation of the region. The so-called fortress found within Stratum II at Megiddo, which shows some signs of violent destruction, is at the center of this archaeological debate. It is not certain whether its construction credit should go to Psammetichus (Necho's father), that is, if it was built while Megiddo was in Egyptian hands for several decades during the early seventh century B.C., or to Josiah, that is, if it was built after he began his northern expansion in the last quarter of the seventh century B.C. It is possible that the "fortress" was instead built even later, by the Persians in the sixth or fifth century B.C. The question has not yet been satisfactorily resolved, despite decades of excavation at the site.[58]

Unfortunately, our murder mystery also cannot be satisfactorily resolved. If Josiah was murdered, it occurred at the hands or at least on the orders of Necho II. That much is clear, but the evidence currently available is insufficient to convict the Egyptian pharaoh. Even the most incompetent lawyer would be able to easily establish "reasonable doubt" in the minds of any jurors summoned to try this case, for it is quite possible that Josiah's death occurred during the heat of battle. Regardless of how he was struck down, with the death of Josiah at Megiddo, the reforms that he had begun soon ground to a halt, thus denying the Western world any possibility of a continued Judean renaissance. In addition, the Judeans were humbled before the might of Egypt once again, but only for a few years this time. The coming of the Babylonians proved to be even worse for the Judeans, for Nebuchadnezzar and his armies destroyed the city of Jerusalem in 597 B.C. and again in 586 B.C., deporting the rulers and leading families of the land. The march to Jerusalem led directly past Megiddo both times, although apparently no battles were fought in the Jezreel Valley during either invasion.[59]

When the Babylonian exile began in 586 B.C., the death knell was sounded for Israel and Judah, the separate kingdoms that had been under siege since the demise of King Solomon and the passing of the United Monarchy so many centuries before. This final blow left the land bereft of all but a small percentage of its former inhabitants for the next sixty years. Only with the liberation of Babylon by Cyrus the Great of Persia and the return of the Judean exiles would the Jezreel Valley be populated and Megiddo inhabited once more. The following Persian period of the city, beginning in 539 B.C. (Stratum I according to the University of Chicago excavators), would be the last time that Megiddo saw the construction of any structures of significance on its ancient mound, and the coming of Alexander the Great in 332 B.C. would be the end of the road for the venerable city, for the tell was never again occupied on a permanent basis after that date.[60]

CHAPTER 5

On the Edge of Empires

But now Vespasian went about other work . . . , and that was to subdue those that had seized upon Mount Tabor, a place that lies in the middle between the great plain and Scythopolis. . . . As therefore there was a great multitude of people gotten together upon this mountain, Vespasian sent Placidus with six hundred horsemen thither.

—Josephus *Jewish War* 4.54

IT IS CLEAR THAT the Ptolemaic forces defending Atabyrium in the Jezreel Valley were lured to their deaths. Antiochus III and his Seleucid army captured the town in 218 B.C. by means of a common stratagem, attacking the fortifications and engaging the defenders, then pulling back and pretending to retreat in apparent confusion. The gullible defenders opened the gates and pursued the "retreating" Seleucid forces, expecting a great slaughter. A gruesome massacre did follow, but it was the defenders who were mercilessly cut down in an ambush, for Antiochus III's generals had positioned additional, concealed troops nearby. Once the defenders of Atabyrium ran by in hot pursuit of the ostensibly fleeing Seleucid soldiers, these hidden men rose up from where they lay concealed and attacked the pursuing Ptolemaic forces from the rear. At the same time, the "fleeing" Seleucid troops abruptly turned in an about-face and charged the surprised Atabyrium defenders, who were now caught between the two Seleucid forces and soon massacred. Returning to Atabyrium, Antiochus III's men quickly captured the town and its remaining defenders, who apparently put up little further resistance, because they were so stunned at the surprising turn of events.[1]

Polybius, the Greek historian who was born only a decade or so after the battle, tells us the story succinctly.

> Antiochus, with his army, . . . crossed the mountainous country and reached Atabyrium, which lies on a conical hill, the ascent of which is more than fifteen stades. By an ambuscade and a stratagem employed during the ascent he managed to take this city too: for having provoked

the garrison to sally out and skirmish, he enticed those of them who were in advance to follow his own retreating troops for a considerable distance down hill, and then turning the latter round and advancing, while those concealed issued from the ambuscade, he attacked the enemy and killed many of them; and finally following close on them and throwing them into panic took this city also by assault. . . . After garrisoning Atabyrium also, he advanced and took Pella, Camus, and Gephrus. (Polybius *Histories* 5.70.1–12)[2]

When the kingdoms of Israel and Judah effectively ceased to exist and the Babylonian exile commenced after the destruction of Jerusalem ca. 586 B.C., Megiddo and the Jezreel Valley became what one might call a "contested periphery."[3] In such a situation, which is both geographical and political, the affected region lies between two larger empires, kingdoms, or polities established to either side of it, and neither of the two sides fighting in the conflict actually lives in the contested area. Such a designation finally gives a name to an observation that historians have been making about Megiddo, the Jezreel Valley, and the region of Israel/Palestine as a whole for more than a century. Fisher, one of the excavators of Megiddo, perhaps said it best in 1929.

> It has long been obvious to all historians that Palestine is a middle ground, a kind of ancient "No-Man's Land," lying between the great military powers encamped on either side of it—in Africa the great civilization of the Egyptian Pharaohs; in Asia the kings of Babylonia, the mighty armies of the Assyrian military empire, or the Macedonian rulers of the East. The armies of these great powers, whether marching from Asia into Africa or the reverse, passed up and down the valleys of Palestine. . . . The famous plain . . . , taking its name from Megiddo (Armageddon) or from Esdraelon (Jezreel), thus became a battlefield where the great powers of neighboring Africa and Asia met in one long struggle after another for thousands of years, to dispute the political supremacy of the Near East. It was inevitable that there should grow up here a stronghold which would command the pass and the plain.[4]

Thus, the battle between Antiochus III and Ptolemy IV at Mount Tabor in 218 B.C. was a conflict over territory considered to lie on the fringes of both the Ptolemaic Empire in Egypt and the Seleucid Empire in Syria—the Jezreel Valley was quite literally a contested periphery—but neither the Egyptians nor the Syrians were actually living in the valley at the time that they were fighting over it. The same is true for the battles still to come in the Jezreel Valley, between the Ikhshidids,

Abbasids, and Hamdanids during the years A.D. 940–46, between the Muslims and the Byzantines in A.D. 975 and the Muslims and the Crusaders in the twelfth and thirteenth centuries A.D., between the Mamlukes and the Mongols in A.D. 1260, and against the Ottomans by both Napoleon in A.D. 1799 and Allenby in A.D. 1918. Only when the state of Israel was founded in 1948 and could defend itself militarily did the battles fought in the Jezreel Valley once again become conflicts in which at least one side actually lived in the region being contested.

Megiddo and the Jezreel Valley's status as a contested periphery actually began during the Neo-Assyrian period and continued through the ensuing Babylonian and Persian periods, when the region was crisscrossed time and again by armies intent on invading Egypt. The Neo-Assyrian king Esarhaddon probably marched past Megiddo during his successful campaign against Egypt in 671 B.C., as I mentioned briefly in chapter 4; the dreaded Neo-Babylonian king Nebuchadnezzar, who had marched by in 597 and 586 B.C., also probably came through the area again during his attempted invasion of Egypt in 569 B.C.; and the Persian king Cambyses undoubtedly also marched through the region while on his way to conquer Egypt in 526 B.C. Even the conflict between Josiah, king of Judah, and the Egyptian pharaoh Necho II back in 609 B.C., just before the end of the kingdom of Judah and the beginning of the Babylonian exile, could perhaps be seen as an early example of a battle in which the Jezreel Valley was a contested periphery, for Josiah was king of Judah, not of Israel, and Josiah's attack on Necho II was essentially incidental to the Egyptians' real campaign in northern Syria, where they intended to assist the Assyrians against the Babylonians.[5]

The coming of the Greeks in 332 B.C. changed the nationality of the invading armies but little else. Alexander the Great and his army, while en route to conquer Syria-Palestine and Egypt, almost certainly passed right by Megiddo, apparently without needing to fight a battle. Following Alexander's death in 323 B.C., the lands that he had conquered were split up among several of his generals. This gave rise to the Antigonid, Seleucid, and Ptolemaic Empires during the ensuing Hellenistic period from 323 to 30 B.C. The Seleucids in Syria and the Ptolemies in Egypt were almost constantly at war with each other, for each had their eye on the other's territory. During this period, in the time of Antiochus III and Ptolemy IV, the Jezreel Valley again began to see bloodshed as a result of its status as a contested periphery.

In an interesting coincidence, Antiochus III ascended to the Seleu-

cid throne in Syria in 223/222 B.C. at exactly the time when Ptolemy IV
ascended the Ptolemaic throne in Egypt. These two young men proceeded to wage war against each other for virtually their entire reigns,
in battles that affected nearly all of Syria-Palestine. In the year 221 B.C.,
Antiochus instigated what is now referred to as the Fourth Syrian War,
in which he attempted to capture Syria-Palestine once and for all from
Ptolemy IV. By 218 B.C., the war had been carried as far south as Mount
Tabor in the Jezreel Valley. After Antiochus III had captured Philote-
ria, on the shores of the Sea of Galilee, and the great city of Scythopolis (the Hellenistic version of Beth Shean/Beisan), he proceeded
toward Atabyrium (also known as Itabyrium or Atabyrion). The town
served as the administrative center of the Jezreel Valley during the Hellenistic period, for the site of Megiddo had long since fallen into ruin,
following the end of the Persian period ca. 332 B.C.

Apart from what Polybius tells us (related earlier in this chapter), we
know little about the battle at Atabyrium. Indeed, the very location of
the events are a matter of some debate. Most scholars consider
Atabyrium to have been either on top of or on the uppermost slopes of
Mount Tabor. It may be that the town lay just north of Mount Tabor,
for the ruins found on Mount Tabor itself, which include remnants of
fortresses and monasteries, seem to date only from the Roman period
and later. But there is a large ruin dating to the Hellenistic period on a
terrace slightly north of the mountain. While this ruin has not yet been
excavated, it may well be the remains of the Hellenistic city of
Atabyrium destroyed by Antiochus III and his Seleucid army.[6]

The conflict between Antiochus III and Ptolemy IV was not resolved
as a result of this battle in 218 B.C. or even after additional battles in
217 B.C. Indeed, not until the Fifth Syrian War, fought between these
same forces from 201 to 198 B.C., would the Seleucids capture most of
Syria-Palestine from the Ptolemies of Egypt.[7] The Seleucids did not
hold on to the region long, though, for not more than thirty years later,
the Jews successfully overthrew their Hellenistic overlords, in the Maccabean revolt ca. 167 B.C. Led by the priest Mattathias and his son Judas
Maccabeus, the rebellion was sparked by King Antiochus IV
Ephiphanes' oppressive religious policies forbidding worship on the
Sabbath, outlawing circumcision, and eliminating dietary restrictions.
The final straw that broke the camel's back and prompted the Jewish
rebellion against the Seleucid rulers was Antiochus's installation of an
altar to Olympian Zeus within the Temple in Jerusalem (see Daniel
11:31; 1 Maccabees 1:20–61; 2 Maccabees 6:2).

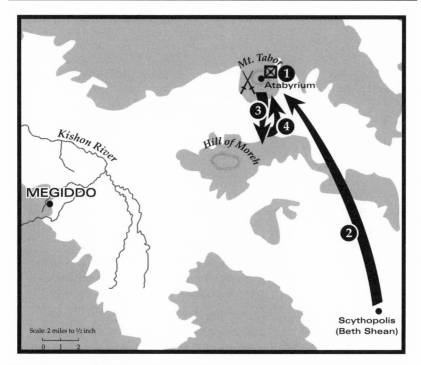

MAP 16. Antiochus III and Ptolemy IV

1. Ptolemaic forces are garrisoned at Atabyrium.
2. Seleucid forces march from Scythopolis (Beth Shean/Beisan).
3. Seleucid forces attack Atabyrium, then pretend to flee, pursued by the Ptolemaic forces.
4. Seleucids ambush Ptolemaic forces, then capture Atabyrium.

Although no battles were actually fought in the Jezreel Valley during the Maccabean revolt ca. 167 B.C. or the following Hasmonaean period of Jewish self-rule until Pompey's siege of Jerusalem in 63 B.C., the valley did see a number of armies crossing its borders and traversing its length throughout this period. These included the three thousand men of Simon, brother of Judas Maccabeus, who came through in 163 B.C. and evacuated the Jews of the area safely to Jerusalem. The three thousand men of Jonathan, successor to Judas Maccabeus, also marched through the Jezreel Valley, and fully two thousand of them were left behind in the Jezreel Valley and western Galilee while the rest marched onward to Ptolemais (Acco) and annihilation in 143/142 B.C.[8]

In addition, the armies of the Hasmonaean John Hyrcanus and of his sons Aristobulus I and Antigonus, as well as the forces of their Seleucid enemy Antiochus IX Cyzicenus, all crisscrossed the eastern end of the Jezreel Valley during the course of their various conflicts. This struggle was finally resolved in a battle fought just south of the valley, between Scythopolis (Hellenistic Beth Shean/Beisan) and Samaria, and by the Hasmonaean capture of Scythopolis itself in 108/107 B.C. Josephus also records that the two Hasmonaean brothers, Aristobulus I and Antigonus, "laid waste all the country that lay within Mount Carmel" (Josephus *Jewish War* 1.66), which may be an oblique reference to the Jezreel Valley.[9]

The forces of Aristobulus I probably then passed through the Jezreel Valley in 104/103 B.C., while en route to their battles against the Itureans in Upper Galilee and further north. Josephus also gives a list of cities that were contained within the kingdom of Alexander Janneus (103–76 B.C.), successor to Aristobulus I, which included Mount Tabor, Scythopolis, and Gadara. This probably implies continued Hasmonaean control of the Jezreel Valley and possible troop movement throughout the area, although this cannot be known for certain.[10]

Thus, although there seems to have been much military traffic, the various opposing forces did not generally stop to fight in the Jezreel Valley itself during the course of more than a hundred years, from ca. 167 B.C. to ca. 63 B.C. Instead, the majority of the battles fought in this general region during the Hasmonaean period took place rather at nearby Scythopolis (Beth Shean/Beisan). Even Pompey's invasion of Palestine in 63 B.C. went by way of Scythopolis, just to the east of the Jezreel Valley. Not until the campaign of Gabinius, Roman governor (proconsul) of Syria, against the Hasmonaean rebel Alexander, son of Aristobulus II and grandson of Alexander Janneus, can a battle be definitely confirmed as having taken place in the Jezreel Valley. The action took place at or near Mount Tabor in 55 B.C.[11]

The revolt of Alexander in 55 B.C. was part of a series of violent uprisings across Palestine against the Romans, which essentially commenced upon Pompey's invasion of Palestine in 63 B.C. and grew in intensity following Gabinius's appointment as governor (proconsul) of Syria in 57 B.C. Alexander's battle against Gabinius is the first of five that would be fought in the Jezreel Valley at various times during the next two thousand years as part of larger, cohesive attempts to establish an independent Jewish kingdom or nation in Syria-Palestine. These battles include not only the two fought in the Jezreel Valley during the Roman period—that of Alexander, son of Aristobulus II, against the Roman governor Gabinius in 55 B.C. and that of the Jewish rebels

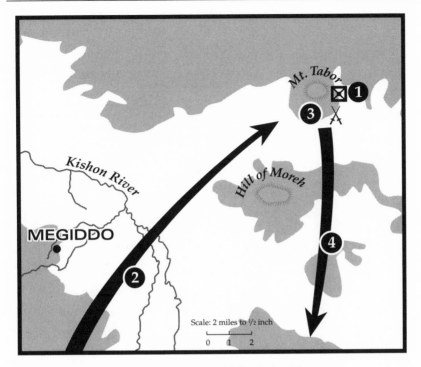

MAP 17. Gabinius and Alexander, son of Aristobulus II
1. Rebellious Jews gather at/near Mount Tabor.
2. Roman forces march from Egypt to Mount Tabor.
3. Battle is fought on or near slopes of Mount Tabor.
4. Romans march to Jerusalem.

against the Roman general Vespasian in A.D. 67—but also the conflicts that took place during the Israeli War of Independence in A.D. 1948, the Six-Day War in A.D. 1967, and the Yom Kippur War in A.D. 1973 (see chap. 9).

According to the historian Josephus, Alexander seized his moment when Gabinius was temporarily occupied with fighting first the Parthians in Mesopotamia and then the Ptolemies of Egypt. Collecting a large army, Alexander quickly captured Jerusalem, Judea, Samaria, and Galilee and began massacring any and all Romans in these areas. Initially, Gabinius sent Antipater to put down the rebellion. Antipater succeeded to a large extent and persuaded many of the inhabitants to accept Roman rule again, but Alexander and some thirty thousand of

FIG. 12. Mount Tabor and the Jezreel Valley (Zev Radovan, Jerusalem)

his men retreated to make a last stand near Mount Tabor. Gabinius himself returned in time to lead the battle against Alexander's forces. Josephus does not describe the battle itself in much detail, but he says that ten thousand of the Jewish rebels were slain and that the rest fled.

> But now, upon Gabinius's absence, the other part of Syria was in motion, and Alexander, the son of Aristobulus, brought the Jews to revolt again. Accordingly, he got together a very great army, and set about killing all the Romans that were in the country; hereupon Gabinius was afraid, (for he was come back already out of Egypt, and obliged to come back quickly by these tumults,) and sent Antipater, who prevailed with some of the revolters to be quiet. However, thirty thousand still continued with Alexander, who was himself eager to fight also; accordingly, Gabinius went out to fight, when the Jews met him; and as the battle was fought near Mount Tabor, ten thousand of them were slain, and the rest of the multitude dispersed themselves, and fled away. So Gabinius came to Jerusalem, and settled the government as Antipater would have it. (Josephus *Jewish War* 1.175)[12]

Josephus elsewhere presents another, somewhat more abridged version of these same events.

> But when Gabinius found Syria in such a state, he sent Antipater, who
> was a prudent man, to those that were seditious, to try whether he could
> cure them of their madness, and persuade them to return to a better
> mind; and when he came to them, he brought many of them to a sound
> mind, and induced them to do what they ought to do; but he could not
> restrain Alexander, for he had an army of thirty thousand Jews, and met
> Gabinius, and joining battle with him, was beaten, and lost ten thousand
> of his men about Mount Tabor. (Josephus *Antiquities of the Jews* 14.101)[13]

Although Josephus reports that the battle took place near Mount Tabor, he does not record the precise location. It may have taken place on the slopes of the mountain itself or on the adjacent Jezreel Valley floor. It would certainly be difficult for Alexander to have positioned thirty thousand men on the mountain itself, which would argue for the battle having taken place on the neighboring plain, but then Josephus's figures of thirty thousand rebels and ten thousand dead in the ensuing battle are themselves somewhat hard to believe and are probably exaggerated.[14] If there were fewer men, the engagement could have taken place on the slopes of the mountain; otherwise, the nearby flat land of the Jezreel Valley, the scene of other past and future battles, including those of Deborah, Gideon, and Napoleon, is a more likely site on which the Jewish and Roman forces could have been successfully deployed.

In any event, the rebellion was crushed and the Roman presence in Syria-Palestine was reinforced. Alexander reportedly had his life spared by Gabinius, only to be put to death by Pompey some six years later.[15] Other small revolts took place in Syria-Palestine during the next few decades, but these did not involve the Jezreel Valley. In fact, for approximately the next century, the valley seems to have remained fairly peaceful and uninvolved militarily, apart from a single incident in A.D. 36 when Vitellius, the Roman official responsible for the province of Palestine, marched his legions through the Jezreel Valley while en route from Ptolemais (Acco) to Transjordan for a confrontation with Aretas IV, king of the Nabataeans.[16] Not until the time of Nero and Vespasian, in the mid–first century A.D., did matters truly come to a head once again, in what is now called the First Jewish Revolt.

Lasting from approximately A.D. 66 to 73, and ending in the famous (although now debated) mass suicide at Masada, the First Jewish Revolt was brought to the attention of the Roman emperor Nero during the early days of the rebellion. Nero dispatched his best general, Vespasian, and three legions to Palestine in an attempt to take control of the rapidly worsening situation. Of the three legions, the Fifth and the Tenth Legions were stationed in Caesarea on the coast at first, while the Fifteenth Legion was headquartered at Scythopolis (Beth Shean/Beisan).[17]

The Jewish rebels were led by their wily general Josephus, the same man who was later to become a historian and apologist and who wrote, among other works, the two books I frequently cite in these chapters: *Antiquities of the Jews* and *The Jewish War.* Josephus tried to prepare the Jews as best he could for the coming battles against the Romans. His preparations included military training for the rebels, who reportedly numbered nearly one hundred thousand at the beginning of the action, and the construction of a number of walls, fortresses, and other means of defense in the Jezreel Valley, Galilee, and what is now the Golan Heights. The most well known of these were the fortifications at Gamla and Jotapata; a wall was also constructed to encircle the top of Mount Tabor.[18]

Vespasian set up his headquarters at Ptolemais (Acco) and quickly engaged Josephus and the rebels. Turning first against Sepphoris and Jotapata in A.D. 67, the Romans enjoyed immediate success and even captured Josephus himself in the process. The surrender of Tiberias, Taricheae, and most of Galilee quickly followed, with only the rebel garrisons at Gischala and on Mount Tabor still resisting. Before undertaking the siege of these minor fortresses, Vespasian and his troops detoured to capture Gamla in the Golan Heights, which had already been besieged for seven months by Agrippa; it took the three Roman legions a further month to capture this stubborn city.[19] The subsequent attack on Mount Tabor would not take nearly as long nor prove nearly as difficult.

It was October of A.D. 67 before Vespasian turned his attention to the Jewish rebels ensconced in the fortress on Mount Tabor.[20] Josephus claims to have built a defensive wall around the top of the mountain, but there may have also been a fortress built by Herod in the same area, which the rebels might have used. Certainly, ruins dated to the Roman period were still visible on Mount Tabor to travelers at the end of the nineteenth century; Kitchener describes these as consisting of "a solid wall built of large drafted stones, flanked at intervals by square towers enclosing a large rectangular space that occupied the whole of the top of the hill."[21]

Josephus gives a fairly detailed description of the battle between the Jewish rebels and the Roman forces at Mount Tabor in A.D. 67.

> And these were the hard circumstances that the people of Gamala were in. But now Vespasian went about other work by the by, during this siege, and that was to subdue those that had seized upon Mount Tabor, a place that lies in the middle between the great plain and Scythopolis, whose top is elevated as high as thirty furlongs and is hardly to be ascended on its north side; its top is a plain of twenty-six furlongs, and all encompassed with a wall. Now Josephus erected this so long a wall in forty days' time, and furnished it with other materials, and with water from below, for the inhabitants only made use of rain water. As therefore there was a great multitude of people gotten together upon this mountain, Vespasian sent Placidus with six hundred horsemen thither. Now, as it was impossible for him to ascend the mountain, he invited many of them to peace, by the offer of his right hand for their security, and of his intercession for them. Accordingly they came down, but with a treacherous design, as well as he had the like treacherous design upon them on the other side; for Placidus spoke mildly to them, as aiming to take them, when he got them into the plain; they also came down, as complying with his proposals, but it was in order to fall upon him when he was not aware of it: however, Placidus's stratagem was too hard for theirs; for when the Jews began to fight, he pretended to run away, and when they were in pursuit of the Romans, he enticed them a great way along the plain, and then made his horsemen turn back; whereupon he beat them, and slew a great number of them, and cut off the retreat of the rest of the multitude, and hindered their return. So they left Tabor, and fled to Jerusalem, while the people of the country came to terms with him, for their water failed them, and so they delivered up the mountain and themselves to Placidus. (Josephus *Jewish War* 4.54)[22]

The exact number of the Jewish rebels defending Mount Tabor is not given, but Placidus, Vespasian's commander to whom the attack had been entrusted, is said to have had only six hundred Roman cavalry. It is not clear whether there were any Roman infantry involved as well; Josephus does not mention any, and the fact that he reports that the Roman forces "were unable to ascend the mountain" may indicate that a goodly number of the Roman attackers were indeed on horseback. Given the standard Roman battle tactics, however, one should probably assume that there were at least some Roman infantry present.

At any rate, the number of men involved on either side seems to have been fairly small, at least relative to the numbers reported by Josephus to have been present at the previous battle between Gabinius and Alexander in this same region.

There are problems with the other figures mentioned in Josephus's account. For example, Mount Tabor is only about three furlongs high, rather than the thirty furlongs that Josephus reports, and the circumference at the top of the mountain is only about six furlongs around, rather than the twenty-six furlongs that Josephus records.[23] It would be nearly impossible to build a wall to encompass twenty-six furlongs (more than three miles) in only forty days as Josephus claims, but a wall encompassing only six furlongs (about two-thirds of a mile) could probably have been built in such a short period. Such problems with Josephus's figures are not uncommon; earlier in this chapter, I noted his probable exaggeration of the number of Hasmonaean defenders during the battle between Gabinius and Alexander, son of Aristobulus II, in 55 B.C. Similar discrepancies and problems with reported heights, distances, and numbers of people involved have been pointed out by other scholars examining Josephus's account of the battle that took place at Masada in A.D. 73, some six years after the defeat of the rebels at Mount Tabor.[24]

Of the three battles (in 218 B.C., 55 B.C., and A.D. 67) that took place in the Jezreel Valley during the Hellenistic and Roman periods, all were fought on or near Mount Tabor, for this mountain and the city of Atabyrium functioned as the administrative capital of the Jezreel Valley during this time. The similarity of the tactics used in two of the three battles (in 218 B.C. and A.D. 67), which consisted of luring the defenders out of their fortifications and into an ambush, should perhaps not be too surprising, since the natural geography of the Mount Tabor region may have lent itself to such tactics, much as, on the opposite side of the Jezreel Valley, Thutmose III and General Allenby followed battle plans eerily reminiscent of each other by marching through the Musmus Pass to Megiddo thirty-four hundred years apart.

However, in both the battle against Antiochus III in 218 B.C. and the battle against Vespasian in A.D. 67, the defenders on Mount Tabor would have benefited from strategic advice given later by the Prussian military genius Clausewitz in his book *Principles of War.*

> The purpose of fortifications is to keep a considerable part of the enemy's army occupied as siege troops, to give us an opportunity to

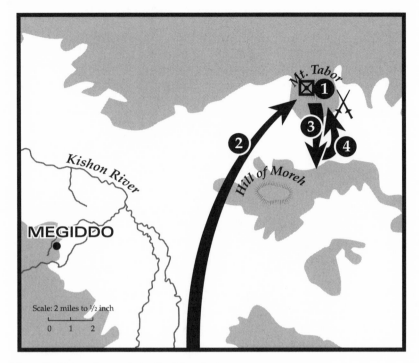

MAP 18. Vespasian and the Jewish rebels
1. Jewish rebels gather on top of Mount Tabor.
2. Romans march to Mount Tabor.
3. Rebels march down to meet Romans, then attack in surprise move.
4. Romans pretend to flee, pursued by Jews, then turn and ambush rebels.

> defeat the rest of his army. Consequently, it is best to fight our battles
> behind our fortifications and not in front of them.[25]

In both battles, instead of remaining behind their fortifications, the
defenders of Mount Tabor allowed themselves to be lured out and were
subsequently ambushed and defeated by their attackers.

The truth of the well-known saying "Geography dictates both history
and battles" is nowhere more self-evident than in the Jezreel Valley,
with its mountains and hills, wadis and rivers, and fertile valley floor. As
Clausewitz wrote in his volume simply entitled *On War:* ". . . geography
and the character of the ground bear a close and ever-present relation
to warfare. They have a decisive influence on the engagement, both as
to its course and to its planning and exploitation." However, Clausewitz

went on to point out that more important than the terrain is the "relative quality of the two armies and their commanders." He concluded, "Great commanders . . . usually preferred to take up a position on open ground."[26] Thus, while it seems clear that the geography of the Jezreel Valley may have dictated the use of similar strategies in the thirty-four battles fought there during the past four thousand years, victory was achieved in a number of these cases through the use of superior strategy that would have worked regardless of the type of terrain on which it was employed. The most obvious example is the strategy of a faked retreat luring the enemy into an ambush, as discussed earlier in this chapter. Not only was this strategy used by Antiochus III in 218 B.C. and Vespasian in A.D. 67, but we shall soon see that it was also used by Zahir al-'Umar in A.D. 1735 and perhaps by the Mamlukes in A.D. 1260.

However, it should be noted that in the battle against Vespasian and the Romans, the Jewish rebels apparently left their defensive stations voluntarily and were proceeding to a conference that the Romans had requested. The rebels were not naive and seem to have intuitively known a warning given by the earlier, Chinese military strategist Sun-Tzu of the fifth century B.C., "When without prior arrangements a cease-fire is requested, this indicates a scheme."[27] Thus, the rebels proceeded to the requested conference, but they bore treachery in their own hearts as well, for they intended to attack the Romans once they were in close quarters. Only after the rebels had initiated the attack did the Romans introduce their own double-cross and pretend to retreat, luring the rebels further out into the plain, where the Roman cavalry could be put to efficient and effective use cutting the Jewish defenders to pieces.

Thus, the Romans defeated the Jewish rebels at Mount Tabor in A.D. 67 and continued relentlessly on their way to capture Jerusalem and destroy the Second Temple three years later. The final vestiges of the revolt were not suppressed until A.D. 73, with the possible massacre/suicide at Masada, but by then the Romans had learned their lesson. Realizing the importance of Palestine overall and of the Jezreel Valley in particular, yet another Roman legion was sent to the region some fifty years later, during the turbulent decade before the Second Jewish Revolt, which began ca. A.D. 132.

The Sixth Roman Legion arrived in Palestine most likely between A.D. 117 and 120, probably in response to increased Jewish antagonism and resistance toward the occupying Romans. Known as Legio IV Ferrata (the "Ironsides"), the legion based its headquarters only a mile from the ancient site of Megiddo, displacing the Jewish village of Kefar 'Otnai. This village, called "Caparcotnei" by the Romans, had been established during the Hasmonaean period or perhaps even earlier, to guard the vital road leading through the Wadi 'Ara (Musmus Pass) and eventually to Jerusalem. The Sixth Roman Legion would be based in this area for the next hundred years or so, guarding the Jezreel Valley in particular. Their very presence seems to have been enough to ensure that no battles were fought in the valley during their century-long stay.[28]

The Sixth Legion eventually gave its name to the city that grew up around the military camp. This metropolis became known as Legio, while the Jezreel Valley as a whole was called the "Campus Maximus Legionis." Major Roman roads led from Legio to Sepphoris, Caesarea, Scythopolis (Beth Shean/Beisan), Ptolemais (Acco), and Jerusalem, now renamed Aelia Capitolina. Unfortunately, the Roman remains at Kefar 'Otnai/Caparcotnei/Legio have yet to be thoroughly explored by archaeologists, and the ensuing Byzantine remains are even less well known.[29]

During the Byzantine period, ca. A.D. 300 to 634, Legio was temporarily renamed Maximianopolis, after either Diocletian's coruler Maximianus Herculius (A.D. 286–304) or Maximianus Galerius (A.D. 305), who was Augustus of the provinces of the Eastern Roman Empire.[30] Happily, the name did not catch on and the locals continued to refer to the city as Legio. This explains the transmutation of the name into the Arabic *Lejjun* or *Lajjun* upon the subsequent arrival of the invading Muslim forces in A.D. 634. This name, *Lejjun* or *Lajjun,* would then be used to refer to the Arabic village located continuously in this approximate area for the next thirteen hundred years, right up until the Israeli War of Independence in A.D. 1948, at which point the village was finally abandoned when the inhabitants fled following the outcome of the war.

CHAPTER 6

Islamic Invaders

> . . . whoever fights in the way of Allah, then be he slain or be he victorious, We shall grant him a mighty reward.
>
> —Koran, Sura 4 ("Women"), 74

WITH THE COMING of Islam to the region of Syria-Palestine, the Jezreel Valley, continuing in its role as a "contested periphery" (see chap. 5), once again became the scene of several military conflicts. The first may have occurred as early as A.D. 634. The battle of Adjnadayn (also known as Ijnadayn) took place on 30 July of that year, between Byzantine and Islamic forces. In that battle, the Islamic army inflicted a tremendous defeat on the Byzantine soldiers. Theodorus, brother of the emperor Heraclius, and the other Byzantine leaders were forced to retreat as far as Damascus, leaving all of Palestine ripe for the taking by the Muslim invaders, who went on to capture and occupy Jerusalem four years later, in A.D. 638. They would occupy this holy city for the next 450 years, until the Crusaders wrested it from their control in A.D. 1099.[1]

Although the Muslim sources say that Adjnadayn was located far to the south of the Jezreel Valley, no place by this name is actually attested anywhere by geographers. There is an outside possibility that the name *Adjnadayn,* which may mean "Two Armies," is the Arabic equivalent of the Latin *legionum* and thus may indicate that the battle was in fact fought at Lejjun in the Jezreel Valley. However, there is not enough data to specifically confirm or deny this possibility, and most modern scholars believe that Adjnadayn had nothing to do with the Jezreel Valley but is instead to be identified with ancient Yarmuth near Wadi al-Samt, some fifteen miles (twenty-five kilometers) to the west-southwest of Jerusalem, in the vicinity of the two villages of al-Djannaba.[2]

Several battles can, however, be certainly confirmed as having taken place in the Jezreel Valley during the centuries of Islamic rule in Syria-Palestine, before the coming of the Crusaders. Two of these occurred only six years apart, one in A.D. 940 between the Ikhshidid dynasty of

Egypt and the Abbasid dynasty of Mesopotamia, and one in A.D. 946 between the Ikhshidids of Egypt and the Hamdanids of Mosul and northern Syria. The third was fought about thirty years later, when the Byzantine emperor John I Tzimisces saw his chance to invade and conquer Palestine. Although few details are available for any of these battles, it is clear that all were fought because the region continued to be a contested periphery.[3]

In July A.D. 935, Muhammad ibn Tughj was appointed governor of Egypt by the Abbasid rulers in Baghdad. Ibn Tughj was the son of a former governor of Damascus and had spent much of his childhood in Syria and Palestine. He quickly set about establishing control in Egypt, and by A.D. 939 he was granted the title *al-Ikhshid*, or "the Servant," a title previously used by princes from Farghana in Central Asia, whence his family originally came. He ultimately threw off Abbasid authority and founded the Ikhshidid dynasty of Egypt, which would last for approximately the next thirty years.[4]

At almost the same time, in late December A.D. 938, a man named Ibn Ra'iq, who had served as the supreme commander of the Abbasid army, was appointed governor of the region of the Upper Euphrates and northern Syria. He promptly undertook a campaign to recapture the rest of Syria, Palestine, and Egypt from the newly founded Ikhshidid regime. He left Baghdad with an army in January A.D. 939 and marched southwest toward Syria-Palestine. In response, Muhammad ibn Tughj made a generous gesture for peace, offering to sign a treaty with Ibn Ra'iq giving him most of Syria and Palestine as far south as Tiberias, as well as an annual tribute of money. Although Ibn Ra'iq may have initially accepted this offer, he did not remain content for long, and by November of that same year, he had abandoned any pretense at peace and sent his army as far south as Ramla in Palestine.[5]

Muhammad ibn Tughj and his Ikhshidid forces promptly marched north from Egypt, intent on repelling the invaders. Although they were defeated in a battle fought near el-Arish in Sinai, Ibn Tughj and his army managed to regroup and ambush Ibn Ra'iq before he could march on Egypt itself. Ibn Ra'iq retreated temporarily to Damascus, while the Ikhshidids made their way back to Egypt to raise another army.[6] The two forces would meet again, this time in the Jezreel Valley, several months later.

The Ikhshidid army made its way north from Egypt once again, at the beginning of the summer in A.D. 940, this time led not by Muhammad ibn Tughj al-Ikhshid himself but by his brother Abu Nasr al-

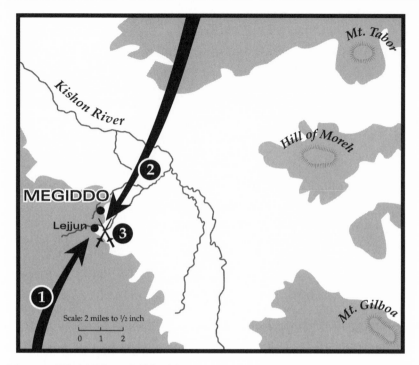

MAP 19. Ikhshidids and Abbasids
1. Ikhshidid army marches north from Egypt.
2. Abbasid army marches south from Damascus.
3. Battle is fought at Lejjun.

Husayn. The Abbasid army that made its way south from Damascus at the same time was once again led by Ibn Ra'iq. The battle took place at Lejjun in the Jezreel Valley on 24 June A.D. 940, during the middle of Ramadan. It is not recorded how large either force was. The precise details of the battle itself are not known either, except for the singular fact that Abu Nasr al-Husayn, leader of the Ikhshidid forces and brother of Ibn Tughj, was killed during the conflict. For this reason, the battle is sometimes considered to have been an Abbasid victory, although the outcome was more of a draw or a tie than an outright victory by either side.[7]

The story is told that Ibn Ra'iq himself discovered Abu Nasr's body and gave it a decent burial. In his sorrow at the death of the Ikhshid's brother, Ibn Ra'iq sent his own son Muzahim as a hostage to Egypt, telling Ibn Tughj to do whatever he wished with Muzahim. Ibn Tughj promptly responded with a simple request to return things to the way that they had been before the most recent fighting. Ibn Ra'iq agreed, and the ensuing peace treaty was sealed by a marriage alliance between Muzahim, the son of Ibn Ra'iq, and Fatima, the daughter of Ibn Tughj. The southern portion of Syria-Palestine, including the area from Tiberias and the Sea of Galilee on down, continued to be ruled by Ibn Tughj and his Ikhshidid forces, while the northern portion, including most of Syria, was given to Ibn Ra'iq and his Abbasid forces. Ibn Tughj also agreed to pay an annual tribute of 140,000 gold coins, making this treaty almost identical to the one he had originally offered Ibn Ra'iq back in A.D. 939.[8]

However, the peace was not destined to last long, for only two years later, in A.D. 942, Ibn Ra'iq was assassinated. His assassination was ordered by Nasir al-Dawla, or "the Defender of the Dynasty," a member of the rival Hamdanid family originally based in Mosul. In A.D. 944, as part of the establishment of his own realm, Nasir al-Dawla sent first his cousin Husayn and then his own younger brother, Sayf al-Dawla, or "the Sword of the Dynasty," to occupy Aleppo and take over the area of Syria previously controlled by Ibn Ra'iq.[9]

By October A.D. 945, after some skirmishes and at least one outright battle, Muhammad ibn Tughj al-Ikhshid of Egypt had agreed to terms of peace with this new power in the region, only to die during the summer of A.D. 946, before the new treaty could be implemented.[10] Thus, in the fall of A.D. 946, Sayf al-Dawla and his Hamdanid forces took advantage of the perceived power vacuum and invaded Ikhshidid-controlled Palestine. An armed struggle ensued between the two rival Islamic powers.

The Hamdanid army advanced south from Syria, under the command of Sayf al-Dawla. The Ikhshidid army advanced north from Egypt, under the command of the rulers of Egypt, Hasan ibn Tughj and Abu'l Qasim Unujur (another brother and the son, respectively, of the recently deceased Muhammad ibn Tughj al-Ikhshid), as well as Kafur, the renowned black eunuch regent of Egypt. The armies met in the Jezreel Valley on 21 December A.D. 946 (24 Jumada I A.H. 335).[11] Some accounts, such as those written by Ibn Zafir and al-Dhahabi, say that the battle took place at Lejjun itself. Other reports, such as the account written by al-Kindi, state that it took place at Iksal, located seven miles (ten kilometers) to the northeast of Lejjun, near Nazareth. The account of Ibn al-Amin, usually considered to be the most accurate concerning Sayf al-Dawla, says that the Hamdanid army marched south with the original intention of intercepting the Ikhshidid army at Lejjun, but that before they could get to the town, the Ikhshidids not only had already reached it but had continued to march north. Thus, he says, the battle took place at Iksal, still in the Jezreel Valley, instead of at Lejjun as planned.[12]

Details about the battle itself are sketchy, but all accounts agree that the Ikhshidid army from Egypt inflicted a crushing defeat on Sayf al-Dawla and the Hamdanid invaders from Syria. The Hamdanid army was forced to retreat far to the north, while Unujur and the Ikhshidid forces proceeded to enter Damascus and Aleppo in triumph. As a result, the Ikhshidid and Hamdanid rulers signed a treaty in A.D. 947, dividing up Syria-Palestine between them. The Hamdanids received the rights to northern Syria and portions of Mesopotamia, while the Ikhshidids continued to rule the region of Palestine as far north as Damascus.[13]

Is it coincidence that after a gap of at least three hundred years (from A.D. 634) and perhaps as much as nine hundred years (from A.D. 67) since the previous conflict had taken place in the Jezreel Valley, two battles were fought at or near Lejjun within six years of each other? It certainly might be, but one should note that the Ikhshidid army was involved in both battles. Moreover, in both cases, the battle fought was either the last or the only battle fought in the war. It is certainly within the realm of possibility to suggest that the Ikhshidid military strategists may have deliberately picked the Jezreel Valley as a logical place to fight both their Abbasid and their Hamdanid foes. Although the Ikhshidid army was only able to fight the Abbasid forces to a draw during the first battle in A.D. 940, Ibn Tughj was still able to procure an immediate truce and secure the safety of Egypt itself. This may have been more than enough motivation for his brother and son to pursue the same strategy in A.D. 946, in a battle that the Ikhshidids did indeed win.

In fact, the battle fought by the Ikhshidids in A.D. 946 is somewhat of an anomaly in the history of the Jezreel Valley. Of the thirteen examples in which the Jezreel Valley was the scene of battles because of its status as a contested periphery and in which neither side lived permanently in the valley, the party who arrived second (i.e., was last to the battlefield) won the battle outright in ten out of the thirteen instances. Two out of the other three battles ended in draws, so the only instance in which the first party to arrive at the battlefield clearly won the ensuing battle is that fought in A.D. 946 by the Ikhshidids, in which they

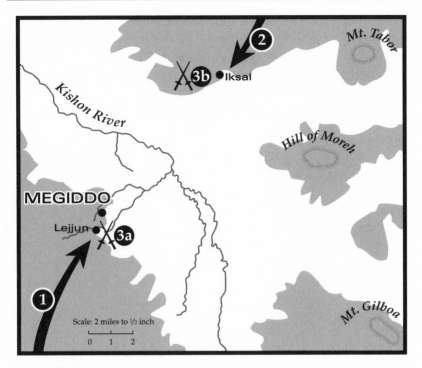

MAP 20. Ikhshidids and Hamdanids
1. Ikhshidid army marches north from Egypt.
2. Hamdanid army marches south from Syria.
3. Battle is fought at either (a) Lejjun or (b) Iksal.

defeated the Hamdanid forces.[14] However, since this was the second battle fought in the Jezreel Valley by the Ikhshidids within a single decade, one might suggest that they had obviously learned a lesson when fighting the Abbasids to a draw in the same region just six years earlier.

The observation that the party arriving last at the battlefield won the battle in ten out of the thirteen cases where both sides were foreign to the Jezreel Valley (i.e., more than 75 percent of the time) seems counterintuitive at first. One might expect that the first party to arrive would win nearly every time, since that party had the opportunity to select the actual locale and the terrain over which the battle was fought and thus to prepare for the battle in an area of their own choosing. However, the army that came to the battlefield second may actually have had the advantage, because they could see the first party's setup and adjust their attack accordingly—much as a coach in modern American football and basketball will sometimes call a play just to see the defensive setup and then will immediately ask for a timeout to adjust the offense before the game resumes.

In A.D. 969, the Fatimid caliphate took over in Egypt and also assumed possession of Palestine, including the Jezreel Valley. The Byzantine emperor John I Tzimisces soon saw his chance to wrestle the region away from Muslim control, and he launched a campaign with the intent of capturing Jerusalem.[15] Leading a force of probably between twenty-five thousand and seventy thousand men and between sixteen thousand and forty thousand cavalry, John set out from Antioch in April A.D. 975. Capturing Baalbek and Damascus in Syria en route, the Byzantine army marched south into Palestine and quickly captured Tiberias, Beisan (Beth Shean), and Nazareth. Mount Tabor was occupied without a fight, and John I Tzimisces proceeded to hold court on the mountain, receiving from Jerusalem and Ramla envoys who promised loyalty and tribute. According to the contemporary chronicle by Matthew of Edessa, John himself wrote the following account of the campaign.

> In the month of April [A.D. 975] we directed ourselves towards Phoenicia and Palestine and advanced into these areas; moreover, we pursued the abominable Africans who had come to the region of Syria. . . . Going forth from there [Damascus], we went to the Sea of Galilee, where our Lord Jesus Christ had performed a miracle with one hundred and fifty-three fish. We were intent on laying siege to the town of Tiberias also, but the townspeople came in submission to our imperial majesty and brought us many gifts like the Damascenes had done and also tribute in the amount of thirty thousand *dahekans,* not counting many other valuable presents. They requested that one of our commanders be put over them and gave us an affirmation of loyalty as had the Damascenes, promising to be subject to us perpetually and to give us tribute ceaselessly. On that basis we left them free of enslavement and did not plunder them because the region was the native land of the holy apostles. We felt the same way about Nazareth where the Theotokos, the Holy Virgin Mary, heard the good tidings from the angel. We also went to Mount Tabor and climbed up to that place where Christ our God was transfigured. While we remained in the place, people came to us from Ramla and Jerusalem to beseech our imperial majesty, looking for compassion from us. They asked that a commander be appointed over them, and became tributary to us, swearing to serve us; all of these things which they asked we indeed did. We also were intent on delivering the holy sep-

ulcher of Christ our God from the bondage of the Muslims. We established military commanders in all the areas which had submitted and
become tributary to our imperial majesty; these were Baisan (called
Decapolis), Genesareth, and Acre (also called Ptolemais), and by a written statement they undertook to give tribute ceaselessly from year to year
and to serve us. We went up to Caesarea, which is on the coast of the
great Mediterranean Sea, and they also submitted and came under our
rule.[16]

This invasion of the Jezreel Valley by the Byzantine emperor John I
Tzimisces and his army in A.D. 975 is one of twenty-one instances of
conflicts during the past four thousand years in which at least one party
actually lived in or was based in the Jezreel Valley. In fifteen of the
twenty-one cases, the invading force, such as John's Byzantine army,
was victorious. The only parties who successfully defended themselves
against their attackers were Biridiya of Megiddo in the fourteenth century B.C., Gideon of Ophrah (modern Afula) in the eleventh century
B.C., and, as we shall see in chapters 7 and 9, the Muslims at Mount
Tabor in A.D. 1217 and the Israelis of Kibbutz Mishmar Haemek in A.D.
1948 and at the Ramat David airbase in A.D. 1967 and 1973.[17]

Why did the invading force usually win? Is it easier to prepare a good
offense than an effective defense? The nineteenth-century Prussian
general and military strategist Carl von Clausewitz suggested an answer,
stating, "Admittedly, an aggressor often decides on war before the
innocent defender does, and if he contrives to keep his preparations
sufficiently secret, he may well take his victim unawares."[18] This may
have been true in a number of the Jezreel Valley battles, such as the
campaigns of Pepi I, Amenhotep II, Shoshenq I (Shishak), John I
Tzimisces, and Saladin. But perhaps more importantly, Clausewitz also
pointed out:

> The one advantage the attacker possesses is that he is free to strike at any
> point along the whole line of defense, and in full force. . . . For the
> attacker it is easier to surround the whole opposing force and cut it off
> than it is for the defender: the latter is tied to his position and has
> thereby presented the attacker with an objective.[19]

One suspects, probably with good reason, that a variety of different
factors were involved in each of the victories enjoyed by the invading
forces in the Jezreel Valley and that no particular element can be
singled out for their nearly 75 percent rate of success (winning fifteen
of twenty-one battles) over the past four thousand years. It would be

interesting to see if this rate of success is similar to that enjoyed by invading forces elsewhere in the world and elsewhere in time. Clearly, for whatever reasons, the invaders of the Jezreel Valley have consistently had far more success than have the valley's defenders during the past four millennia, despite constant changes in technology, tactics, and techniques.

Following his successful occupation of the Jezreel Valley and a triumphant return to Constantinople, Emperor John I Tzimisces died suddenly on 10 January A.D. 976. He was most likely a victim of typhoid fever, although rumors persisted that he had actually been poisoned by his wife and the man who ultimately succeeded to the Byzantine throne, Basil II. John's conquests in Palestine, including those in and around the Jezreel Valley, were only fleeting, but his campaign as a whole was a taste of what was to come when the Crusaders came to recapture the land just over a century later, in A.D. 1099.[20]

CHAPTER 7

The Coming of the Crusaders

This, then, was the state of affairs in the kingdom, and meanwhile the greater part of the army was assembled at Sephorie. During this time Saladin, after much deliberation, had summoned his forces from the lands beyond the Euphrates and with all the cavalry which he could gather from every source entered the frontiers of the realm, followed by his great host armed to the teeth.

—William of Tyre

"IF YOU HAD BEEN there, your feet would have been stained up to the ankles with the blood of the slain. What more shall I tell? Not one of them was allowed to live. They did not spare the women and children"—thus wrote Fulcher of Chartres, describing the capture of Jerusalem during the First Crusade in A.D. 1099.[1] The story of Pope Urban II's call in A.D. 1096 for a Crusade to rescue the Holy Land from the Muslims and of the subsequent history of the additional Crusades and of the Crusaders in that land from A.D. 1099 to 1291 is well known and has been extremely well documented by historians. Megiddo and the Jezreel Valley first enter the picture about a decade after the success of the First Crusade, when the Muslims began a series of counterattacks designed to win back the Holy Land from the Crusaders. Among the first to be involved was Maudud of Mosul, who launched four separate campaigns at the beginning of the twelfth century A.D. It was his attack in A.D. 1113 that first affected the Jezreel Valley.[2]

During this, the last of his four campaigns, Maudud allied himself with Tughtigin of Damascus, who had been having problems with Crusaders raiding his lands. Their joint Muslim army first marched down the east side of Lake Tiberias, where they met and defeated King Baldwin and his Crusader army at a battle near al-Sannabra on 28 June 1113. Baldwin lost twelve hundred infantry and thirty knights, out of his original force reportedly numbering four thousand infantry and seven hundred knights, but after crossing the Jordan River south of Tiberias, he was able to meet up with reinforcements in the form of Roger of Antioch and Pons of Tripoli, together with their armies. The

Crusaders retreated to an unnamed hill west of Tiberias, where they remained besieged by Maudud and Tughtigin and suffering from a lack of water for the next twenty-six days. During this time, when Muslim raiding parties were roaming at will across the Jezreel Valley, Galilee, and Samaria, the three Christian monasteries on top of Mount Tabor were captured and destroyed by Maudud and his forces. Unfortunately, no further details regarding the fighting at Mount Tabor are available, although reportedly both Nablus and Beisan (Beth Shean) were also destroyed during the same series of raids. Eventually the Iraqi forces in Maudud's army insisted on returning home. Maudud allowed them to do so and dismissed the rest of his men at the same time, so the Muslim siege of the Jezreel Valley and surrounding areas was lifted at the end of the summer in A.D. 1113.[3]

This turned out to be Maudud's final campaign in Palestine, for he returned to Damascus with Tughtigin on 5 September 1183 only to be assassinated there on the following 2 October. Maudud's death was probably ordered by his erstwhile ally Tughtigin, who wanted to control these regions of Palestine by himself. However, if he is indeed guilty, Tughtigin's plan backfired, for although he was never charged with Maudud's murder, he was the obvious suspect and subsequently lost favor with his superiors in Baghdad. Tughtigin was ultimately forced to sign a treaty with the Crusaders and end his raiding activities in Palestine. The Jezreel Valley was then at peace for nearly seventy years, until the coming of Saladin.

Best known for his almost total annihilation of the Crusader forces at the battle of Hattin near Tiberias in A.D. 1187 and for his capture of Jerusalem two years later, Saladin began his rise to power during the interval between the Second and Third Crusades, having sworn to take back the Holy Land from the Crusaders. The Jezreel Valley was the scene of several forays by Saladin and his men in the years before and after the battle of Hattin, for Saladin proceeded to repeat the tactics used so successfully by Maudud of Mosul before him. Not once but at least four separate times within the same decade, Saladin's army crossed the Jordan River and marched into the Jezreel Valley via the same "Tiberias gateway" used by Maudud. The Crusaders became very familiar with Saladin during these years. Indeed, the costly debacle at the Horns of Hattin in A.D. 1187 might have been avoided altogether and the history of the Crusades may have followed a different path if the Crusaders had only heeded a lesson they learned at the battle of

'Ayn Jalut (the "Spring of Goliath"), which took place during Saladin's invasion of the Jezreel Valley in A.D. 1183.[4]

The story of the Crusaders versus Saladin in the Jezreel Valley actually begins a year earlier, in A.D. 1182, when Saladin's men conducted two separate raids in June and July.[5] The first of these was led by Saladin's subordinate Farrukh-Shah, who led the Islamic troops from Damascus in June 1182. According to the historian William of Tyre, who is our main source for these events, the action then unfolded as follows:

> They crossed the Jordan near the sea of Galilee, that is, near Tiberias, and furtively entered our land. After overrunning a part of Galilee, they came to a place at the foot of Mt. Tabor called Buria [Daburiya], near the ancient city of Nain. The people of those parts were as yet unaware that the truce had been broken. Accordingly, in complete reliance upon it, they did not take measures to protect themselves. As a result the enemy fell upon them stealthily by night and completely surrounded the place so that the besieged could not escape to the mountains which rose above them.[6]

Thus, crossing the Jordan River, Farrukh-Shah attacked the town of Daburiya (biblical *Daberath*), which lay at the foot of the western slopes of Mount Tabor. He and his men surrounded the town before dawn, as was the usual strategy for the Islamic invaders. When the townspeople awoke, they found themselves already surrounded. The defenders of Daburiya retreated to a tower, but their defense was quickly undermined, and within four hours some five hundred people were reportedly captured. Although William of Tyre says, "Then the Turks again crossed the Jordan and returned, safe and sound, to their own land," Saladin states that Farrukh-Shah actually continued on as far west as Acre (Acco) on this raid and killed or captured one thousand men and women and twenty thousand head of cattle and oxen before returning across the Jordan River.[7]

Saladin's second raid took place in July 1182 and was led by Saladin himself. His army left Damascus on 11 July and took little more than a day to reach the Sea of Galilee. By the evening of 12 July, they were threatening the city of Tiberias. The Crusaders in Tiberias, under the command of Raymond of Tripoli, who had married the Lady of Tiberias, sent for reinforcements from the nearby castles of Safad and Kaukab. These additional men reached the town later on the night of

12 July and safely slipped inside the defenses. On the morning of 13 July, Saladin was informed of the arrival of these reinforcements and decided to provoke a battle by sending out his left wing under the command of Farrukh-Shah. The Crusaders, however, could not be enticed to emerge for battle. Therefore, that evening Saladin marched south to attack Beisan (Beth Shean), hoping to provoke the Crusaders into emerging from Tiberias in response. By 14 July, Beisan was captured and being ravaged by Saladin's forces, although the garrison was still resisting fiercely. This finally prompted the Crusaders in Tiberias to move, which is precisely what Saladin had hoped they would do.[8]

According to William of Tyre, the Crusaders marched south, with the Jordan River on their left, and reached the Jezreel Valley between Beisan and Forbelet (modern Taiyiba) on the evening of 14 July. They spent the night camped on a hillside for protection. When dawn broke on the morning of 15 July, the Crusaders found themselves faced by Saladin's men, who had broken off their attack on Beisan (Beth Shean) when they heard that the Crusaders had left Tiberias. Saladin's forces numbered twenty thousand fighting men and apparently represented the largest Muslim army seen since the beginning of the Crusades, at least according to William of Tyre. The Crusaders themselves were led by a number of Frankish nobles, including the Ibelin brothers, Baldwin of Ramlah and Balian of Nablus, as well as Hugh the Younger, stepson of the count of Tripoli, but numbered barely seven hundred cavalry and an unknown quantity of infantry.[9]

The Crusaders were hemmed in on three sides by Saladin's forces, with Farrukh-Shah to the west, Taqi al-Din to the east, and Saladin himself to the south in the center. William of Tyre reports that the Crusaders "drew up their lines according to the rules of military science and with their usual courage advanced upon the foe." He continues, "Firmly they resisted the attacks against them and, although to their own everlasting disgrace many Christians . . . ignominiously fled from the heat of battle, yet in that conflict we proved superior to our foes."[10] According to the Muslim sources, however, the events and outcome of the battle were actually somewhat different. The Frankish cavalry charged but were quickly repulsed by the Muslims, who then proceeded to attack the Frankish infantry. After fierce fighting, the Crusaders were forced to retreat north up the hillside, in the only direction left open to them, and withdrew to the nearby castle of Forbelet. Although William claimed that the Crusaders had won the battle, it seems that Saladin's forces triumphed that day. Saladin and his men

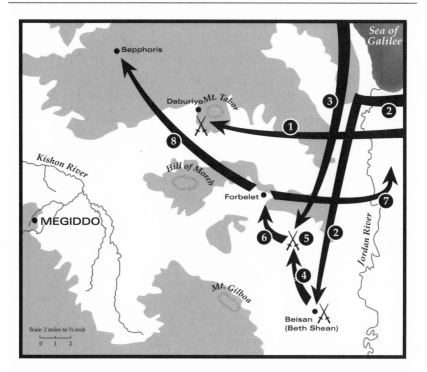

MAP 21. Saladin and the Crusaders, A.D. 1182

1. Islamic troops cross Jordan River and capture Daburiya in June 1182, then continue on to Acre (Acco).
2. Saladin threatens Tiberias in July 1182, then marches to attack Beisan (Beth Shean).
3. Crusaders march from Tiberias to the Jezreel Valley, south of Forbelet.
4. Saladin marches to meet Crusaders.
5. Crusaders charge Muslim army but are turned back.
6. Crusaders retreat to castle at Forbelet, followed by Saladin's forces, who camp nearby.
7. Saladin gives up siege, recrosses Jordan River, and returns north.
8. Crusaders march to Sepphoris to recover in peace.

then spent the night of 15 July by Forbelet, perhaps contemplating a siege of the castle and the Crusaders within, but broke camp a day or so later. By 18 July, Saladin had recrossed the Jordan and returned north, leaving the Crusaders to retrench at Sepphoris and lick their wounds in relative peace.[11]

In addition to everything else, the intense July heat had apparently taken its toll during the battle. Saladin complained that the noonday

sun had robbed him of complete victory, while William of Tyre records
that as many people died of heatstroke as were killed in the actual battle. The exact number of dead is not known. Of the Crusader forces,
William says that "only a few of our knights fell . . . but of the people
many perished." The Muslims apparently lost about one thousand
men, although this number is only approximate, since Saladin's men
carried away the bodies and secretly buried them during the night.[12]

Just over a year later, in mid-September A.D. 1183, after having captured the Syrian city of Aleppo and various cities in Mesopotamia in the
duration, Saladin and his army returned to the Jezreel Valley. They left
Damascus on 17 September, but did not cross the Jordan River south of
Lake Tiberias until 29 September. They found the city of Beisan empty,
the inhabitants having fled to Tiberias, and proceeded to sack and
burn the town. It is unclear just how many men were in Saladin's army,
but the Arab historians reported them to be "in vast numbers" and said
that they included troops from Aleppo and from across the Euphrates,
as well as the Turkoman cavalry and a large number of volunteers and
auxiliaries.[13] In the meantime, the Crusaders had received word that
Saladin was on the march again, and they began to assemble their own
forces in the city of Sepphoris.

The Crusaders numbered some thirteen hundred knights and more
than fifteen thousand well-armed infantry, according to both William
of Tyre and 'Imad al-Din, chroniclers of the two opposing sides. Their
numbers were also swelled by Italian sailors, merchants, and pilgrims
from Pisa, Lombardy, Venice, and Genoa, who left their ships in Acre
(Acco) to join the rapidly growing army. Even so, they were still outnumbered by the Muslim force advancing under Saladin. All of the
Crusaders were placed under the command of Guy de Lusignan,
brother-in-law of young King Baldwin IV of Jerusalem. The king himself could not command, because of his leprosy, which was to take his
life in Nazareth all too soon. Guy's control of the army was apparently
resented by a number of the other Crusader leaders. According to
William of Tyre, these included wealthy visiting Crusaders, such as God-
frey III, duke of Brabant; Henry, duke of Louvain, from the kingdom of
the Teutons; and Ralf de Maleine, a warrior of great renown from
Aquitaine. Also participating in the battle were most of the local Crusader nobles, including Raymond of Tripoli, grand master of the Hospitallers; Reynald of Châtillon, lord of a domain beyond the Jordan,
who had formerly been prince of Antioch; the Ibelin brothers, Baldwin
of Ramlah and Balian of Nablus; Reynald of Sidon; Walter of Caesarea;

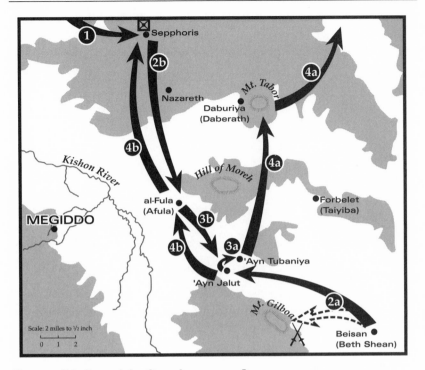

MAP 22. Saladin and the Crusaders, A.D. 1183

1. Crusaders from Acre (Acco) join others already in Sepphoris.

2a. (Primary arrow) Saladin marches from Beisan (Beth Shean) to ʿAyn Jalut on 30 September, (secondary arrow) while Islamic detachment ambushes Crusaders marching to Sepphoris.

2b. Crusaders from Sepphoris march to al-Fula (Afula) on 30 September.

3a. Saladin moves unexpectedly to ʿAyn Tubaniya on 1 October.

3b. Crusaders march and camp at ʿAyn Jalut on 1 October.

4a. Saladin marches to Mount Tabor on 6 October and then back to Damascus.

4b. Crusaders march back to al-Fula (Afula) on 6 October and then back to Sepphoris.

and Joscelin de Courtenay, seneschal of the king. They apparently considered Guy to be an incompetent leader; William reports that they regarded him as "an obscure man, wholly incapable and indiscreet."[14]

On 30 September 1183, Saladin's men marched westward some ten miles up the Jezreel Valley and camped at ʿAyn Jalut (the "Spring of Goliath"). Today located just west of the modern village of Gidona, at the foot of the northwestern corner of Mount Gilboa, the spring is either the same as or at least in the same general area as the Well of

FIG. 13. Ein Harod/ʿAyn Jalut (Zev Radovan, Jerusalem)

Harod, where Gideon gathered his forces to fight the Midianites and Amalekites more than two thousand years before. While en route to ʿAyn Jalut, an advance guard led by the Islamic commanders Chauli and ʿIzz al-Din Jurdik ran across a detachment of Crusaders under the authority of Humphrey IV of Toron, who were marching from the castles of Kerak and Shaubak to the city of Sepphoris to join the rest of the Crusader army. The small force of Crusaders was ambushed on the slopes of Mount Gilboa, and all of them were either killed or captured, while the Islamic advance guard reportedly lost only one man.[15]

On this same day, 30 September, the Crusaders who had assembled at Sepphoris finally made their move. William of Tyre reports:

> they crossed the mountains where lies Nazareth, the city of Our Lord, and went down into the great plain, the ancient name of which was Esdraelon. Thence, with troops arranged in battle formation, fittingly disposed according to the rules of military science, they directed their course toward the springs of Tubania [actually, Jalut], where Saladin with a strong force of picked knights distinguished for their prowess had established himself near the waters.[16]

The Crusaders camped that night at al-Fula (modern Afula), in the Crusader castle known as La Feve, or "the Bean," now buried underneath modern Kibbutz Merhavya. On the morning of the next day, 1 October, the Crusader forces moved directly toward those of Saladin at 'Ayn Jalut. Saladin unexpectedly backed off, moving his men about a mile out into the valley, away from 'Ayn Jalut and into open country, by the spring of 'Ayn Tubaniya. The advance guard of the Crusaders, led by Constable Amalric, was attacked by five hundred Muslim soldiers during this march. Perhaps Saladin was testing the Crusaders by sending out these five hundred skirmishers and thus moved his forces onto the open ground by 'Ayn Tubaniya to use his cavalry if he were given the chance. However, the Crusader advance guard was rescued by the timely arrival of reinforcements led by the Ibelin brothers, Baldwin and Balian. Saladin was thus unable to deploy his cavalry against the massed Crusader formation and was forced to bid his time and wait for a future opportunity. The remainder of the march was made without incident, and the Crusaders immediately took the opportunity to camp at 'Ayn Jalut themselves, settling in by the spring, with their backs to Mount Gilboa and within earshot of Saladin's forces only a mile away.[17]

Saladin's men proceeded to sally forth each day, intent on ravaging the countryside. William of Tyre records that the Greek convent on top of Mount Tabor was attacked but that the Muslims were repelled by the monks, aided by refugees from the surrounding countryside. William reports: "It is a fact . . . that for seven or eight successive days the enemy remained without opposition in our territory in the vicinity of the Jordan and daily, with impunity, wrought much evil upon our army." During these raids, the village of Zarin, located by the ancient site of Jezreel only two miles from 'Ayn Jalut, was attacked, and Forbelet (Taiyiba), where the Crusaders had taken refuge from Saladin back in July 1182 during his previous raid into the area, was destroyed. Other small forts in the area were reportedly also besieged, and the inhabitants of Nazareth claimed to have seen Muslim soldiers staring down into their city from the nearby heights. However, no major encounters were reported during the next five days, while the two armies stood face-to-face and toe-to-toe, each daring the other to make the first move.[18]

The Muslims also succeeded in cutting the supply lines of the Crusaders, so that hunger quickly set in at the camp by 'Ayn Jalut. The knights and foot soldiers had come supplied with provisions, but the sailors, merchants, and pilgrims who had left their ships in the harbor of Acre (Acco) and joined this mini-Crusade on the spur of the moment had come with virtually no food at all, expecting the encounter to last only a few days. William of Tyre reports that a minor miracle occurred and fish were suddenly discovered in the springs, where they had not been before.

> A certain event worthy of record happened during the time when our army was waiting at the spring of Tubania. Up to that time it was thought that this spring and the streams flowing from it contained few or no fish, but during the Christians' sojourn there it is said to have furnished a supply sufficient for the whole army.

Enough fish were found to feed the entire army, only to disappear once again after supply columns broke through the Muslim blockade and ended the threat of famine.[19]

Meanwhile, Saladin's forces were also facing a shortage of provisions after failing for nearly a week to lure the Crusaders into a battle on their own terms. Saladin therefore began marching toward Mount Tabor on 6 October, apparently hoping that the Crusaders would pursue him. The Crusaders did break camp, but only to march back to al-Fula (Afula) and then to their base in Sepphoris, having successfully faced down the invaders. By 8 October, Saladin had recrossed the Jordan; by 13 October, he and his massive army were back in Damascus.[20] Thus, the confrontation of A.D. 1183 at ʿAyn Jalut was in fact a non-event, but that fact in itself favored the Crusader forces.

William of Tyre reports that many in the Crusader army were furious at the battle plan followed by Guy de Lusignan. They thought that Guy should have attacked Saladin rather than remaining inactive; Guy was in command of the largest Crusader army that had been assembled within living memory, yet he allowed Saladin to raid Frankish territory with impunity. They accused Guy of cowardice and worse, but, in fact, patiently waiting until Saladin's supplies were exhausted and he had to retreat was probably the most sensible plan for the Crusaders to have pursued. While Guy may have followed this stratagem purely out of indecision or perhaps because he could not get the other jealous Crusader leaders to coordinate an attack, remaining inactive was exactly what he had been advised to do by Raymond of Tripoli, as well as by the Ibelin brothers, Baldwin and Balian. That the tactics succeeded and that Saladin was forced to withdraw without inflicting serious damage on the Jezreel Valley rendered this engagement, or rather nonengagement, both a draw and a qualified victory for the Crusaders.[21] Although it ended with a whimper rather than a bang—hardly an encounter about which later epics could be written, as indeed they were not—the Crusaders had learned a valuable lesson in their ongoing fight with Saladin and his Muslim forces, somewhat along the lines of Alexander Pope's aphorism "Fools rush in where angels fear to tread."

At any rate, Guy de Lusignan and the Crusaders had the opportunity to apply this lesson and follow the same defensive strategy four years later, at the Horns of Hattin by the Sea of Galilee just to the north of the Jezreel Valley, on 3–4 July 1187. The consensus by later historians is that had they done so, Saladin would again have been eventually forced to withdraw once more. However, Guy foolishly elected to fight this time. The abuse that he had received for failing to engage Saladin in A.D. 1183 may well have been the driving force underlying his foolhardy plan of attack at Hattin in A.D. 1187. This time, Guy de Lusignan and the Crusaders followed a disastrous offensive policy, resulting in the massacre of the Crusader forces, the capture of Guy himself, the beheading of Reynald of Châtillon, and the most lopsided victory by the Muslim forces during the entire history of the Crusades.[22] The Crusaders' days in the Holy Land were numbered from that moment on.

Immediately following the battle at Hattin, Saladin captured Mount Tabor, by then known in Arabic as "Qalat al-Tur." Few details are known, apart from the fact that Mount Tabor was not the only Crusader stronghold in the Jezreel Valley to be captured at this time, for Daburiya, Zarin (Jezreel), and the castle at al-Fula (modern Afula) also fell to Saladin. Indeed, the Crusaders defended few, if any, of their fortifications between Acre and Tiberias; other fortresses lost to Saladin included those of Nazareth, Caesarea, Haifa, and Sepphoris. It was said that everything within the Crusader fortresses was plundered and that enough booty was removed to fill a vast plain.[23]

Thirty years later, after the Third Crusade, with Richard the Lion-Hearted, had failed to dislodge Saladin and the Muslims from the Holy Land, and after the Fourth Crusade had massacred the inhabitants of Constantinople instead of those of Jerusalem, the Fifth Crusade began. King Andrew II of Hungary, among others, responded to the call of the pope to recapture the stronghold at Mount Tabor. However, Andrew distinguished himself while on the Fifth Crusade in A.D. 1217 not by his fearsome conduct in battle but rather by the number of relics and saintly body parts that he collected religiously while in the Holy Land. For example, he acquired the heads of both St. Stephen and St. Margaret and procured the right hands of both St. Thomas and St. Bartholomew. He also obtained part of the rod of the biblical Aaron and one of the water jugs used at the marriage feast at Cana recorded in the New Testament, or at least so Andrew was led to believe.[24] He brought all these items back to Europe the following year, having abandoned the Crusade before it had barely begun, but not before the Crusaders had tried mightily but unsuccessfully to capture the Muslim fortress on Mount Tabor.

Earlier, in A.D. 1211, Saladin's brother, the sultan al-'Adil, and the sultan's son al-Mu'azzam, both members of the Ayyubid dynasty in Egypt founded by Saladin, had begun building a solid fortress on top of Mount Tabor, where previously the Christian monastery marking the spot of Christ's transfiguration had stood. This was the same monastery, one of three on top of Mount Tabor, that had been attacked previously by both Maudud of Mosul and Saladin himself. The conversion of this monastery into a Muslim fortress sparked the Fifth Crusade. Pope Innocent III had, in April A.D. 1213 at the Fourth Lateran Council, called for a Crusade to destroy this stronghold on top of Mount Tabor, as well as to rescue the thousands of Crusaders who had been captured during previous Crusades and who were now languishing in Muslim prisons.

> And in addition to the former great and grave injuries which the treacherous Saracens have inflicted on our Redeemer, on account of our offences, the same perfidious Saracens have recently built a fortified stronghold to confound the Christian name on Mount Thabor, where Christ revealed to his disciples a vision of his future glory; by means of this fortress they think they will easily occupy the city of Acre, which is very near them, and then invade the rest of that land without any obstructive resistance, since it is almost entirely devoid of forces or supplies. (Pope Innocent III's proclamation for the Fifth Crusade)

The Fifth Crusade's additional objective of attacking Damietta in Egypt may have been a proposal cooked up by the Crusader forces already in Palestine, rather than by the pope himself, who had a rather more limited goal in mind.[25]

The Crusade began in A.D. 1217, despite the death of Innocent III the previous year, for his successor Honorius III took responsibility for seeing Innocent's project through to the end. Apart from enthusiastically collecting relics, however, Andrew does not seem to have personally accomplished much during his time in the Holy Land. After landing at Acre (Acco), he and his Hungarian troops linked up with Duke Leopold of Austria and John de Brienne, king of Jerusalem, along with

FIG. 14. Mount Tabor (Zev Radovan, Jerusalem)

their men. They launched an expedition immediately, on 3 November 1217, and marched from Acre eastward through the Jezreel Valley.[26]

Oliver of Paderborn, a participant and eyewitness who wrote a chronicle of the events that occurred during the Fifth Crusade, tells best what happened, or rather what did not happen.

> The Patriarch of Jerusalem, with great humility on the part of the clergy and the people, reverently lifted up the wood of the life-giving Cross, and set out from Acre on the sixth day after the feast of All Saints. . . . With such a standard, we advanced in orderly array, through the plain of Faba [Al-Fula, modern Afula] as far as the fountain of Tubania, toiling much on that day; and when we had sent scouts ahead, seeing the dust that was being stirred up by our enemies, we were uncertain whether they were hastening to attack us or to flee. On the following day we set out through the mountains of Gilboa, which were on our right, with a swamp on the left, to Bethsan [Beth Shean/Beisan] where the enemy had pitched camp; but fearing the arrival of the army of the living God, that was so numerous, and was proceeding in so orderly a way, they broke camp and fled, leaving the land to be devastated by the soldiers of Christ. Thence,

> crossing the Jordan . . . we washed our bodies at leisure in it, and we rested throughout two days in the same place, finding an abundance of food and fodder; then on the shore of the Sea of Galilee we made three days' rest, wandering through places in which Our Savior deigned to work miracles, and conversed with men in His corporal presence. We looked upon Bethsaida, . . . and thus we returned to Acre, carrying our sick and our needy brethren through Capharnaum on beasts of burden.

Apparently, the Egyptian sultan al-'Adil had decided not to attack the marauding Crusaders and had ordered his son al-Mu'azzam to likewise restrain himself, probably for the simple reason that they were outnumbered by the Crusaders, who may have had as many as four thousand knights in their army. Some sources say there were a total of fifteen thousand men or more in the Crusader army, but this may be an exaggeration. At any rate, Sultan al-'Adil and his Muslim forces retreated across the Jordan River before the advancing Crusaders, the Muslims being prepared to attack only if the Crusaders showed intentions of heading toward either Nablus or Jerusalem, which did not happen.[27]

Participation in this first foray through the Jezreel Valley and beyond was pretty much the extent of Andrew's active involvement in the Fifth Crusade. His men engaged in at least one more sortie north into Syria, with unfortunate results. But Andrew remained in Acre, enjoying the relative luxury, until he left with King Hugh of Cyprus to attend the wedding of Count Bohemond IV to Hugh's half sister Melisend in Tripoli, on the coast of Syria. Following Hugh's sudden death at the age of only twenty-three in Tripoli on 10 January 1218, Andrew decided to return to Europe with his collection of relics, heads, and hands of various saints. He promptly marched overland back to Hungary via Tripoli, Antioch, Armenia, and Constantinople, despite first the threat and then the actuality of excommunication by the patriarch of Jerusalem for not having completed the Crusade and for taking his men home with him, thus leaving the remaining Crusader forces in Acre seriously depleted, if only temporarily.[28]

Meanwhile, however, following the first ineffective sortie, which returned to Acre ca. 14 November 1217, John de Brienne, king of Jerusalem, had decided to take matters into his own hands. Giving his men only two weeks' rest, John marched out again from Acre through the Jezreel Valley on 30 November A.D. 1217, determined to capture Mount Tabor and thus fulfill one of the original objectives of the Fifth Crusade. His force was much smaller this time, but their first attack on the fortress, on 3 December, was almost successful, despite the fact that the fortress, built with fully seventy-seven towers and manned by two thousand Muslim troops, was nearly impregnable.

The Crusaders made their approach undetected, thanks to thick cloud cover blanketing the top of the mountain. They were helped by a local Muslim boy, whom they baptized, and who agreed to show them a path up to the fortress. As Oliver of Paderborn reports, the patriarch of Jerusalem (Ralph of Merencourt) proceeded at the head of the Crusader forces, leading the way up the mountain, holding fragments of the True Cross and accompanied by bishops and clergy who sang and prayed. While marching uphill in the thick fog, the Crusaders surprised a small force of Muslim defenders outside the fortress, who quickly retreated back inside for safety. Heavy fighting then ensued at the walls of the fortress itself.

John himself personally killed the Muslim emir and commander of the garrison, then he suddenly and inexplicably gave his men orders to desist and to march back down the mountain. Why John gave these orders remains one of the great mysteries of this conflict. James of Vitry (the bishop of Acre at the time) cites a lack of siege engines, such as battering rams, scaling ladders, and other heavy machines of assault. Oliver of Paderborn wrote:

> But the King then lost as much in merit by descending as he had gained by ascending; for in descending on the same Sunday and making others descend, he gave courage to the infidel by the space of time that was granted to them; but we do not know by what judgment of God or by what plan of the leaders the army of the Lord descended then and withdrew ingloriously.

It is possible that John did not know how close he was to winning the battle and so retreated to wait for siege engines and similar weapons of war or at least to wait for reinforcements. His decision later came under heavy criticism, for, probably unbeknownst to him, the Muslim garrison was just about to surrender when the Crusaders withdrew on John's orders.[29]

A second attack two days later failed, despite additional forces comprised of Hospitallers and Templars who had arrived to beef up the Crusaders' strength. This time, the Crusaders managed to carry a huge scaling ladder up the mountain and place it against the fortress walls, but the Muslim defenders counterattacked. Splashing the Crusaders with "Greek fire" (the napalm of that era), the Muslims set the scaling ladder on fire and killed virtually the entire party of men manning it.

Moreover, the Muslims then went on the offensive, having decided to fight to the death this time, for they had all heard the stories of how Richard the Lion-Hearted treacherously executed nearly three thousand of their brethren who had surrendered to the Crusaders in good faith after relinquishing Acre (Acco) during the earlier Third Crusade. Discouraged by the Muslims' stout resistance, the Crusaders gave up the siege and returned to Acre (Acco) on 7 December, leaving the Ayyubid forces still manning the fortress on top of Mount Tabor.[30]

The Crusaders then abandoned their efforts in the Jezreel Valley and turned their attention toward their additional objective of besieging Damietta in Egypt—which they would successfully capture some eighteen months later. Almost immediately after the Crusaders moved on to Egypt, Sultan al-'Adil ordered his son al-Mu'azzam to destroy the Muslim fortress on top of Mount Tabor, in part because he could no longer spare the men needed to defend this outpost. He was correct in thinking that it would be better for the fortress to be destroyed by his own men than for it to fall into the hands of the Crusaders, for Crusader control of the fortress would have posed a threat to the rest of Galilee. Within six months of the Crusaders' ignominious retreat from Mount Tabor, therefore, the fortress that they had been unable to capture was torn down by the Muslims themselves.[31]

After it was razed by al-Mu'azzam, the sultan's son and Saladin's nephew, in A.D. 1218, the Muslim fortress on Mount Tabor remained in ruins for the next decade, until A.D. 1229, at which time it was partially restored by Hungarian monks. In A.D. 1241, it once again came into Crusader hands, as a result of a peace treaty signed by Richard of Cornwall. However, in the late spring of A.D. 1247, the fortress was again captured by the Muslims. This time, they were led by a new actor on the world stage, the Ayyubid ruler as-Salih Ayyub. Ayyub had appeared on the scene as sultan in Egypt after ousting his younger brother in A.D. 1240. Since then, he had been busy fighting, mostly in battles against his uncle, as-Salih Isma'il of Damascus, and his cousin an-Nasir Da'ud of Kerak, but also in battles against the Crusaders, including a battle that proved a major victory against the combined forces of all three of these enemies at Harbiyya (La Forbie), a few miles northeast of Gaza, far to the south of the Jezreel Valley, in A.D. 1244.[32]

In the late spring of A.D. 1247, having vanquished his uncle and cousin, Ayyub sent an army north to the Jezreel Valley and Galilee.[33] Commanded by his general Fakhr al-Din ibn al-Shaykh, Ayyub's Egyptian army attacked Tiberias first, on 16 June 1247, and then captured

Mount Tabor, Belvoir, and Kaukab soon afterward. The Crusaders put up little fight for either Mount Tabor or the other fortresses, for they were too lacking in able-bodied men to defend themselves properly. Ayyub and his army moved on to besiege and capture Ascalon and then marched on Damascus.[34]

The Jezreel Valley was saved from further incursions by Ayyub, however, because he was stricken by a fatal disease and died soon thereafter. The fortress on top of Mount Tabor reverted once again to Crusader hands in A.D. 1255, when the Hospitallers petitioned Pope Alexander IV and received permission to repair the fortress and man it with forty knights. Less than a decade later, however, the fortress was captured by the Muslims yet again. This time, the Mamluke sultan Baibars from Egypt took control of Mount Tabor, after his justly famous defeat of the Mongol army at the battle of ʿAyn Jalut, right across the valley at the foot of Mount Gilboa.[35]

CHAPTER 8

Dreams of Glory

All the armies of the world could maneuver their forces on this vast
plain. . . . There is no place in the whole world more suited for war than
this. . . . [It is] the most natural battleground of the whole earth.

—Napoleon Bonaparte (?), supposedly as he
contemplated the Jezreel Valley in 1799

THE MONGOL HORDE roared out of their homelands in the Asian
steppes, killing, burning, looting, and pillaging anything and everything that lay in their way. They were an inexorable force, at first
spreading like an inkblot across the Middle East and then steamrolling
their way into Syria-Palestine, intent on dominating an ever increasing
empire. They were the heralds of a new era, as the thirteenth through
the eighteenth centuries A.D. saw the spread of empires across the
region—including those of the Mongols and Mamlukes, the Ottomans,
and Napoleon, to name but a few whose dreams of glory affected the
Jezreel Valley during the second millennium A.D.

On 3 September A.D. 1260, the Jezreel Valley was the site of a fierce
conflict waged by two relative newcomers to the world scene, the Mongols and the Mamlukes. They met that day in a hotly contested battle at
'Ayn Jalut (the "Spring of Goliath") in the Jezreel Valley, the same location where Saladin and the Crusaders had stood and glared at each
other in a standoff more than seventy-five years earlier. The Mamlukes
prevailed in this conflict, inflicting on the Mongols their first major
defeat ever, and saving Syria-Palestine and Egypt from Mongol domination in the process. The details of this battle are fairly well known,
thanks to a number of contemporary and near-contemporary accounts,
some of which are based on eyewitness descriptions. However, since we
have records from both pro-Mongol and pro-Mamluke sources, several
variations of the course of the battle and of the fate of some of the participants exist. Substantial questions therefore abound: Was there an
ambush of the Mongol troops, as the Persian historian Rashid al-Din
claims? Was the Mongol leader Kitbuqa killed in the heat of battle, or
did he have his head chopped off afterward? How important was the

outcome of the battle for the history of the Middle East and for the Western world as a whole?[1]

The Mongols had been expanding westward from the steppes of Asia since the time of Genghis Khan in the early thirteenth century. Having overrun Iran, Mesopotamia, Armenia, Georgia, Anatolia, and Iraq by A.D. 1258, they looked toward Syria-Palestine and Egypt for their next conquests. In late December 1259, a Mongol army under the command of Hülegü, a grandson of Genghis Khan and younger brother of the ruling Great Khan Möngke, crossed the Euphrates and attacked Aleppo in Syria. The size of his army is debated—estimates have ranged from 60,000 to 300,000 men—but was probably about 120,000 soldiers. Aleppo quickly fell to the invaders, but events back in the Mongol homelands necessitated a change in Hülegü's plans. Word that the Great Khan had died and that Hülegü's two older brothers were quarreling over the succession prompted Hülegü to move back with the bulk of his army, northeast to Azerbaijan, near Tabriz. He may also have been concerned that there was not enough pasture land in Syria to support his huge army and all of their cavalry for an extended period of time.[2]

Before he left in late April 1260, or perhaps after he was already en route to Azerbaijan, Hülegü sent an embassy to Egypt, demanding that the Mamluke sultan either submit to the Mongols and become a vassal or else face the wrath of their army. The letter, which contained verses from the Koran alongside insults aimed at the Egyptian sultan, suggested that resistance would be futile, that the Mongols' right to rule the world was heaven-sent, and that all rebels would be destroyed if they did not submit peacefully. The sultan was urged: "Hasten your reply before the fire of war is kindled. . . . You will suffer the most terrible catastrophes, your countries will become deserts, . . . and we will kill your children and your old men together."[3]

The Mongol invasion of lower Syria, Palestine, and Egypt was left to one of Hülegü's most trusted generals, Kitbuqa. However, since Hülegü had taken the majority of the army with him back to Azerbaijan, Kitbuqa was left with no more than ten thousand to twelve thousand Mongol soldiers. Even if local recruits swelled the ranks to twenty thousand soldiers as several ancient sources report, this was not a very large force.[4] Why he was left with so few troops is not completely clear, but it seems that Hülegü and the Mongols had underestimated the Egyptian forces in terms of both their exact numbers and their willingness to fight. This may have been based on faulty intelligence data deliberately fed to them by Syrian captives. Be that as it may, Kitbuqa quickly went on the offensive, capturing both Damascus and Sidon by August 1260, and sending an advance force into Palestine as far as Gaza, to reconnoiter the lay of the land while also pillaging, looting, and burning wherever and whenever possible.

Meanwhile, in Cairo, the Mamluke sultan Qutuz had received and read the threatening message sent by Hülegü. His reaction was swift: the Mongol ambassadors who had brought the letter were executed, by being cut in half, and their heads were nailed up on the Zuwaila Gate of Cairo.[5] Preparations were begun to defend Egypt against the inevitable Mongol attack, now guaranteed by this act of defiance.

Qutuz himself was a relatively new player on the political scene. He had seized power in Egypt in November 1259, only a few months before Hülegü's message arrived. He was a Mamluke, one of the slave-soldiers so favored by the Egyptian sultans of the thirteenth century. These Mamlukes were almost all of Turkish origin. They were slaves who had been bought as children and brought to Egypt. There they were converted to Islam, given the name *Ibn Abdullah* ("son of Abdullah"— Abdullah having been the father of Muhammad), and raised under the strict tutelage of a Mamluke army sergeant. Upon reaching adulthood, they were given their freedom in exchange for serving in the Egyptian army. They were greatly feared, and usually fiercely loyal, warriors.

Qutuz had been a trusted commander of the army under the previous Egyptian sultan Aybak. When Aybak was assassinated in A.D. 1257, his son Ali was only fifteen years old, so Qutuz was appointed regent to help the young man rule. By the end of 1259, however, Qutuz had overthrown Ali and was proclaimed as sultan in his place. Qutuz used the encroaching Mongol army and Egypt's need for a strong leader as the excuse for his actions. The Mamlukes had realized that they were now both numerous enough and powerful enough that they could rule Egypt as well as or better than their previous patrons, the Ayyubid sultans.

Deciding to anticipate the impending Mongol attack and take the offensive, Qutuz rallied the Egyptians via fiery orations and quickly raised a force of Mamluke soldiers and other assorted troops. He may have believed that the best chance of defending Egypt lay in marching northward and forcing a confrontation with the Mongols in a region far from the borders of Egypt. That way, even if his forces were initially defeated, they would be able to fall back and fight several more times before the Mongols actually crossed into Egypt. If the Egyptian forces were to stay in Cairo and wait for the Mongols to come to them, there would be no fall-back position if they lost the initial battle. Moreover, Qutuz may have feared that his forces would lose heart as the Mongol army approached Cairo and might not fight as well as they would if they took the offensive against a force that Qutuz now knew was only a small portion of the Mongol army that had originally invaded Syria.[6]

The number of soldiers in this Mamluke Egyptian force is debated; originally modern scholars thought that there might have been as many as 120,000 men, but this seems to have been a figure arrived at only because of an error introduced in translating an original Arabic source into French and then into English. No exact numbers are given in any of the Mamluke sources, but there were probably only about twelve thousand Mamluke soldiers in this force. In addition to the Mamlukes themselves, the army also consisted of refugee Syrian troops and assorted other fighting men who had fled the Mongol advance in the northern countries. These may have swelled the numbers of the Egyptian army to as many as twenty thousand men, but almost certainly no more than that; it is unlikely to have "numbered over 100,000 men" as some have claimed. In short, the Mongol and the Mamluke armies that were to meet at ʿAyn Jalut were probably of approximately the same size, with between ten thousand and twenty thousand men in each.[7]

The Mamluke army left Cairo on 26 July 1260 and headed for Sali-hiyya, a staging area approximately seventy-five miles (120 kilometers) northeast of Cairo. Here Qutuz was forced to use his oratory powers again, to persuade the reluctant Egyptian leaders that they should con-tinue to advance northward. He was able to shame them into doing so, it is reported, by yelling at one point, "I am going to fight the Mongols alone!" Their resolve stiffened, the advance guard of this Egyptian army, led by the Mamluke commander Baibars, left for Gaza and defeated the small Mongol force posted there. The few Mongol sur-vivors fled to the safety of Damascus and reported the turn of events to Kitbuqa and the Mongol generals.

The rest of the Egyptian army, under the command of Qutuz him-self, followed Baibars and the advance guard to Gaza and then, after resting for only one day, marched up the coast and camped outside the Crusader city of Acre (Acco). There, Qutuz entered into negotiations with the Frankish Crusaders, who were caught in the cross fire between the Mamlukes and the Mongols. The Franks elected to remain neutral but allowed the Egyptian army to pass through their territory and pro-vided them with food and supplies.

As soon as Kitbuqa heard that the Egyptian army was heading north, he prepared to break camp and lead the Mongol army south to meet them. However, reportedly, a revolt broke out in Damascus at just that time, and Kitbuqa was forced to delay long enough to quell the rebellion.[8] This allowed Qutuz and the Egyptians to reach Acre (Acco) untouched. The Mongol forces finally marched south from Damascus, crossed the Jordan River, and pitched camp in the Jezreel Valley toward the end of August or in early September 1260. Here, at ʿAyn Jalut by Mount Gilboa, some ten miles into the Jezreel Valley, where Saladin and the Crusaders had faced each other in the previous century, the Mongols awaited the Mamlukes.

Why did the Mongols choose this particular spot, in the Jezreel Valley, for their battleground? Several potential factors for their choice can be ascertained. First, the area offered water and good pasture for their horses and fairly good conditions for cavalry warfare, since it was late summer or early fall. In fact, some authorities insist that this was the final, southernmost point that offered such advantages along the route from Damascus to Egypt. Second, the floor of the Jezreel Valley, which measures fully seven miles wide at some points, narrows to only three miles wide at ʿAyn Jalut and could thus be easily controlled or even completely blocked by a large army. Third, both Mount Gilboa and the nearby Hill of Moreh could be used as vantage points, and Mount Gilboa could also be used to anchor the Mongol flank during the coming battle. Fourth, the Mongols may have thought that the Mamlukes would come from the south and send their army through the Wadi ʿAra pass, emerging into the Jezreel Valley by the ancient site of Megiddo, much as Thutmose III had done twenty-five hundred years earlier, and as General Allenby would do again some seven hundred years later. In that case, they could attack the Mamluke army while it was still coming through the pass and deployed in marching mode, stretched out in a thin line several miles long and vulnerable to exactly the sort of ambush that Thutmose III's generals had warned him against. However, as I mentioned earlier in this discussion, the Mamlukes had instead already marched further north, up the coast to Acre (Acco), and would be proceeding south and east across the Jezreel Valley toward the Mongol position at ʿAyn Jalut.[9]

Qutuz exhorted his Mamluke army camped outside Acre (Acco), giving them a rousing speech recalling past Mongol atrocities; invoking the need to protect their families, property, and way of life; and emphasizing the need to defend Islam against the infidels. He then sent his

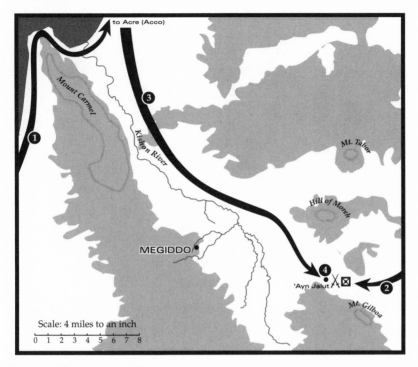

MAP 23. Mamlukes and Mongols

1. Mamlukes march north from Egypt via Salihiyya and Gaza to outside Acre (Acco).
2. Mongols move south from Damascus, cross Jordan River, and camp at 'Ayn Jalut.
3. Mamlukes advance from Acre (Acco) toward 'Ayn Jalut.
4. Battle is fought at 'Ayn Jalut on 3 September; Mamlukes are victorious.

trusted commander Baibars ahead with the Mamluke advance guard and led the rest of the army slowly out of Acre (Acco) and toward the Mongols.[10]

There are at least two differing accounts of the events that unfolded next at the battle of 'Ayn Jalut: the account of the pro-Mongol Persian historian Rashid al-Din written in the fourteenth century and that of the pro-Mamluke fifteenth-century Egyptian historian al-Maqrizi, who paints quite a different picture. Until recently, the pro-Mongol account of Rashid al-Din was believed to be the more accurate of the two, but recent research utilizing additional sources, including some eyewitness accounts, has changed the picture dramatically. Now the pro-Mamluke

FIG. 15. Jezreel Valley floor in the vicinity of ʿAyn Jalut, with Mount Gilboa in the background (Zev Radovan, Jerusalem)

accounts of the battle, such as that written by al-Maqrizi, are thought to be generally more reliable, but overall it appears that the true unfolding of the events at the battle lies somewhere between the descriptions of Rashid and al-Maqrizi, a compromise that is perhaps not too surprising.[11]

When the Mamluke advance guard under Baibars ran into the first Mongol scouts, they fought a series of inconclusive, small skirmishes. Rashid al-Din claims that Baibars and his small band retreated little by little before the onslaught of the Mongols, until they led the Mongol troops into an ambush. Rashid records that Qutuz and the rest of the Mamluke army, who had hidden themselves in a favorable position, promptly attacked and decimated Kitbuqa's forces, just as Antiochus III had done to Ptolemy IV centuries before. However, there is no corroboration for Rashid's account, and it may be that he took a few liberties with the facts. Instead, it appears that these small skirmishes took place the day before the actual battle and that when Baibars and the advance guard ran into the first Mongol scouts, Baibars simply sent word back to

Qutuz and briefly retreated to await reinforcements. He did not have to wait long, for Qutuz and the rest of the Mamluke army were only a day's march behind, riding east from Acre (Acco) along the Jezreel Valley. Soon after sunrise of the next day, then, on the morning of 3 September 1260, the battle of 'Ayn Jalut officially began.

At the outset, the armies seem to have been drawn up facing each other somewhere in the plain slightly to the north or northwest of the spring at 'Ayn Jalut, with each army arrayed in a north-south line stretching across the valley. The Mongols, who had arrived and positioned themselves at the battlefield first, quickly attacked and demolished the left wing of the Mamluke army, which may have been left deliberately weak by Qutuz and his generals. Qutuz rallied his men, removing his helmet so that he could be recognized and riding straight at the enemy while shouting, "O Islam!" at the top of his voice. Moving his men around like chess pieces, he launched a counterattack that outflanked the oncoming Mongols and evened the battle. If there was, as Rashid claims, an ambush at any point during the battle, it can be said to have occurred at this moment, but only if it is argued that Qutuz deliberately allowed his left wing to collapse to lure the Mongol troops in and surround them in a pincher movement. The Mamlukes took heart, fighting fiercely, and the Mongols began to flee headlong, only to be cut down as they ran.

However, calling to his men, Kitbuqa made a last desperate charge and, in so doing, nearly reversed the events of the day. The Mamlukes were saved only by Qutuz once again inspiring his troops, this time by bellowing, "O God, give us victory!" while charging across the battlefield.[12] The Mamlukes followed their fearless leader in a final bold onslaught, during which they overwhelmed the Mongol forces and chopped them to pieces. Al-Maqrizi's account says that Kitbuqa was galloping "backwards and forwards in front of his men shouting that it was their duty to die where they stood" when he was cut down and killed.[13] Rashid, however, says that Kitbuqa was not killed in battle but instead captured after the loss of his horse and brought before Qutuz. Rashid reports that a violent argument ensued, with words and insults exchanged between the two leaders, and that, threatened with decapitation, Kitbuqa told the Mamluke leader:

> Do not be too much elated with your momentary victory. If I perish it is by the hand of God, and not by yours. As soon as the news of my death shall reach the ears of Khulagu Khan, his wrath will boil over like an

angry sea. From Azerbaijan to the gates of Egypt the whole land shall be trodden under by the hoofs of Mongol horses, and our soldiers will carry off in the sacks of their horses the sands of Egypt. Khulagu Khan has among his followers 300,000 warriors equal to Kitbuqa. My death will only make them one less. . . . Make haste and put an end to me that I may no longer hear your reproaches.[14]

According to Rashid, Qutuz then made good his threat: Kitbuqa was summarily dispatched, and his severed head was sent to Cairo posthaste. Either way, whether he was killed in battle or executed immediately afterward, it is clear from both accounts that Kitbuqa's head was cut off and sent back to Cairo as vivid proof of the Mamluke victory.

After their defeat, the few Mongol survivors fled in different directions. Many scrambled up a nearby hill, only to be pursued by Baibars and his men and slaughtered where they stood. Others were killed by local villagers, and still others, hiding in fields of reeds, were flushed out and killed when the Mamlukes set the fields on fire. The last remaining survivors fled north to Syria, where their women and children were still camped, and there were chased and defeated once more by Baibars and his advance guard of Mamlukes. There is no good record of exactly how many Mongol warriors died that day at ʿAyn Jalut. One report that the entire Mongol army perished is probably exaggerated; another report gives the figure of fifteen hundred dead, which may be closer to the truth.[15] There are no figures recorded at all for the number of Mamluke casualties.

Unfortunately for him, the Egyptian sultan Qutuz did not have long to enjoy his victory. He continued to lead the rest of the Mamluke army north after the battle and captured both Damascus and Aleppo, bringing Syria under Mamluke rule and creating a new political and military force in Syria-Palestine, with which the remaining Crusaders would have to contend in the future. In October, he set off once again back to Egypt, intending to celebrate the Mamluke victory once safely home. However, a few miles outside Cairo, in the desert between el-Arish and Salihiyya, he was assassinated by a group of conspirators headed by none other than his trusted commander Baibars. It was 22 October 1260; Qutuz had been sultan for less than a year. Baibars, who may have been angered by Qutuz's refusal to appoint him governor of Syria, proclaimed himself sultan and was duly installed as such upon reaching Cairo the next day.[16]

The importance of the battle fought at ʿAyn Jalut that day in September 1260 cannot be overestimated. It was the first time that the Mongols had been defeated by any foe in a pitched battle anywhere. The defeat made it clear that they were vulnerable after all. The myth of Mongol invincibility had been shattered. The battle affected the very course of Western civilization, not only halting the westward advance of the Mongols and saving Egypt and Syria-Palestine from Mongol domination, but also marking the beginning of Mamluke influence in the region, starting with the reign of Baibars, who is considered to be the "real founder of Mamluke power."[17]

For whatever reasons (still not completely understood), the Mongols never made a serious effort to avenge their defeat at ʿAyn Jalut. A token force was sent in November 1260, perhaps in part to test the resolve of the new Mamluke sultan Baibars, but it was defeated at Homs in Syria. Additional invasions were launched in A.D. 1281, 1299, 1300, 1303, and 1312, but with only one exception—in A.D. 1300, when the Mongols momentarily occupied Syria again—these all seemed halfhearted and, in the end, were no more successful than the efforts of Kitbuqa and his forces had been on that fateful day at ʿAyn Jalut in the Jezreel Valley.[18]

When Baibars and his Mamluke followers assumed control of Egypt in A.D. 1260, they also inherited the associated territories in Syria-Palestine. Baibars' policy in these regions was dominated by the continued threat posed by the Mongols during the next half-century. In particular, Baibars sought to ensure continued and safe passage for his Mamluke armies from Cairo to Damascus, a route that went through Palestine via the Jezreel Valley.[19] Therefore, when the Hospitallers set about restoring the ruined Muslim fortress on top of Mount Tabor, which they had been given by Pope Alexander IV in A.D. 1255, and proceeded to man it with forty knights (as mentioned in chap. 7), Baibars saw this as a direct and immediate threat to his military lifeline stretching from Cairo to Damascus.

Baibars therefore attacked and destroyed the partially refortified Crusader outpost on top of Mount Tabor early in A.D. 1263.[20] There are few details available for the battle, perhaps because the Hospitallers seem to have evacuated the castle upon seeing Baibars approaching and may have given it up without a fight. Baibars then continued on to sack Nazareth and Acre in April A.D. 1263, using his camp at Mount Tabor as a base for these and other raids. In retaliation, perhaps, the

Hospitallers and the Templars united to attack and capture Baibars' small fortress at al-Lejjun near Megiddo in January A.D. 1264. Again, few details are available for the battle, and it is said that "such fruitless excursions only served to irritate the sultan."[21]

Undoubtedly, other battles occurred in the Jezreel Valley during the next several centuries, for Syria-Palestine was anything but peaceful during those years, and the Jezreel Valley was no exception. For instance, in a situation similar to that found during the Neo-Assyrian through Persian periods, the Jezreel Valley saw a number of armies traversing its length and width during the early Ottoman period. Sultan Selim I and his Ottoman army marched through the Jezreel Valley, known in Arabic as the "Marj Ibn 'Amir," on their way from Istanbul to Jerusalem and Cairo and back again, during their victorious campaign against the Mamlukes in A.D. 1516/1517. This campaign broke the back of the Mamlukes and established the Ottoman Empire, which then took control of the area for the next four hundred years, until World War I. Selim I and his men stayed twice at Khan Lejjun, the fortified *caravanserai* located by the town of Lejjun and ancient Megiddo—once on 24 December 1516 during the journey to Cairo, and again on 30 September 1517 during the journey back to Istanbul. Selim I's men also fought a major battle on 24 December 1516 near Beisan (Beth Shean), inflicting a severe defeat on the Mamluke forces, but this is the closest that they ever got to fighting in the Jezreel Valley itself.[22]

Additional battles must have been fought in the Jezreel Valley during the first several centuries of Ottoman rule, but it is not until the local Palestinian ruler Zahir al-'Umar appears on the scene during the eighteenth century A.D., replete with dreams of glory, that we get the next recorded instances of such conflicts.[23] Beginning his career rather inauspiciously, as the youngest son of a bedouin tax-collecting family named Zayadinah, Zahir al-'Umar quickly gained control of most of Galilee and ruled it with an iron fist. Born about 1690, Zahir began to establish his mini-empire from his stronghold at Tiberias in the 1720s. By the time of his death in A.D. 1775, he controlled an area extending from Tiberias and the Jordan River in the east to Acre (Acco) and the Mediterranean in the west, including both Safad and Nazareth, and was the confidant of such powerful rulers as 'Ali Bey of Egypt, the Russian emperor, and the Ottoman sultan.[24] As a result of Zahir's aggressive attempts to expand his mini-empire and of attempts by others to contain him, the Jezreel Valley was the scene of at least two battles during the lifetime of Zahir al-ʿUmar.

In the first instance, Zahir was faced with a hostile alliance of the sheikhs of Nablus and the Bani Saqr bedouin tribe in A.D. 1735. The Nablusites feared that Zahir would interfere in the affairs of Nazareth, which they controlled at the time. The Bani Saqr nursed a deep-seated hatred of Zahir for his having established a relative peace in the Jezreel Valley, which prevented them from pursuing their chosen vocation as bandits and brigands preying on travelers passing through the territory. Thus, the Nablus-Saqr alliance against Zahir al-ʿUmar was born.[25]

Zahir had originally been counting on having some three thousand Bani Saqr cavalrymen to help him fight against the sheikhs of Nablus. When he heard that the two forces had allied against him, he realized that a change of plan and drastic new tactics were necessary. He called together a council of his family, the Zayadinah, and enlisted the aid of his brother Saʾd along with other family members. Since there was no time to gather more recruits, they decided to plan an ambush of the Nablus-Saqr alliance forces at a site known as al-Rawdah, located in the Jezreel Valley some distance to the west of Lejjun and Megiddo.[26]

Zahir led his main force of two thousand men directly at the Nablus-Saqr soldiers, as scripted. Upon engaging in fierce battle, he and his men then retreated in apparent confusion, as if they had been routed and severely defeated. The Nablus-Saqr soldiers ran after them, in gleeful pursuit. Two separate and additional forces of Zahir's men, numbering five hundred soldiers each and under the command of Zahir's brother Saʾd and other leaders, promptly rose up and trapped the Nablus-Saqr forces between them, as Zahir's own two thousand men halted their fake retreat, turned as one, and closed the circle around the enemy soldiers. History thus repeated itself, as Zahir duplicated tactics used earlier in the Jezreel Valley by Antiochus III in 218 B.C., Vespasian in A.D. 67, and possibly the Mamlukes in A.D. 1260 (as just discussed). And indeed, the tactics were once again successful. Some accounts claim that Zahir's victory was so overwhelming that nearly eight thousand men were killed in the battle. So many bones were left lying on the battlefield that, reportedly, it was not able to be cultivated for the next twenty years.[27]

Zahir's power and reputation continued to grow following this battle, and despite numerous attempts to rebel against him, including attempts by his own sons, Zahir managed not only to retain control but

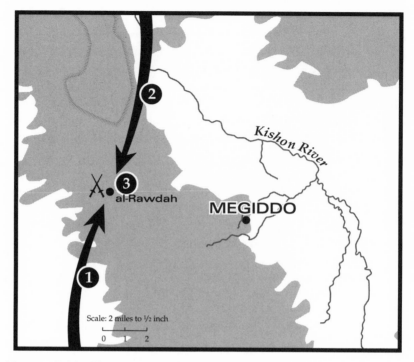

MAP 24. Zahir al-ʿUmar and the Nablus-Saqr alliance
1. Nablus-Saqr army marches to al-Rawdah.
2. Zahir al-ʿUmar advances to al-Rawdah and attacks Nablus-Saqr forces.
3. Zahir's soldiers pretend to flee, pursued by Nablus-Saqr army, then turn and trap the Nablus-Saqr forces in an ambush.

to expand his holdings in Galilee and the Jezreel Valley during the ensuing decades of the mid–eighteenth century. At this time, the Jezreel Valley was the most fertile area in all of Palestine, famous for its grain, tobacco, watermelons, and, above all, cotton.[28] It is by no means surprising, particularly also given the Jezreel Valley's continuing strategic importance along the trade routes leading to Damascus, that Zahir al-ʿUmar spent most of his rule in conflict with other forces who desired to take over his lands.

The second occasion that Zahir al-ʿUmar fought in the Jezreel Valley seems to have been during the course of his campaign in A.D. 1771–73, when he was attempting to capture Nablus, located some distance to the south of the valley. It is reported that he used cannons against the town of Lejjun, destroying much of the village, although precise details of the battle are not available. During this same period, a number of different armies marched through the Jezreel Valley. Some actually stopped and camped near Megiddo, Lejjun, and other locations. However, all were either en route to or retreating from battles fought outside the valley itself.[29]

Zahir's mini-empire quickly collapsed upon his death. He was murdered—probably on the orders of the Ottoman sultan, and perhaps at the hands of his own men—outside of Acre (Acco) in A.D. 1775 while battling Ottoman forces in a futile attempt to protect his holdings.[30] However, the Jezreel Valley would not long be without hostilities, for the region played host to Napoleon Bonaparte's dreams of glory less than a quarter-century later.

During Napoleon's ill-fated attempt to liberate Egypt and Syria-Palestine from the Ottoman Empire ca. A.D. 1798–1801, he led an expedition to Syria-Palestine in 1799. The principal objectives were, first, to intercept and defeat the Turkish army being assembled in Syria by the Ottoman sultan for the invasion and liberation of Egypt and, second, to capture the city of Acre (Acco).[31] The expedition is frequently deemed a failure by scholars and military historians because Napoleon was unable to capture the city of Acre (Acco), even after a prolonged siege. However, other scholars consider the expedition to have been a success, solely because of the so-called Battle of Mount Tabor that took place on 16 April 1799. As a result of this battle, fought in the Jezreel Valley near the modern city of Afula, Napoleon scattered the Turkish "Army of Damascus." This army had assembled in Syria and was one of two forces—the other was the "Army of Rhodes"—that the Ottoman sultan was planning to send against Napoleon in an attempt to liberate Egypt from the French.[32] Reports abound that Napoleon won the "Battle of Mount Tabor" simply by firing two cannons across the rear of the Turkish army, at which point the Ottoman forces fled in terror. Could this really be what happened? It seems most unlikely, yet with Napoleon, one must always expect the unexpected.

During the late autumn and early winter of A.D. 1798, Napoleon received word that preparations were being made by the Ottoman sultan to recapture Egypt, which Napoleon had invaded and captured earlier that year. On the assumption that the best defense is a good offense, and following the same reasoning as the Ikhshidids and the Mamlukes before him, Napoleon gathered together thirteen thousand men and prepared to meet the Turkish Army of Damascus before it could cross the desert from Palestine and attack Egypt proper. He also wished to capture the city of Acre (Acco), on the coast of Palestine, which was governed by Ahmed Pasha, better known as El Jezzar, or "the Butcher." Details about the overall campaign and about the battle fought at Mount Tabor in specific are available from a number of sources, including Napoleon's own correspondence with the Executive Directory back in France and his later memoirs, the reports that Napoleon's chief of staff General Berthier sent to the minister of war back in Paris, and various eyewitness accounts, including General Kléber's written report to Napoleon after the battle.[33]

Leaving some sixteen thousand men behind to guard Egypt in his absence, Napoleon led his small force of thirteen thousand to Suez in December 1798 and made his final arrangements for the invasion of Palestine. His men were split into four infantry divisions numbering nearly ten thousand soldiers, commanded by Generals Kléber, Regnier, Bon, and Lannes. There was also a division of eight hundred cavalry commanded by General Murat, an artillery division commanded by General Dommartin, and a division of engineers commanded by General Caffarelli.

By 18 March 1799, after a series of battles at el-Arish, Jaffa, and other sites, Napoleon reached Acre (Acco) and laid siege to the city. At the same time, he sent various detachments to capture the fort at Safad, to occupy Nazareth, and to capture Tyre. All of these missions were successfully accomplished. In early April, word was received that the Army of Damascus was on the move and was headed toward Galilee and the Jezreel Valley. Several minor battles and skirmishes were subsequently fought between the French forces and various detachments of the Turkish army and their allies during the week of 8–15 April.

On 15 April, General Kléber found himself in Nazareth with some two thousand men under his command. He had heard that Turkish forces had established a position at Mount Tabor and in the nearby town of el-Fuleh (modern Afula) in the Jezreel Valley. Kléber decided to stage an all-night march to mount a surprise attack on the morning of 16 April. They left at 10 P.M. that evening, expecting to arrive at their destination some four hours later, at about 2 A.M. in the morning. Unfortunately, however, unlike Gideon in a similar situation twenty-nine hundred years before him, Kléber had not personally reconnoitered the route beforehand and was seriously misled as to the distance involved, the difficulty of the terrain at night, and the time that it would take to make the journey. He and his two thousand infantrymen marched east from Nazareth; turned south once they had passed

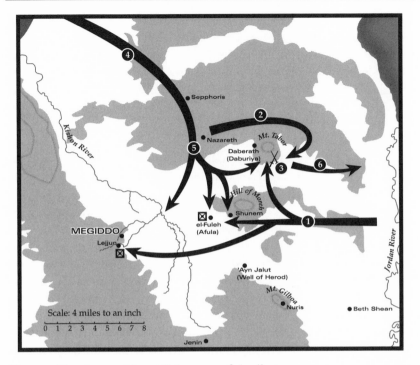

MAP 25. Napoleon at Mount Tabor, 15–16 April 1799

1. Ottoman forces gather at el-Fuleh (Afula), at Lejjun and at the base of Mount Tabor.
2. Kléber marches from Nazareth on the night of 15/16 April.
3. French forces, surrounded by Ottoman army, fight against overwhelming odds on 16 April.
4. Napoleon marches, via Sepphoris, to Kléber's rescue.
5. General Rambaud's Thirty-second Brigade heads directly for the battle; Generals Bon and Vial's Eighteenth Brigade continues toward Mount Gilboa; the division of the Foot Guides continues toward Jenin; and the cavalry turns and attacks the Mamluke base camp by Lejjun.
6. Ottoman forces scatter and flee; many drown while trying to cross the Jordan River.

Mount Tabor, in order to go around the mountain; and only then headed west again up the Jezreel Valley in the shadow of Mount Tabor. They finally arrived at the designated site four hours later than expected, at about 6 A.M. on the morning of 16 April. It had taken them a full eight hours to march nearly fifteen miles (twenty-five kilometers). They instantly found themselves surrounded by twenty-five thousand cavalry and ten thousand infantry, all belonging to the Pasha of Damascus. Kléber had successfully located the Army of Damascus but had lost the critical element of surprise.[34]

According to Kléber's own report to Napoleon, written after the battle, he immediately captured a nearby "fort" (probably the ruins of the Crusader castle known as La Feve, near el-Fuleh [Afula]) that was inaccessible to cavalry. By 7 A.M., he had staffed it with one hundred men, intending to use it as a point of support and a place for retreat if necessary. Kléber quickly formed the remainder of his men into two squares, a tactic favored by Napoleon, and gallantly faced wave after wave of attacking Ottoman horsemen. One participant reports that the battle had been joined so quickly that the French forces had not had time to eat their morning meal or to drink from a nearby lake that was tantalizingly visible from their vantage point throughout the day. Outnumbered at a ratio of seventeen to one, Kléber and his men were forced to fight a purely defensive battle, which they did for the rest of the morning. At noon, Kléber ordered his men to combine their two squares into one and to begin conserving their ammunition. They continued fighting into the early afternoon, with the situation becoming increasingly hopeless. Suddenly, at about 1 P.M. or perhaps a little bit later, they heard two French cannons fired to the south of the battlefield.[35] These were the two cannons of legend, the earliest "shots heard around the world," or at least across the fertile plain of the Jezreel Valley.

It seems that Napoleon had suspected that Kléber might find himself in a difficult situation. Therefore, he, too, had begun to march toward Mount Tabor on 15 April, leaving only General Lannes and his division to continue the siege of Acre (Acco). Napoleon took with him General Bon's infantry division, as well as General Murat's entire cavalry division and eight cannons from General Dommartin's artillery division. Camping overnight by Sepphoris, they began marching again at dawn on 16 April. By 9 or 10 A.M., using field glasses and looking from the heights around Nazareth, they could see Kléber's men in the far distance, at least three and perhaps as many as nine miles away. They appeared to be in two squares and were surrounded by clouds of swirling smoke, valiantly defending themselves against the charging cavalry of the Army of Damascus. By marching directly south at this point, to the west of Nazareth and down into the Jezreel Valley, rather than to the east and behind Mount Tabor as Kléber's men had done, Napoleon and his forces quickly covered the remaining distance.[36]

Upon approaching the rear of the Turkish army, Napoleon fired two shots from his cannons.

According to Kléber and Napoleon themselves, the Turkish army then broke and fled "in all directions, towards the mountains and into the valleys." Kléber and Napoleon reported, "The French who watched this from a distance rejoiced at the spectacle and broke into peals of laughter."[37] However, as is usual in such stories, especially those worthy of being told and retold around campfires and in bars and taverns, if it sounds too good to be true, it probably is. And this story is no exception, for it seems that it was, at one and the same time, both an abbreviated and an exaggerated version of what actually transpired. Not surprisingly, it took more than two cannon shots to scare off thirty-five thousand Ottoman troops. Other sources, including several participants in the battle, give a more detailed account of the final hours of fighting, which I paraphrase in the paragraphs that follow.[38]

Although Napoleon's troops, in marching rapidly to the battlefield, could see the fighting from the mountains as early as 9 or 10 A.M. on the morning of 16 April (only a few hours after the fighting had begun), the distance to the battlefield was still great. Moreover, the troops had been marching since first light and over the mountainous terrain that had just afforded them this view of the battlefield, and Napoleon therefore judged that they needed a rest to be fresh when they finally joined in the fray. So, against the wishes of his men, Napoleon ordered a halt of several hours duration. When the march resumed and Napoleon elected to fire the two cannons, it was already at least 1 P.M. According to several eyewitnesses, it may have been even later in the afternoon. Napoleon fired the two cannon shots both to alarm the enemy and to announce to Kléber's beleaguered men his imminent arrival with reinforcements. Immediately upon hearing the shots, Kléber's men began fighting with renewed vigor, shouting, "It is Bonaparte! It is Bonaparte!"[39]

Napoleon and his men then advanced rapidly against the Ottoman Army of Damascus. Having positioned themselves earlier by marching to the west of the enemy troops, the French were now able to attack the rear of the Ottoman forces and thus trap the enemy between Kléber's and Napoleon's men. One eyewitness, an artillery lieutenant named Jean-Pierre Doguereau, who later rose to the rank of general in the French army, reports that Napoleon split General Bon's infantry division in two and sent the two halves in different directions, so as to form, with Kléber's men, the three sides of a triangle, with the enemy caught in the middle. Other sources report that Napoleon in fact divided his men into four units, with half a mile (eight hundred meters) separating one unit from another. The high wheat growing in the valley apparently shielded the French forces and prevented them from being seen by the Ottoman soldiers until the last minute.[40]

When Napoleon's men began their final charge toward the enemy, General Rambaud's Thirty-second Brigade headed directly for the battle in progress, while the Eighteenth Brigade of Generals Bon and Vial continued in the direction of Mount Gilboa. The Foot Guides proceeded toward Jenin, while the cavalry unit turned to the right and attacked the base camp of the Mamluke portion of the Ottoman army, which was situated near Lejjun. So, Napoleon not only threw some of his forces directly into the battle but also sent some to attack the enemy's camp and still others to cut off potential lines of retreat, thus utilizing psychological as well as physical tactics against the Ottoman army.[41]

After initial resistance, the Turkish forces gave way and the panicked soldiers began to flee toward the Jordan River and the nearby mountains. The French forces followed, capturing the village of el-Fuleh (modern Afula) and massacring much of the Army of Damascus; the rest were dispersed to the four winds. One participant in the battle stated,

> we no longer thought of drinking but only of killing and of dyeing the lake red with the blood of those barbarians, who only a moment before had hoped to cut off our heads and drown our bodies in that very same lake, where they themselves were drowned and which was filled with their corpses.[42]

The battle was finally over by about 4 P.M. in the afternoon, fully ten hours after it had begun. The tall tales do not end here, however, for according to General Kléber's report, when roll call was taken after the battle, supposedly only two of his own men had been killed and sixty wounded; he does not mention how many of the men brought by Napoleon were slain. On the other side, at least five thousand men of the Army of Damascus reportedly died, including two thousand who drowned while fleeing and trying to cross the Jordan River following the battle itself.[43] The numbers seem rather outrageous, particularly since Kléber's two thousand men had been fighting against thirty-five thousand enemy cavalrymen and infantrymen for a good part of the day, while Napoleon's additional troops had also been involved in the final phase of the fighting. Indeed, one would do well to remember the nineteenth-century Prussian military strategist Carl von Clausewitz's observation that "casualty reports on either side are never accurate, seldom truthful, and in most cases deliberately falsified."[44]

One French participant, named Bernoyer, wrote a letter home reporting specifically that "the battle of Mount Tabor cost the enemy more than six thousand men, whereas we lost hardly two hundred." Napoleon's own memoirs, written while he was a prisoner on St. Helene years later, corroborate this larger figure, reporting that "Kléber had 250 to 300 killed or wounded men; the column of [Napoleon] had 3 or 4." This seems a much more reasonable total for the French losses, although perhaps even still a bit too low, considering that they had fought for ten full hours while being outnumbered seventeen to one for most of the battle. However, no matter how many were actually killed or wounded, the French strategy of using disciplined infantry formed in squares to counter disorganized mass cavalry attacks by the enemy clearly proved to be the superior tactic in the Jezreel Valley that day.[45]

That night, Napoleon and his troops reportedly slept at Mount Tabor, although this story may also be a later fabrication, since the mountain was probably a fair distance from the site of the actual battle. Napoleon's camp may actually have been located quite a bit nearer to the ancient site of Jezreel and ʿAyn Jalut (the "Spring of Goliath"), closer to Mount Gilboa than to Mount Tabor. Kléber kept Napoleon company in his tent until early in the morning of 17 April, when he left to rejoin his division and lead them to stand guard at the Jordan River against further infiltration by the Ottoman forces and their allies. Upon arising, Napoleon's troops captured and burned the village of Nuris on Mount Gilboa and the city of Jenin even further south, outside the Jezreel Valley, before returning to camp and then proceeding in a relaxed march as far north and west as Nazareth. During their march back to Nazareth, they apparently also burned down the village of Shunem in the Jezreel Valley. Napoleon and his men then spent the night of 17 April in a monastery at Nazareth, returning to Acre (Acco) the following day.[46]

Napoleon was compelled to lift the unsuccessful siege of Acre (Acco) soon thereafter, due in part to an outbreak of bubonic plague

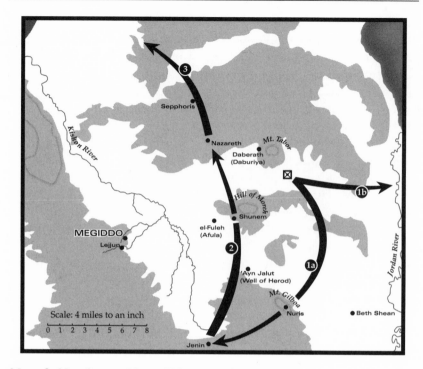

MAP 26. Napoleon at Mount Tabor, 17–18 April 1799

1a. French forces burn Nuris on Mount Gilboa and Jenin on morning of 17 April,

1b. while Kléber and his men assume guard duty at the Jordan River.

2. Napoleon's men march back to Nazareth, burning Shunem en route, later on 17 April.

3. Napoleon makes a final triumphant return to Acre (Acco) on 18 April.

that was ravaging his forces. On 20 May 1799, in a rousing speech to the army before they left Acre (Acco) later that day, Napoleon declared:

> Soldiers! You have crossed the desert that separates Africa from Asia with more speed than an Arab army. The army that was marching to invade Egypt has been destroyed. You have taken its general, its campaign equipment, its luggage, its goatskin bottles, its camels; you have seized all the fortified towns that defended the wells of the desert; you have dispersed on the field of Mount Tabor this swarm of men who came from all parts of Asia in the hope of plundering Egypt.[47]

He then withdrew his men and marched back to Egypt to face the Army of Rhodes, the other half of the Ottoman sultan's allies who were attempting to recapture Egypt from the French forces.

Although he had failed to capture Acre (Acco), admittedly one of the primary goals of his Palestinian expedition, Napoleon had successfully defeated and dispersed the Turkish Army of Damascus at the "Battle of Mount Tabor." Indeed, although he had not accomplished all that he had set out to do, his main objective of destroying the Turkish army before it could cross the desert and attack Egypt itself had been accomplished. Having met at least this goal, Napoleon, the acknowledged master of propaganda, therefore declared his expedition to Syria-Palestine and the Jezreel Valley to have been a great success and staged a triumphal march through Cairo on 14 June A.D. 1799.

Napoleon's battle at Mount Tabor would be the last fought in the Jezreel Valley for more than a century, until the coming of World War I. The man who succeeded him as the victor in the next conflict, General Edmund H.H. Allenby, knew all about Napoleon and the battle at Mount Tabor, for by A.D. 1918, Napoleon's victories were standard reading material in the textbooks at the Royal Military College at Sandhurst and the Staff College where Allenby studied.[48] Allenby, a descendant of Oliver Cromwell, was a voracious student of ancient history and previous military tactics. I have already discussed in chapter 1 how he put his knowledge of the violent history of the Jezreel Valley to good use in leading the British army and their allies to victory over the Ottomans at Megiddo on 20 September 1918. I therefore turn to a time exactly thirty years after Allenby's triumph—to a period when the British had relinquished their rights to Palestine and when the fledgling state of Israel was fighting for its very life—to find the next conflict fought on the blood-soaked soil of the Jezreel Valley.

CHAPTER 9

The Struggle for Survival

We have a long thorny path ahead of us. The day after the State of
Israel was established, Tel Aviv was bombed by Egyptian planes. . . . We
have also received reports that our country is being invaded from the
north, east, and south by the regular armies of the neighbouring Arab
States. We face a troubled and dangerous time. . . . It is the responsibility of each one of us, and of every municipal body, to take appropriate
defensive measures, such as constructing air raid shelters, digging
trenches, etc. We must concentrate in particular on building up a military striking force capable of repulsing and destroying enemy forces
wherever they may be found.

—Prime Minister David Ben-Gurion,
Broadcast to the nation of Israel on 15 May 1948

THE BABY DIED INSTANTLY on the shattered second floor of the
children's house when the Arab artillery shell pierced the concrete kibbutz building. The mother, who had tried to protect her infant, died a
few hours later on a makeshift operating table set up in the shower
room of the ruined building. They were the first casualties of the attack
on Mishmar Haemek, a kibbutz located a few miles northwest of
Megiddo in the Jezreel Valley. The attack began with an initial one-
thousand-shell barrage striking the Jewish settlement without warning
at about teatime on the afternoon of 4 April 1948.[1] It lasted for two
hours and left most of the buildings in ruins, even those built of concrete. Fortunately, most of the defenders were able to seek shelter in
the deep trenches crisscrossing the kibbutz.

The battle of Mishmar Haemek lasted for nine days, from 4 to 12
April 1948, with the Jewish settlers suffering heavy casualties and fighting for their very lives against overwhelming odds the entire time.[2] It
had been exactly thirty years since Allenby fought against the Ottomans
at nearby Megiddo in A.D. 1918. Now the attack by the Arab Liberation
Army (ALA) was led by Fauzi el-Kaukji, formerly a Syrian officer with
the Ottoman army. He was determined to capture Mishmar Haemek
while the main forces of the young Jewish army were concentrating

their efforts on Operation Nachshon, the opening of the Tel Aviv–Jerusalem road that was officially conducted from 6 to 15 April. A victory at Mishmar Haemek would provide a vital link in the supply lines for the Arab forces, a means by which to disrupt Jewish communications along the Haifa–Tel Aviv road, and an opportunity for Kaukji to restore his name and reputation, which had been tarnished by a defeat at Tirat Zvi south of Beth Shean (Beisan) back in February.[3]

During the War of Independence in A.D. 1948, two separate sets of battles, occurring six weeks apart, were fought in the Jezreel Valley between Arab and Israeli forces, as part of the effort by the Israelis to establish the new state of Israel and by the Arabs to rid Palestine of the unwanted interlopers. For both sides, it was quite literally a fight for survival. In the first series of battles, which took place from 4 to 12 April, the Arabs were the aggressors, attacking the Jewish settlement of Kibbutz Mishmar Haemek. In the second series, which took place from 28 May to 4 June, the shoe was on the other foot, for the Israelis were the aggressors against Arab villages and defensive outposts, including Zarin, Megiddo, Lejjun, and, ultimately, further south and outside the Jezreel Valley, the town of Jenin.

Kaukji was in charge of more than one thousand men, including the Dadisia Battalion, the Hittin Battalion, and units from the First Yarmuk Battalion. These he marched west from Nazareth on 3 April 1948. On the morning of the following day, 4 April, he deployed his men around the kibbutz in a loose ring that could be tightened at any time. Kaukji also had about a dozen three-inch mortars, several armored cars, and, most importantly, seven pieces of artillery, both 75-millimeter and 105-millimeter guns, which had been given to him by the Syrian army, and which were the first to be used in the war. These he placed in the hills above Mishmar Haemek.[4]

Defending the kibbutz were the armed settlers of Mishmar Haemek, consisting of approximately three hundred men, women, and children, led by their commander, Yehuda Yevzori. They had been reinforced by a small detachment from the Haganah, a branch of the Israeli defensive forces. Together, the defenders had available at the beginning of the battle only one heavy machine gun, a three-inch mortar, two two-inch mortars, two light machine guns, and about fifty rifles. However, they had been preparing their defenses for nearly two months and had erected barbed wire and dug deep connected trenches across the grounds of the kibbutz. They also had stockpiled a month's supply of food.[5]

The infantry attack that immediately followed the artillery barrage at teatime on 4 April 1948 was only barely repulsed by small-arms fire and grenades at the perimeter fence of the kibbutz as evening fell. That night, in the early hours of 5 April, a company from the Golani Brigade of the Haganah arrived to reinforce the besieged defenders at Mishmar Haemek. Unbeknownst to them, Kaukji and the Arab forces were well aware of the arrival of the reinforcements and could have fired on them at any time during their approach to the kibbutz. Instead, Kaukji decided to let the Israelis slip into the kibbutz unmolested so that there would be more Jewish defenders to kill.[6]

On the morning of 5 April, however, the expected offensive by the Arab forces did not materialize. This was due to an unexpected cease-fire, negotiated and instigated at the insistence of British officers from the Third Hussar Regiment, who were stationed only about two miles away from the fighting. On the next day, 6 April, though, sporadic fighting resumed and the kibbutz came under heavy shelling for most of the daylight hours. On the morning of 7 April, a second cease-fire was arranged, this time at the request of Lieutenant Colonel Peel of the British army, who demanded that the wounded and children of the kibbutz be allowed to move to safety. That night, more Jewish reinforcements, in the form of the First Battalion of the Palmach led by Major Dan Laner, readied themselves in the nearby village of Ein Hashofet for a surprise counterattack against the Arab forces surrounding Mishmar Haemek. It was ironic, and perhaps even deliberate, that the First Battalion of the Palmach came to the rescue, for it was at Mishmar Haemek that the newly formed Palmach (i.e., the "Assault Companies" established by the Haganah) had held its first intensive training sessions back in 1942, with six hundred recruits. The graduates had learned sabotage and reconnaissance, among other skills, and had trained in the forests surrounding Mishmar Haemek. Thus, it was very familiar terrain to many of the soldiers in the First Battalion.[7]

On the morning of 8 April, Major Laner and the First Battalion attacked Kaukji's Arab forces. The battle raged for the next five days, with both sides trying to capture Arab villages and positions in the hills surrounding Mishmar Haemek. Some areas were fought over repeatedly, falling into Arab hands during the day and being recaptured by the Jewish forces during the night. These days of fighting also saw the first appearance of the fledgling Israeli Air Force, in the form of the "Galilee Squadron" of the Aerial Service, which, at that time, consisted of two Piper Cubs and three pilots. The pilots, who had flown recon-

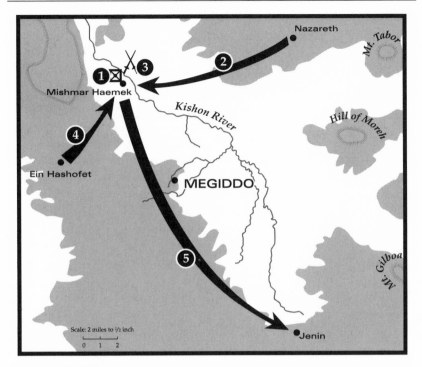

MAP 27. The War of Independence: Mishmar Haemek (April 1948)

1. Israeli settlers fortify Kibbutz Mishmar Haemek in preparation for Arab attack.
2. Arab forces march west from Nazareth to Mishmar Haemek.
3. Attack on Mishmar Haemek begins on 4 April.
4. Israeli reinforcements arrive during the night of 4/5 April and on 8 April.
5. After eight days of fighting, Arab forces retreat to Jenin, Jerusalem, and Jaffa.

naissance flights over the kibbutz on 5 April and dropped supplies of ammunition packed in rags on 7 April, finally attacked the Arab forces directly on 9 April. Their "bombs" consisted of irrigation pipes with a screw top at one end and a fuse lit by a match on the other end. These were dropped on Kaukji's men and particularly on the gun emplacements in the hills overlooking the kibbutz.[8]

On 11 April, as it became clear to Kaukji that the First Battalion of the Palmach was gradually gaining the upper hand in the fighting, he sent a telegram to the Druze Battalion, headquartered in the village of Shfar-Am. The Druze had formed a mercenary force willing to fight on the side of the highest bidder but owed no allegiance to either the Arabs or the Jews. Kaukji wrote: "I turn to you Sons of Maruf. I am in trouble. If you do not help me, my complaint will be to God." In response, the Druze immediately attacked two nearby Arab villages that the Jewish forces had previously captured. However, facing fierce resistance, the Druze soldiers withdrew without gaining any advantage in the operation. Eventually, they decided it would be more beneficial to fight on the side of the Jews in the future.[9]

On 12 April, Kaukji attempted to attack Mishmar Haemek directly once again, but his forces were ambushed in the forests surrounding the kibbutz before they could launch their attack. At the same time, the Israeli Haganah soldiers also captured two Arab villages behind and to the east of Kaukji and threatened to encircle his forces and cut off their lines of communication. Kaukji quickly sent a desperate cable to the Arab League, announcing, "10,000 Jews have cut Mishmar Haemek off and are closing in from all sides." He then abandoned the campaign against Mishmar Haemek and retreated to Jenin, sending his precious artillery south to Jerusalem and a portion of his troops to Jaffa. The Haganah forces followed in hot pursuit, reaching almost to the mouth of the Wadi ʿAra (Musmus Pass) by Megiddo.[10]

Kaukji had failed, suffering what he considered to be yet another humiliating defeat hard on the heels of his previous setback at Tirat Zvi back in February. Indeed, following his loss, far from regaining his honor, reputation, and good name at Mishmar Haemek, Kaukji was apparently referred to as a "dog," a "thief," and a "traitor" in cables sent by the king of Transjordan and the president of Syria. At least one Arabic newspaper, though, in Beirut, erroneously reported that Kaukji had been victorious. Many of the Arab inhabitants of the villages surrounding Mishmar Haemek were expelled southward, to Jenin and beyond, and several of the villages themselves, such as ʿAyn al-Mansi, were blown up, razed, or otherwise destroyed during the period from 8 to 19 April.[11]

The successful defense of Mishmar Haemek was an extremely important and very inspiring event for the Israelis, particularly coming as it did at the same time as the successful opening of the Tel Aviv–Jerusalem road under the auspices of Operation Nachshon.[12] Approximately one month later, on 14 May 1948, the Declaration of the Establishment of the State of Israel was proclaimed. On the next day, the Arab nations officially declared war on Israel and the stage was set for the next series of battles fought in the Jezreel Valley.

The second round of fighting took place some six weeks after the battle at Mishmar Haemek and two weeks after the official beginning of the War of Independence. The battles, most of them fought initially at night, took place from 28 to 31 May 1948. At stake this time were a number of towns and villages in the Jezreel Valley, including Zarin, Lejjun, and Megiddo. However, the ultimate goal of the offensive movement was an assault on Jenin, located further to the southwest, along the pass leading to the Dothan Valley.

The village of Zarin, some six miles (ten kilometers) north of Jenin, is located near Mount Gilboa, by the ancient site of Jezreel. This village was picked as the first target of the offensive. A company from the Golani Brigade of the Israeli forces was given the order to proceed from el-Fuleh (Afula) on the evening of 28 May 1948. By the morning of the next day, 29 May, the village of Zarin had been captured, despite a lack of artillery support and a breakdown of the Israeli communication system.[13] Later the village would be shelled by Iraqi artillery and an attempt at a counterattack would be made by the Arab irregulars, but Zarin remained in Israeli hands.

Resting during the day of 29 May, the same company from the Golani Brigade set out again that evening, with the objective of capturing two more villages, al-Mazar and Nuris, one at the top and one at the foot of Mount Gilboa (known in Arabic as "Mount al-Mazar"). Again, by the time the night was over and the sun had risen the next morning, on 30 May, these villages and all of Mount Gilboa were in Israeli hands.[14]

The attack against first the ancient site of Megiddo and then the nearby Arab village of Lejjun was launched on the night of 30 May by other units from the Golani Brigade. The settlement of Ein Hashofet, where the First Battalion of the Palmach had gathered before entering the battle at Mishmar Haemek back in April, was the starting point for the attack. The Arab forces defending Megiddo were apparently taken completely by surprise, and the ancient site was captured after only a minor skirmish. The Iraqis launched a counterattack the next day, but Megiddo remained in Israeli hands.[15]

The capture of Lejjun, however, was not quite as simple. The fighting at nearby Megiddo had alerted the Arab defenders of Lejjun to the impending attack, and they had taken the opportunity both to prepare their defenses inside the police station and to radio for reinforcements, primarily in the form of armored cars. When the Golani infantry forces reached Lejjun in the early morning hours of 31 May (after the attack on Megiddo had been successfully concluded), they found themselves

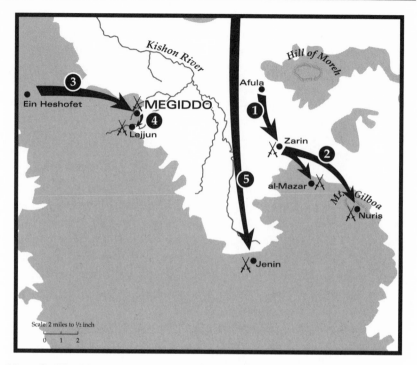

MAP 28. The War of Independence: Zarin, Megiddo, and Lejjun (May–June 1948)

1. Golani Brigade forces march to Zarin on evening of 28 May and capture it the next morning.
2. Israelis continue advance, marching to al-Mazar and Nuris on evening of 29 May, and capturing them by the next morning.
3. Additional Golani Brigade forces march to Megiddo on evening of 30 May and capture it by the next morning.
4. Israeli forces continue on to Lejjun in the early morning of 31 May and capture the town after fierce fighting.
5. Offensive against Jenin by battalions from the Israeli Carmeli and Golani Brigades commences on 1 June and ends with victory on 4 June.

under fire from both the armored vehicles parked outside and the defenders stationed inside. However, the Israeli troops quickly captured the police headquarters nevertheless. With the help of their own armored cars and a Renault tank, all of which arrived later, the Israelis then proceeded to hold off a fierce Iraqi counterattack for the rest of the day and were able to mine the roads later that evening, thus preventing further Arab attacks.[16]

The offensive against Jenin followed the next day, on 1 June, and was conducted by two northern battalions from the Carmeli Brigade aided by a single battalion from the Golani Brigade. The Carmeli forces passed through the Jezreel Valley, now securely held by the Golani Brigade, on their way to Jenin.[17] Jenin and the surrounding hills were then captured after a fierce battle lasting until 4 June. The success of this brief campaign in late May and early June paved the way for the next phase of the Israeli offensive outside the Jezreel Valley, later in the summer of 1948.

Some material remains from the 1948 battles can still be found at the site of Megiddo. Excavations in 1994 just outside the entrance to the ancient city revealed a three-foot-deep trench at the perimeter of the lower mound. At the bottom of the trench were found spent bullets, strands of wire (both barbed wire and wire for a field telephone), and pieces of wood planking. These remains and others found elsewhere on the site can be attributed either to the Arab forces who were defeated on the night of 30/31 May by the Israeli Golani Brigade or to the Israeli forces who were preparing later, in June, for the July offensive against Kaukji and the ALA known as Operation Dekel.[18]

The following year, in January 1949, the settlement of Kibbutz Yosef Kaplan was established approximately a third of a mile (half a kilometer) to the northeast of the former village of Lejjun. This settlement was later renamed Kibbutz Megiddo, in honor of the ancient site next to whose prominent mound the kibbutz—featuring not only an air-conditioned bed-and-breakfast setup and an Olympic-size swimming pool but also the more traditional pursuits of agriculture and dairy farming—is still located today. It would be less than twenty years, however, before Megiddo and the Jezreel Valley came under attack once more and the inhabitants were forced to fight again for their very survival.

The events that took place in the Jezreel Valley during the Six-Day War in 1967 were totally unlike any of the previous thirty-two military confrontations that had taken place in this region. Until this war, advances in technology do not seem to have much affected the techniques used in the Jezreel Valley battles during the past four thousand years, apart from the replacement of the chariot and horse by the tank and armored personnel carrier. Success on the battlefields of the Jezreel Valley seems to have frequently depended more on superior strategy and tactics than on superior numbers and technology. Examples of such superior strategy and tactics include Kléber forming his few men into squares against the overwhelmingly large but undisci-

FIG. 16. Bullets found in trench at Megiddo (Eric H. Cline)

plined Ottoman cavalry; Thutmose III and Allenby both unexpectedly sending their forces through the Wadi ʿAra (Musmus Pass); Deborah and Barak's infantry overcoming Sisera's nine hundred iron chariots in their battle in the valley; and Antiochus III, Vespasian, and Zahir al-ʿUmar all trapping the enemy in well-planned and well-executed surprise ambushes.

However, now the invention of the airplane and the long-range artillery gun dramatically changed the way that battles were fought in the Jezreel Valley. First used in the region almost as a novelty during the War of Independence back in 1948 (as mentioned earlier in this chapter), airplanes and long-range artillery were the basis of the military tactics used in the Jezreel Valley in 1967. This new technology meant that for the first time in the history of the Jezreel Valley, the fighting was conducted solely by long-range weapons, without the participants ever confronting one another face-to-face within the valley itself. The principal, and indeed virtually the only, target of the attacks in the Jezreel Valley by Jordanian, Syrian, and Iraqi forces during the Six-Day War was the Ramat David airfield located near Megiddo. This

FIG. 17. Barbed wire found in trench at Megiddo (Eric H. Cline)

was the largest Israeli Air Force base north of Tel Aviv and was considered vital for the nation's defense.[19]

The hostilities started on Monday, 5 June 1967. Beginning at 9:00 A.M. in the morning and continuing for approximately the next two hours, a Jordanian artillery crew located at Yamun, to the northwest of Jenin in the Dothan Valley, sporadically fired their battery of American-made Long Tom 155-millimeter long-range guns at the Ramat David airbase in the Jezreel Valley. A volley of shells landed between 10:00 and 10:15 A.M., damaging installations at the base and, more importantly, pockmarking the runways with deep holes. The incoming shells and the resultant craters began to pose serious problems for the Israeli aircraft, threatening to put the airbase out of action just when it was needed to help on the Syrian front by providing air support for the Israeli infantry troops stationed in Upper Galilee.[20]

In response, Israel began large-scale ground operations against the Jordanian positions in Jenin and further south. Jenin and the surrounding area were defended by the Jordanian Twenty-fifth Infantry Brigade, under the command of Lieutenant Colonel Khalidi. His men fired the

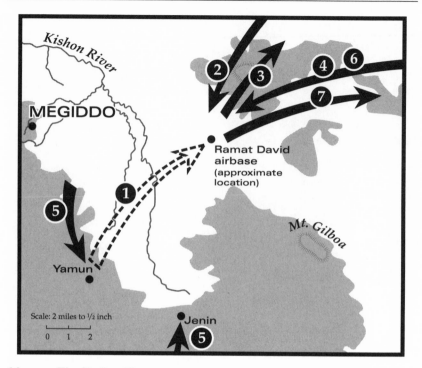

MAP 29. The Six-Day War

1. Jordanian artillery shells fired from Yamun hit Ramat David airfield on morning of 5 June.
2. Syrian MiGs attack Ramat David airfield just before noon on 5 June.
3. Israeli aircraft immediately bomb Syrian airfields in retaliation.
4. Iraqi aircraft attack Ramat David airfield at 2 P.M. on 5 June.
5. Israeli ground forces attack Jenin and Yamun from both north and south on afternoon of 5 June; battle lasts until early evening; victory ensures that there will be no further artillery fire against Ramat David airfield.
6. Iraqi airplane attacks Ramat David airfield on morning of 6 June.
7. Israeli aircraft conduct several retaliatory raids against Iraq on 6 June and destroy Habbaniyah Airbase on Kirkuk oil pipeline.

battery of Long Tom 155-millimeter long-range guns at the Ramat David airbase. Several Israeli army units, including an armored brigade under Colonel Uri Ram, proceeded through or across the Jezreel Valley on their way to engage the Jordanians. Other units approached Jenin from the south. In addition, Israeli aircraft began a continuous assault on the gun battery shelling the Ramat David airfield.[21]

In the meantime, however, the airfield suffered from additional air strikes sent by two other enemy forces. Shortly before noon, Syrian aircraft were sent to attack the Ramat David airbase, bomb oil refineries at Haifa, and hit other positions near Tiberias. Ironically, the three Syrian MiGs that attacked Ramat David mistakenly bombed a nearby runway for crop dusters that was decorated with a dummy combat plane, rather than the precious runways of Ramat David airfield itself. At least one and possibly two of the MiGs were shot down during the attack. The Israelis retaliated immediately, launching attacks against most of the Syrian airfields and destroying the majority of the Syrian Air Force. Some two hours after the Syrian raid, around 2:00 P.M., Iraqi aircraft also attacked the Ramat David airbase. Revenge would be postponed until the following day, when the Israeli Air Force could be assured of air supremacy all the way to Iraq.[22]

The battle for Jenin and the surrounding area, to the southeast of Megiddo and the Jezreel Valley, did not begin until after 3:00 P.M. on 5 June. It was 7:30 P.M. before a battalion of Israeli armed infantry, approaching from the southwest up the Dothan Valley under the command of Lieutenant Colonel Moshe Bar Kochva, entered the village of Yamun.[23] Although the Jordanian troops under Colonel Khalidi fought fiercely elsewhere in the Jenin area, the soldiers manning the battery of Long Tom guns reportedly retreated after only a few shots had been fired. The 155-millimeter guns were captured intact by the Israeli forces, ensuring that the Ramat David airbase would no longer be threatened by the Jordanian long-range artillery.

On the morning of 6 June, six Israeli aircraft were preparing to take off from the Ramat David airfield on a retaliatory strike against the Iraqis, aiming for the H-3 Airbase at Habbaniyah on the Kirkuk oil pipeline. Minutes before they were due to depart, an Iraqi TU-16 Tupolev bomber, flying without markings or camouflage, approached the Ramat David airbase on an attack run. Seconds after the big bomber's gunner opened fire on the base, two Israeli Mirages closed in on the Iraqi plane. One Mirage fired its guns, the other fired a missile, and the Iraqi bomber went down in flames. Unfortunately, it crashed into a military camp located near Megiddo, killing twelve Israeli soldiers and injuring many more. The Israelis retaliated immediately, sending four Vautours and two Mirages to fly the five hundred miles to Iraq and bomb the Habbaniyah Airbase. As it happened, the Israelis surprised ten Iraqi aircraft at the base and destroyed them all before they could take off from the ground. Two additional attacks were made against the Iraqi airbase later that same day.[24]

Thus, by the evening of 6 June 1967, the Israeli aircraft based at Ramat David airfield in the Jezreel Valley were freed from the menace of further Jordanian, Syrian, or Iraqi attacks for the remainder of the Six-Day War. Not until the Yom Kippur War of 1973 would the Ramat David airbase come under fire again. At that time, Syrian long-range FROG surface-to-surface missiles were fired into the Jezreel Valley on 7–8 October. The Syrians were attempting to hit the Ramat David airfield, but their inaccurate aim endangered the civilian population throughout the entire Jezreel Valley and Central Galilee. Once again Israeli reaction was almost immediate. Beginning on 9 October 1973, Israeli aircraft began systematically bombing Syrian ports, storage facilities, electric power plants, and industrial facilities throughout the country, in retaliation. The Syrian artillery attacks against Ramat David airfield and Central Galilee then ceased, and the Jezreel Valley saw no further action for the remainder of the Yom Kippur War.[25] The fight for survival had once again ended in a victory for the Israelis.

Since 1973, the Jezreel Valley has been fairly quiet, apart from various acts of terrorism, mostly bombings, that took place from 1994 to 1998 in the modern city of Afula as part of the uprising known as the Intifada. These bombings do not qualify as battles in their own right but may be a harbinger of things still to come in this area located so close to Jenin and the West Bank. Indeed, a goodly portion of the world's population presently awaits, with varying degrees of anxiety, dread, and awful anticipation, the "Mother of All Battles"—the final battle of Armageddon predicted by John in the biblical Book of Revelation—which is supposed to take place at Megiddo and the Jezreel Valley some time in the future.

CHAPTER 10

The Battle between Good and Evil

... the victory shall be ours, and it shall be won as we have already won
so many victories, by clean and honest fighting for the loftiest of causes.
We fight in honorable fashion for the good of mankind; fearless of the
future; unheeding of our individual fates; with unflinching hearts and
undimmed eyes; we stand at Armageddon, and we battle for the Lord.

—Theodore Roosevelt, address to the
Republican Convention in Chicago on 17 June 1912

APOCALYPSE, JUDGMENT DAY, the End Time, Armageddon, the
cataclysmic battle between the forces of good and the forces of evil—
evocative, powerful, and frightening, the concept of the original
"Mother of All Battles" has gripped the imagination of Judeo-Christians
since John wrote the New Testament's Book of Revelation in the first
century A.D. The battle of Armageddon predicted in the Bible has been
portrayed in countless medieval and modern paintings, discussed in
endless popular and scholarly articles and books, featured on television
and in numerous Hollywood movies, and made the subject of endless
sermons by televangelists. The public reaction to the concept of
Armageddon has reached a crescendo with the coming of the twenty-
first century, replete with intense, interesting, and basically unanswer-
able questions about the nature of good and evil, the end of the world,
and millennial hopes and fears—to mention only a few of the more
pervasive issues. But will it happen? Will there be a battle of Armageddon? And if so, when and where will it take place? Such questions have
been long debated and will undoubtedly continue to be hotly discussed
for the foreseeable future, until the event itself actually transpires,
whenever that might be. At the very core of the discussion is Megiddo,
considered by most scholars, laypeople, and tour guides as the site destined to lie at the epicenter of Armageddon.

Armageddon is, perhaps surprisingly, only mentioned once in the
entire Bible, including both the Old and the New Testaments as well as
the Apocrypha. It appears only in the Book of Revelation, where it is
said:

> And I saw three foul spirits like frogs coming from the mouth of the dragon, from the mouth of the beast, and from the mouth of the false prophet. These are demonic spirits, performing signs, who go abroad to the kings of the whole world, to assemble them for battle on the great day of God the Almighty. . . . And they assembled them at the place that in Hebrew is called Armageddon. (Revelation 16:13–16)

What is the relationship between Armageddon and the site of Megiddo? Literally, Megiddo *is* Armageddon, or rather Armageddon *is* Megiddo. The very word *Armageddon* comes from the Greek Ἀρμαγεδών, which in turn is most likely derived from the Hebrew *Har Megiddon,* meaning "Mount of Megiddo." The corruption of *Har Megiddon* to *Harmageddon* and thence to *Armageddon* is readily seen, especially in early versions of the New Testament where the Greek is frequently spelled with an aspirant, or "H," at the beginning of the word, that is, as Ἁρμαγεδών (transliterated "Harmagedon"). The Greek word also occasionally has a second delta added to render Ἁρμαγεδδών (transliterated "Harmageddon"), a spelling very close to the original Hebrew *Har Megiddon.*[1] Thus, a proper translation of Revelation 16:16 should actually read, "And they assembled them at the place that in Hebrew is called 'Mount of Megiddo.'"

The Book of Revelation was written by John while on the island of Patmos. This much is told to us in the opening chapter of the book (Revelation 1:1–11). John may well have been the man we know as John the Apostle, but despite a slew of learned books and articles, scholars have been unable to determine whether the author was in fact the apostle or someone else named John. Whoever the author was, internal references indicate that the Book of Revelation was probably written in the first century A.D., during the reign of the Roman emperor Domitian.[2] Despite the dizzying array of symbols, numbers, psychedelic images, and dream sequences found in the Book of Revelation, the events leading up to Armageddon, the battle itself, and the ensuing events are actually set out in a fairly plain and straightforward manner.

However, it is by no means clear whether the details spelled out in the Book of Revelation are meant to be only symbolic, as per many, if not most, apocalyptic visions described in the Old and the New Testaments, or if they are meant as an actual prophetic foretelling of the future. If they are purely symbolic, we cannot take the description found in Revelation 6–21 as an accurate prediction of the events before, during, and after the battle of Armageddon and cannot begin to discuss the details of the battle. If, however, there is even the slight-est possibility that the details are meant to be taken literally as a prophecy of what is to come—as John himself may have thought, and as many televangelists and recent best-selling authors on this topic seem to feel—then it behooves us to look closely at the description in Revelation 6–21.[3] Since the issue remains debated, and since there is at least an off chance that John's vision is indeed a prediction of what is to come, I proceed cautiously through the scholarly and religious minefield to discuss this possibly impending conflict in the same man-ner as I have discussed the previous thirty-four battles fought in the Jezreel Valley.

Even if we assume for argument's sake that this battle is indeed going to occur as a real historical event, we must still keep in mind that John's description of the events during the battle was written during the first century A.D. That was a time nearly two thousand years ago, when only thirteen battles had been fought in the Jezreel Valley and fully twenty-one more were yet to take place. Thus, John's description of the battle is couched in terms more familiar to the first century A.D. than to the twenty-first century A.D. and reflects the political and tech-nological realities of that earlier era, when the Romans ruled the civi-lized world.

Details about the events that will immediately precede the battle of Armageddon are given in Revelation 6–16:15. These include great earthquakes (6:12–17; 8:5; 11:13, 19); thunder and lightning (8:5, 11:19); hail and great fires (8:7, 11:19, 16:8–9); a comet or asteroid (8:10–11); partial eclipses, both solar and lunar (8:12); a plague of locusts (9:3–11); one-third of all humankind killed, with blood flowing for two hundred miles (9:15, 14:20); troops of cavalry numbering two hundred million (9:16); a plague of foul and painful sores (16:2); the death of all living things in the sea (16:3); the turning of all water in rivers and springs into blood (16:4); total darkness (16:10); and the drying up of the great river Euphrates to prepare the way for the kings from the east (16:12). Which of these events should be taken literally and which should be taken figuratively are matters of great discussion. Some say that a number of these events have already occurred or are occurring in the world today, particularly given the eclipses and the spate of earthquakes and volcanic activity that took place during the summer and fall of A.D. 1999.[4]

According to John, once these events have occurred, the combatants will then assemble for the catastrophic battle. It is at this point that

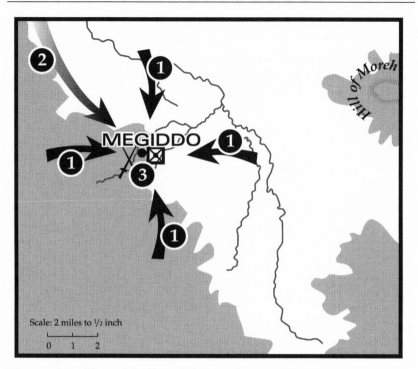

Map 30. Megiddo and the Jezreel Valley at Armageddon

1. The "kings of the whole world" and their armies are assembled for battle at Armageddon by three foul spirits coming from the mouths of a dragon, a beast, and a false prophet (Rev. 16:13–16).
2. The armies of heaven led by the "rider on the horse" fly from heaven for the battle of Armageddon (Rev. 19:11–16).
3. Defeated by the armies of heaven, the beast and the false prophet are thrown alive into the lake of fire, the "kings of the earth with their armies" are killed by the sword of "the rider on the horse," and the dragon (Satan) is bound and thrown into a pit, which is then locked and sealed for one thousand years (Rev. 19:19–20:3).

Armageddon is mentioned for the first and only time in the Bible. John reports that he saw three foul spirits, shaped like frogs, come out of the mouths of a dragon, a beast, and a false prophet. These spirits go to "the kings of the whole world" to assemble them for battle "at the place that in Hebrew is called Armageddon" (Revelation 16:13–16). Thus, the "kings of the whole world" and their armies are called to war by the evil spirits. As has been pointed out by many "dispensationalist" authors and theologians (called "dispensationalist" because they view history as a sequence of dispensations from God), the human armies are therefore going to be fighting on the side of evil rather than the side of good.[5] They will be fighting for the Antichrist and against the new Messiah, which comes as a surprise to most people, who wrongly assume that humans will be on the side of good, not evil, in this battle. Confirmation comes from the scant details given of the actual battle in Revelation 19–20.

> Then I saw heaven opened, and there was a white horse! Its rider is called Faithful and True, and in righteousness he judges and makes war. His eyes are like a flame of fire, and on his head are many diadems; and he has a name inscribed that no one knows but himself. He is clothed in a robe dipped in blood, and his name is called The Word of God. And the armies of heaven, wearing fine linen, white and pure, were following him on white horses. From his mouth comes a sharp sword with which to strike down the nations, and he will rule them with a rod of iron; he will tread the wine press of the fury of the wrath of God the Almighty. On his robe and on his thigh he has a name inscribed, "King of kings and Lord of lords." . . . Then I saw the beast and the kings of the earth with their armies gathered to make war against the rider on the horse and against his army. And the beast was captured, and with it the false prophet who had performed in its presence the signs by which he deceived those who had received the mark of the beast and those who worshiped its image. These two were thrown alive into the lake of fire that burns with sulfur. And the rest were killed by the sword of the rider on the horse, the sword that came from his mouth; and all the birds were gorged with their flesh. Then I saw an angel coming down from heaven, holding in his hand the key to a bottomless pit and a great chain. He seized the dragon, that ancient serpent, who is the Devil and Satan, and bound him for a thousand years, and threw him into the pit, and locked and sealed it over him, so that he would deceive the nations no more, until the thousand years were ended. After that he must be let out for a little while. (Revelation 19:11–20:3)

According to the Book of Revelation (20:4–6), in the aftermath of the battle, when the forces of evil have been defeated, those humans who had previously died as martyrs will be restored to life and reign with Christ for a period of one thousand years. It is a matter of fierce debate whether this era will follow the return of Christ, as the so-called premillennialists believe, or whether it is ongoing at the present time, perhaps in heaven rather than on earth, as the so-called amillennialists hold.[6] When that period of time expires, Satan will be released from prison and will once again deceive the nations of the earth. These nations, including those of Gog and Magog, who are also mentioned in Ezekiel 38–39 and whose identities have been much debated,[7] will then march against Jerusalem and the army of the saints, only to be defeated once again in a final conflict between good and evil (Revelation 20:7–10). At this point, Judgment Day will take place, with all of the dead resurrected and then judged according to what they have done (20:11–15), and a new era will begin (21:1–8).

Thus, contrary to popular belief, the battle scheduled to be fought at Armageddon is in fact destined to be not the last battle ever fought but rather the penultimate one, taking place during the first phase of the final conflict. The second battle, the one to be fought at Jerusalem after an intervening thousand-year period of peace (Revelation 20:7–10), will be the final battle in the conflict between good and evil. Where exactly in or around Jerusalem this final battle will take place is debated, but the Valley of Jehoshaphat is thought to be the most likely location, based on possibly related references in Ezekiel 38–39 and Joel 3:1–16.[8]

Some authors, preachers, and believers, however, apparently either misinterpret or take substantial liberties with the text as found in the Book of Revelation. Some embellish the simple description of the battle of Armageddon by detailing the horrors of the preceding events as if they were part of the battle itself. Others apparently conflate the two battles, separated by a thousand years, into a single battle and argue that Armageddon will take place in the Valley of Jehoshaphat by Jerusalem, that Armageddon will start at Megiddo but end in Jerusalem, or that the Valley of Jezreel and the Valley of Jehoshaphat are one and the same. Still others—many others—pull into their discussion of Armageddon details from prophecies found in the Books of Ezekiel, Daniel, Zechariah, and Joel, prophecies that may or may not be related.[9]

The objection is sometimes made that there is no true mountain at Megiddo, which is certainly a problem if the word *Armageddon* is indeed derived from the Hebrew *Har Megiddon* and refers to the "Mount of Megiddo." Some scholars suggest that the reference must be to a mountain somewhere in the vicinity of Megiddo, such as Mount Carmel or perhaps Mount Gilboa or Mount Tabor. Others suggest instead that Armageddon should be translated as "Mount of Assembly" rather than "Mount of Megiddo" and is thus a reference to Mount Zion in Jerusalem rather than to Megiddo.[10]

However, Megiddo is indeed a mount, albeit a human-made one.

The mound of ancient Megiddo rises nearly seventy feet above the surrounding plain and is an imposing site in many regards and from many angles. It reached its present height already during the Iron Age, in the early first millennium B.C., and would have been even higher by the Hellenistic and Roman periods. It would also have appeared even taller initially, since the valley floor surrounding Megiddo was lower at that time than it is now; a good deal of colluvium has been deposited in the past two thousand years, perhaps as much as ten feet of soil and debris as a result of flooding and related events.[11] At any rate, there is no doubt that Megiddo would certainly have been seen as a "mount" at the time that John wrote the Book of Revelation in the first century A.D., and thus there is no problem in interpreting the word *Armageddon* as coming from *Har Megiddon* and therefore as referring to Megiddo and, by extension, the surrounding Jezreel Valley.

But why did John pick Megiddo and the Jezreel Valley as the site for this cataclysmic battle? Why not Jerusalem, or Rome, or even Athens? The most likely explanation probably goes back to the death of Josiah, the Judean king who was the last effective (i.e., nonpuppet) ruler to be descended from the House of David. Josiah was killed in battle at Megiddo in 609 B.C. by Pharaoh Necho II of Egypt. The wrong done to this good and just king, viewed by many as a "second King David," needed to be avenged, and what better place for vengeance was there than the site where he had been killed? Moreover, just as Josiah's death at Megiddo had ended the era of the kingdom of God in the form of the House of David ruling over first the United Monarchy and then the southern part of the Divided Monarchy from ca. 1000 to 600 B.C., so the battle of Armageddon to be fought at Megiddo would open a new era and reestablish the Kingdom of God anew.[12] John, the author of the Book of Revelation, would certainly have been familiar with the story of Josiah and his death at Megiddo, which is reported in two places in the Bible (II Kings 23:29–30 and II Chronicles 35:20–24) as well as by Josephus, as I discussed in chapter 4.

John would probably also have been familiar with the Old Testament prophecies found in the Book of Zechariah, which mention Megiddo in the context of the restoration of Davidic Jerusalem: "On that day the mourning in Jerusalem will be as great as the mourning for Hadad-rimmon in the plain of Megiddo" (Zechariah 12:11). Zechariah's prophecies in this book are also concerned with the final battle between God and "all the nations that come against Jerusalem" (12:9). This point would not have been lost on John and may have influenced the placement of the final battles in his own prophecies as recorded in the Book of Revelation.[13]

In addition, already by the first century A.D., a goodly number of battles had been fought at Megiddo and in the Jezreel Valley (four at Megiddo itself, four at Mount Tabor, one at Mount Gilboa, one at the Hill of Moreh/Endor, one at the city of Jezreel, and two in the general Jezreel Valley). While John could not possibly have known of all these battles, he undoubtedly knew those reported in the Bible, that is, those of Deborah, Gideon, Saul, and Josiah. He probably also knew of those fought nearer to his own era, that is, those during the Hellenistic and Roman periods, such as the battles at Mount Tabor in 218 B.C., 55 B.C., and 67 A.D., the last two of which were recorded and published by Josephus. It may have seemed logical that a region that had seen so many previous battles and so much past bloodshed would be an appropriate location for the penultimate "Mother of All Battles."

Thus, we might reconstruct John's thinking process as follows: First, it was clear that the battle of Armageddon had to be fought in Palestine, because this was where Jesus had lived and died. But where in Palestine would it be fought? More battles had been fought in the Jezreel Valley—where at least seven occurred as far as John knew—than anywhere else in Palestine, so that would be a logical place. Then, in choosing a specific locale within the valley itself, and faced with a choice of Mount Tabor (where Christ's transfiguration had occurred), Mount Gilboa, the Hill of Moreh, and the ancient sites of Megiddo and Jezreel, the mound of Megiddo stands out because of the death of Josiah popularly associated with that unique location and perhaps also because of the mention of Megiddo in Zechariah's prophecies. It would indeed be fitting if the dawning of a new era occurred at precisely the spot where the last effective ruler descended from the House of David had died and where the final flickering of the shattered United Monarchy established by David and Solomon had ultimately been extinguished. Thus, according to John's calculations, the penultimate battle between good and evil was most likely to occur "at the place that in Hebrew is called Armageddon"—at the "Mount of Megiddo."

So when, if ever, will the battle of Armageddon take place? Current notions that it should occur, or should have occurred, at the turn of the millennium are unfounded, if only because the beginning of the new millennium quietly came and went several years before it was expected by most people. When the monk Dionysius Exiguus of the sixth century

A.D. tried to figure out the precise year of Christ's birth and indirectly created the beginning of the calendars used today and the B.C./A.D. reckoning system, he miscalculated by several years. As a result, Christ's birth is today considered to have taken place in 4 B.C., rather than in the break between the year 1 B.C. and the year A.D. 1 as Dionysius had intended. If our calendars were to be properly readjusted, we would need to add four years to our present date. Thus, the new millennium actually came and went with the change from 1996 to 1997, with apparently no ill or lasting effects. Despite the dire predictions made by numerous "dispensationalist" authors and others who profess to see signs that the events preceding Armageddon have already occurred or are occurring in the world around us at this very moment,[14] there is in fact no clear indication as to when (or even whether) Armageddon will ever take place. However, given the military history of Megiddo and the Jezreel Valley over the past four thousand years, it is probably only a matter of time before the next battle does indeed take place in this region.

What is it about this area that attracts battles and has prompted such a continuous state of warfare over the past four thousand years? At the beginning of this book, I compared the Jezreel Valley to the meeting place of two tectonic plates, where the stress and strain frequently result in cataclysmic events whose reverberations are felt far away, both geographically and temporally. I said then that only continued study of the region would yield answers to such questions. Now that we have looked in detail at the military history of Megiddo and the Jezreel Valley, can we come to any conclusions as a result of our examinations? What lessons, if any, can we learn from the thirty-four battles that have been fought in the Jezreel Valley over the past four thousand years?

My presentation here will serve only to initiate the discussion, rather than to end it. That is how it should be in all debates of such magnitude. Nevertheless, a few pithy remarks can be made at this point. To begin with the most obvious of observations, although Megiddo and the Jezreel Valley were valuable in their own right, what made them even more valuable was the fact that they were literally always in the way of anyone or anything wishing to proceed from north to south or from south to north, regardless of the period or era in question. The Jezreel Valley was, in short, always a major crossroads, for it also commanded routes leading from east to west and west to east. Thus, whoever controlled the Jezreel Valley, whether it was through occupation of

Megiddo, Jezreel, Mount Tabor, or any of the other prominent cities and towns that rose and fell through the millennia, by default also controlled the trade and traffic through the area, be it merchants or warriors, nomads or kings.

There is also something about this valley, a geographical je ne sais quoi, that seems to bring great conquerors together through time in a way that no other circumstance has or can. As Napoleon may have aptly said, "There is no place in the whole world more suited for war than this. . . . [It is] the most natural battleground of the whole earth." Indeed, few other areas of the world can claim to have seen so many different armies and so many famous leaders march through their lands. Perhaps only the Trojan plain and the neighboring regions bordering the Hellespont, or the plain and valley dominated by Boeotian Thebes in Greece, can be mentioned in the same breath, but even these areas pale in comparison to the veritable parade of military conflicts that make up the gory past of the Jezreel Valley. In part, this is because of the Jezreel Valley's unique location on the outskirts of Egypt, on the edge of empires, and in the path of dreams of glory.

To end on an upbeat note, I would like to close with two succinct observations concerning the battle of Armageddon as prophesied by John in the New Testament's Book of Revelation. First and foremost, I would note that during the battle Megiddo and the Jezreel Valley will once again be a "contested periphery"—for this will be an area fought over by the forces of good, on the one hand, and the forces of evil, on the other, neither of which actually live in the valley itself. Given the past history of the Jezreel Valley, in which nearly a third of the battles fought there were the result of its status as a contested periphery, this should come as no surprise. Even more importantly, I have already pointed out (in chap. 6) that of the thirteen previous battles in which neither party lived permanently in the Jezreel Valley, the party who arrived second (i.e., was last to the battlefield) won the battle outright in ten out of the thirteen instances. This is good news indeed, since according to John the forces of heaven will attack at the battle of Armageddon only after the "kings of the whole world" have already gathered in the Jezreel Valley. Thus, I might risk a quite unscholarly yet most welcome prediction (perhaps with a 75 percent degree of confidence, if the previous battles fought in the valley are any indication), that the forces of good from heaven are the odds-on favorite to defeat the forces of evil, if only because they will be the last to arrive at the battleground of Megiddo in the Jezreel Valley.

At any rate, assuming that human nature does not change in the near future, there is a very real possibility that, for whatever reasons, additional battles will take place in the Jezreel Valley sometime between now and the final battle of Armageddon. In preparing for the eventuality of such future battles, and especially in attempting to avoid them, the present-day inhabitants of the Jezreel Valley, and indeed the world as a whole, would do well to remember the bloody history of this little valley and to keep close at hand the famous statement, attributed to George Santayana, "Those who cannot remember the past are condemned to repeat it." In the case of Megiddo and the Jezreel Valley, the list of doomed participants repeating the past over and over again is already far longer than it is for any other place on earth. It remains to be seen how many more participants and how many additional battles have yet to be added to this list before Armageddon is at our door.

Notes

CHAPTER 1

The epigraph translation follows Pritchard 1969, 237.

1. Unless otherwise noted, translations from the Bible follow the New Revised Standard Version (specifically, as found in *The New Oxford Annotated Bible*).
2. Finkelstein and Ussishkin 1994, 28. See now also Silberman et al. 1999.
3. E.g., Lindsey 1970; Loasby 1989; Shea 1980.
4. Cf. Smith 1931, 380–83.
5. Rogerson 1985, 151; Davies 1986, 7–8; Halpern 2000.
6. Allenby, dispatch of 31 October 1918. For the following description and discussion of the battle, I am indebted to the accounts found in Pirie-Gordon 1919; Nelson [1913] 1920; Savage 1926; Wavell 1929; Falls 1930; Wavell 1941; Falls 1964; Gardner 1965; Newell 1991; Hughes 1996; Duncan and Opatowski 1998.
7. Newell 1991, 375.
8. Cf. Newell 1991, 377–79.
9. Duncan and Opatowski 1998, 113.
10. Cf. Newell 1991, 379.
11. Breasted 1943, 306–7.
12. Falls 1964, 35–36.
13. Wavell 1941, 194–95. These volumes included Myres 1911 and Hogarth 1914.
14. Wavell 1929, 3.
15. Smith 1931, 390.
16. Cline 1994a, 1994b.
17. For the following description and discussion of the battle, I am indebted to the accounts found in Petrie 1904; Breasted 1906; Nelson [1913] 1920; Faulkner 1942; Fuller 1954; Pritchard 1969; Yadin 1963; Davies 1986; Aharoni et al. 1993; Finkelstein and Ussishkin 1994; Duncan and Opatowski 1998.
18. Albright 1944, 27; Davies 1986, 52–55; Pritchard 1969, 234, 237–38.
19. Nelson [1913] 1920, 6.
20. Nelson [1913] 1920, 6; Aharoni et al. 1993, text to map 27; Duncan and Opatowski 1998, 1.
21. The translation follows Pritchard 1969, 235.

22. The translation follows Pritchard 1969, 235.
23. Nelson [1913] 1920, 41–43; Faulkner 1942, 7–8; Davies 1986, 52; Aharoni et al. 1993, text to map 27; Duncan and Opatowski 1998, 1.
24. Nelson [1913] 1920, 45–54; Faulkner 1942, 15; Yadin 1963, 103; Pritchard 1969, 236; Davies 1986, 53–55; Duncan and Opatowski 1998, 2.
25. The translation follows Pritchard 1969, 236.
26. Pritchard 1969, 237.
27. The translation follows Pritchard 1969, 237.
28. Leonard and Cline 1998, 5; Kempinski 1989, 67–68; Loud 1948, 5.
29. Aharoni et al. 1993, map 30.
30. Fuller 1954, 6; Gonen 1987; Finkelstein and Ussishkin 1994, 32–33; Duncan and Opatowski 1998, 3. Cf. Pritchard 1969, 238.
31. Nelson [1913] 1920, i.
32. Nelson [1913] 1920, i.
33. Smith 1919, 389–409. In fact, the 1919 edition still mistakenly identified the site of Lejjun as ancient Megiddo; cf. Smith 1919, 152, 380, 386–88.
34. Smith 1931, vii–viii. In this, 1931 edition, Smith also finally identified Tell el-Mutesellim, rather than Lejjun, as the site of ancient Megiddo; cf. Smith 1931, 150, 385–87, 390, 411–12.
35. Gardner 1965, 127.
36. Trotter 1894, 452; cf. Smith 1894, 380–409.
37. The *Geographical Journal* articles by Maunsell (1908) on the Hejaz Railway and by Masterman (1917) on Palestine's resources and suitability for colonization would probably also have been of interest to Allenby.
38. Wavell 1941, 195.
39. Faulkner 1942, 15.
40. Breasted 1943, 246–50. I am indebted to Dr. Gary Oller of the Classics Department at the University of Akron for suggesting that I consult the autobiographies and biographies of James Henry Breasted and Sir William Flinders Petrie to see whether they mentioned Allenby. His suggestion led to the finding of this published journal entry.
41. Liddell Hart 1934, 553.

CHAPTER 2

The epigraph translation follows Moran 1992, 297.

1. For the following description and discussion of the battle, I am indebted to the accounts found in Breasted 1906; Hayes 1953; Gardiner 1961; Breasted 1969; Lichtheim 1973; Aharoni 1979; Grimal 1992; Aharoni et al. 1993.
2. Lichtheim 1973, 18–22.
3. The translation follows Aharoni 1979, 135–37.
4. Breasted 1906, 140; Hayes 1953, 126; Gardiner 1961, 96; Pritchard 1969,

228 nn. 10–11; Aharoni 1979, 137; Aharoni et al. 1993, text to map 21.

5. Aharoni 1979, 137; Aharoni et al. 1993, text to map 21.

6. Gardiner 1961, 96; Pritchard 1969, 228 n. 12; Lichtheim 1973, 22 n. 7; Aharoni 1979, 137; Aharoni et al. 1993, text to map 21.

7. Kempinski 1989, 10, 30.

8. Weinstein 1981.

9. For the following description and discussion of the campaign, I am indebted to the accounts found in Albright 1944; Aharoni 1960; Malamat 1961; Aharoni 1967; Yeivin 1967; Pritchard 1969; Rainey 1973; Aharoni 1979; Rainey 1981; Weinstein 1981; Spalinger 1983; der Manuelian 1987; Aharoni et al. 1993.

10. Aharoni 1979, 168; Spalinger 1983, 95–96.

11. Malamat 1961, 219; Spalinger 1983, 97–98.

12. The translation follows Rainey 1981, 62*–63*.

13. Albright 1944, 27; Malamat 1961, 218–26; Rainey 1973, 73–74; Aharoni 1979, 169; Rainey 1981, 62*–63*; Weinstein 1981, 12–13; Spalinger 1983, 98; Aharoni et al. 1993, text to map 32.

14. Pritchard 1969, 245.

15. The translation follows Pritchard 1969, 246–47.

16. Aharoni 1960, 181; Malamat 1961, 223; Aharoni 1967, 212–15; Spalinger 1983, 90–91; der Manuelian 1987, 73–74; Aharoni et al. 1993, text to map 32.

17. The translation follows Pritchard 1969, 247.

18. Aharoni 1960, 182; Malamat 1961, 224; Yeivin 1967, 128; Aharoni 1979, 168; Rainey 1981, 61*–62*; Spalinger 1983, 89–90.

19. The translation follows Pritchard 1969, 247, as emended by Aharoni 1960, 182.

20. Maisler 1953, 81; Aharoni 1960, 182–83; Malamat 1961, 223; Yeivin 1967, 127–28; Aharoni 1979, 168; Spalinger 1983, 89–90; der Manuelian 1987, 75.

21. Maisler 1953, 81; Malamat 1961, 224–25; der Manuelian 1987, 75.

22. Epstein 1963, 49–56; Weinstein 1981, 13.

23. For the following description and discussion of Labayu's efforts, I am indebted to the accounts found in Campbell 1964; Reviv 1966; Aharoni 1971; Aharoni 1977; Ahituv 1978; Aharoni 1979; Na'aman 1981; Davies 1986; Na'aman 1988; Kempinski 1989; Moran 1992; Aharoni et al. 1993; Hess 1993; Finkelstein and Ussishkin 1994; Giles 1997.

24. Izre'el 1990; Moran 1992.

25. This and all subsequent translations from the Amarna Letters follow Moran 1992 except where otherwise noted.

26. Aharoni 1979, 176; Davies 1986, 60; Miller and Hayes 1986, 65–67; Aharoni et al. 1993, text to map 35.

27. Horowitz 1996; Halpern 2000.

28. Cf. Aharoni et al. 1993, text to map 35.

29. See Amarna Letters EA 234, 246, and 365. Cf. Campbell 1964, 97; Rainey 1978, 28–31; Adamthwaite 1991; Giles 1997, 48.

30. See Amarna Letters EA 8 and 248. Cf. Lapp 1967, 4; Aharoni 1979, 172; Kempinski 1989, 12; Moran 1992, 16–17; Aharoni et al. 1993, text to map 35.

31. Albright 1947, 59; Campbell 1964, 103–4; Moran 1992, xxxi, xxxvi–xxxvii; Giles 1997, 52, 255; O'Connor and Cline 1998, v.

32. Shipton 1939, 4, 11, 50; Kenyon 1969, 59; Gonen 1987, 91, 94, 96; Kempinski 1989, 10, 72–74; Leonard and Cline 1998, 6.

33. Singer 1988.

34. Aharoni 1977, 831; Aharoni 1979, 176–81; Aharoni et al. 1993, text to maps 37–38.

35. Papyrus Anastasi I. The translation follows Pritchard 1969, 477–78; Yadin 1963, 111. Cf. Yadin 1963, 242–43; Aharoni 1977, 831; Davies 1986, 10; Kempinski 1989, 13; Aharoni et al. 1993, text to map 41; Finkelstein and Ussishkin 1994, 33.

36. Loud 1948, 29. Cf. Gonen 1987, 94–96; Singer 1988–89, 101–2, 109–10; Kempinski 1989, 10, 67, 72, 74–76, 160; Ussishkin 1995, 240–46; Finkelstein 1996, 171; Leonard and Cline 1998, 7.

37. The translation follows Aharoni et al. 1993, text to map 42; see also discussion therein.

CHAPTER 3

1. For the following description and discussion of the battle, I am indebted to the accounts found in Albright 1936; Engberg 1940; Whiston 1957; Yadin 1963; Kochavi 1965; Mayes 1969; Malamat 1971a; Freedman 1975; Aharoni 1979; Rainey 1981, 1983; Halpern 1983a, 1983b, 1988; Stager 1989; Na'aman 1990; Aharoni et al. 1993; Herzog and Gichon 1997; Duncan and Opatowski 1998.

2. Maisler 1953, 83–84; Yadin 1960; Malamat 1971a, 135–36; Kaufmann 1985; Miller and Hayes 1986, 61–62, 71–72; Aharoni et al. 1993, text to maps 61–62; Na'aman 1994, 256–60, 268–69; Herzog and Gichon 1997, 57–64, map 4; Duncan and Opatowski 1998, 11.

3. See Josephus *Antiquities of the Jews* 5.199–209; Whiston 1957, 157–58; Feldman 1986, 115–28. Some scholars feel that the prose account is the "true basis for the geography of the battle" (Rainey 1981, *63). For discussion of this problem, see Malamat 1971a, 137; Freedman 1975, 4; Rainey 1981, *63; Halpern 1983a, 47–49; Halpern 1988, 76–103; Na'aman 1990, 433.

4. For arguments on whether to follow the poem or the prose, see Albright 1936, 26, 29; Albright 1937, 25; Kochavi 1965, 90–91; Malamat 1971a,

137; Freedman 1975, 3, 13; Rainey 1981, *63–*64; Rainey 1983, 48; Halpern 1983a, 47–49; Halpern 1983b, 394–96; Halpern 1988, 76–103; Bal 1988, 1; Stager 1988, 224; Stager 1989, 52; Na'aman 1990, 433; Albright 1994, 13.

5. Smith 1931, map VII; Yadin 1963, 255; Kochavi 1965, 91–92, with references; Rainey 1981, *64; Rainey 1983, 46–48; Na'aman 1990, 425, 427–32; Aharoni et al. 1993, text to maps 61–62; Lindars 1995, 177–78; Herzog and Gichon 1997, 65; Duncan and Opatowski 1998, 11–12.

6. Boling 1975, 100; Halpern 1983b, 381, 386–87, 390, 393; Halpern 1988, 80–81; Lindars 1995, 187; Herzog and Gichon 1997, 67.

7. Malamat 1971a, 139; Freedman 1975, 15–17; Stager 1988; Stager 1989, esp. 53n, 62.

8. Kochavi 1965, 92–94; Rainey 1981, *63–*64; Rainey 1983, 46–48, fig. 1; Rogerson 1985, 136; Halpern 1988, 91–94; Na'aman 1990, 429 and nn. 19–21; Gal 1994, 44; Lindars 1995, 185; Margalit 1995, 630. Cf. Aharoni 1971, 114–17, on the geography of the territory controlled by the Israelite tribes.

9. Malamat 1971a, 139.

10. The translation follows Na'aman 1990, 426. See Caquot 1986, 54–55; Na'aman 1990, 423–26.

11. Na'aman 1990, 434.

12. Aharoni et al. 1993, text to maps 61–62.

13. Maisler 1953, 83–84; Malamat 1971a, 135–36; Halpern 1983a, 49; Halpern 1983b, 391–92; Halpern 1988, 89–91; Aharoni et al. 1993, text to maps 61–62; Lindars 1995, 165; Duncan and Opatowski 1998, 11.

14. Halpern 1988, 89, 93; Herzog and Gichon 1997, 66–67.

15. Cf. Lindars 1995, 193. Sisera apparently did this of his own accord, for despite an elaborate recent reconstruction of the battle by Herzog and Gichon (1997, 64–71, maps 5–6) in which they suggest that a second Israelite force was involved in the battle and was responsible for drawing the Canaanites into the desired area, there is no indication in either the prose account or the poetic version that such a second Israelite contingent under an unnamed additional commander actually existed. It is clear that the "I" who will draw out Sisera and give him into Barak's hand (Judges 4:7) is the Lord, rather than Deborah herself, contrary to Herzog and Gichon's recently proposed reconstruction of the battle.

16. Yadin 1963, 256; Malamat 1971a, 140, 316 n. 35; Boling 1975, 113; Aharoni 1979, 225; Rogerson 1985, 136; Hobbs 1989, 169–70; Aharoni et al. 1993, text to maps 61–62; Lindars 1995, 265–67; Herzog and Gichon 1997, 69; Duncan and Opatowski 1998, 12.

17. The translation follows Huang 1993, 79.

18. On the dates of the rainy season, see Kempinski 1989, 9. The month-by-

month breakdown of the known dates for the twenty-four battles is as follows: January: Hospitallers/Templars; January–March: Baibars; April: John
I Tzimisces, Napoleon, Israelis (1948); May: Thutmose III, Israelis (1948);
late spring/early summer: Necho II; June: Ikhshidids versus Abbasids, Saladin (1182), Ayyub, Israelis (1967); June/July: Maudud; July: Saladin
(1182 and 1187); summer: Jehu; September: Mongols, Allenby; Septem-
ber/October: Saladin (1183); October: Vespasian, Syrian attack on Ramat
David airfield in 1973; November: Amenhotep II; November–December:
Fifth Crusade; December: Ikhshidids versus Hamdanids.

19. Cf. Malamat 1971a, 136–37; Halpern 1988, 89, 93.

20. This translation follows Halpern 1988, 81 (the New Revised Standard Version is not particularly faithful to the original Hebrew in these verses).

21. Boling 1975, 97–98; Halpern 1983a, 47; Halpern 1983b, 388–90; Halpern
1988, 81–82.

22. Halpern 1983a, 47–49; Halpern 1983b, 389–90, 393–94; Halpern 1988,
76–103; Na'aman 1990. Cf. Rainey 1981, *63.

23. Malamat 1953, 61; Malamat 1971a, 140; Freedman 1975, 12.

24. Lapp 1967, 8–9, 15–16; Malamat 1971a, 136; Rast 1978, 7, 15; Lindars
1995, 267. Cf. Finkelstein 1998, 209–10, 215–16.

25. Albright 1936, 1937, 1940; Engberg 1940; Mayes 1969, 354–55; Malamat
1971a, 136; Aharoni 1979, 228–29; Dothan 1982, 70; Davies 1986, 69;
Gonen 1987, 96; Kempinski 1989, 10, 76–77; Aharoni et al. 1993, text to
maps 61–62; Lindars 1995, 267; Ussishkin 1995, 242, 246, 260; Finkelstein 1996, 171–72; Leonard and Cline 1998, 8, 11.

26. Malamat 1953, 61–62; Herzog and Gichon 1997, 72–73; Duncan and
Opatowski 1998, 13.

27. Cf. Aharoni 1989, 263; Rogerson 1985, 182; Aharoni et al. 1993, text to
maps 75–76; Herzog and Gichon 1997, 73.

28. For the following description and discussion of the campaign, I am
indebted to the accounts found in Tolkowsky 1925; Malamat 1953; Whiston 1957; Whitley 1957; Yadin 1963; Malamat 1971a; Aharoni 1979;
Miller and Hayes 1986; Aharoni et al. 1993; Herzog and Gichon 1997;
Duncan and Opatowski 1998.

29. Thucydides 2.19–23, 2.55–57, 3.1, 3.26. The translation follows Crawley
1910; cf. Hanson 1998, 131–35.

30. Josephus *Antiquity of the Jews* 5.222.

31. Cf. Malamat 1953, 65.

32. Malamat 1953, 65 n. 10; Malamat 1971a, 143–44; Aharoni et al. 1993, text
to maps 75–76; Herzog and Gichon 1997, 78–79; Duncan and Opatowski
1998, 14.

33. Josephus *Antiquities of the Jews* 5.215.

34. Tolkowsky 1925, 73; Malamat 1953, 62; Herzog and Gichon 1997, 73.

35. Yadin 1963, 256–57.

36. Cf. Wavell 1948, 164; Malamat 1953, 62–63; Malamat 1971a, 144; Yadin 1963, 257; Herzog and Gichon 1997, 73–75; Duncan and Opatowski 1998, 13.

37. Cf. Tolkowsky 1925, 70–74.

38. Tolkowsky 1925, 73; Wavell 1948, 166; Malamat 1953, 63–64; Yadin 1963, 257.

39. Yadin 1963, 259; Malamat 1971a, 146.

40. Cf. Aharoni et al. 1993, maps 75–76; Herzog and Gichon 1997, 74, map 7; Duncan and Opatowski 1998, map 9.

41. Clausewitz 1942, 26.

42. For the following description and discussion of the battle, I am indebted to the accounts found in Whiston 1957; Tsevat 1979; Feldman 1982; Miller and Hayes 1986; Hobbs 1989; Aharoni et al. 1993; Herzog and Gichon 1997; Duncan and Opatowski 1998.

43. Tsevat 1979, 74; Miller and Hayes 1986, 144; Aharoni et al. 1993, text to maps 95–97; Herzog and Gichon 1997, 93–94.

44. Josephus *Antiquities of the Jews* 6.327–7.6; cf. translation by Whiston 1957, 200–205.

45. Cf. Mauchline 1971, 181; Klein 1983, 269; Aharoni et al. 1993, text to maps 95–97.

46. I.e., modern Ein Jezreel—perhaps, but by no means certainly, to be identified with ʿAyn Jalut. Cf. Mauchline 1971, 184; Klein 1983, 276.

47. Cf. Whiston 1957, 204–5; Feldman 1982, 77.

48. Tsevat 1979, 74; Miller and Hayes 1986, 144–45; Hobbs 1989, 147; Herzog and Gichon 1997, 93–94.

49. Yadin 1963, 284–87.

50. Cf. Malul 1996, 534; Duncan and Opatowski 1998, 7.

51. Clausewitz 1976, 423, 537–38.

52. Klein 1983, 288; Herzog and Gichon 1997, 94.

53. Cf. Whitelam 1979, 100–105; Klein 1983, 287–88; Malul 1996.

54. Cf. Miller and Hayes 1986, 144–45; Aharoni et al. 1993, text to maps 95–97.

55. Miller and Hayes 1986, 146; Aharoni et al. 1993, text to map 98.

56. Chambers 1985, 154; Rogerson 1985, 157; Davies 1986, 73–74; Kempinski 1989, 13; Herzog and Gichon 1997, 105; Duncan and Opatowski 1998, 17.

Chapter 4

1. Breasted 1929, ix, xii; Fisher 1929, 12, 60–61, figs. 7A–B; Guy 1931, 44; Lamon and Shipton 1939, 60–61, fig. 70; Larson 1990, 2–3; Ussishkin 1990, 71–72, fig. 1.

2. Noth 1960, 239–40; Mazar 1986, 139; Barnes 1991, 60 n. 8; Aharoni et al. 1993, text to map 120; Clayton 1994, 182; Herzog and Gichon 1997, 116–17.

3. Breasted 1929, xi–xii; Fisher 1929, 14–16, 60–61, figs. 8–9; Larson 1990, 2–3; Ussishkin 1990, 71–72, fig. 2.

4. The translation follows Kitchen 1989, 33.

5. Larson 1990, 2; Ussishkin 1990, 71–73; cf. Naaman 1992, 84 n. 11.

6. Breasted 1906, 348–51; Hughes and Nims 1954, viii–ix, pls. X, XI; Mazar 1957, 59; Mazar 1986, 141–44; Rohl 1995, 121, 124.

7. Cf. Mazar 1986, 147; Rohl 1995, 125.

8. For the following description and discussion of the battle, I am indebted to the accounts found in Breasted 1906; Mazar 1957; Yadin 1963; Herrmann 1964; Aharoni 1979; Davies 1986; Kitchen 1986; Mazar 1986; Kitchen 1989; Ussishkin 1990; Barnes 1991; Na'aman 1992; Aharoni et al. 1993; Clayton 1994; Finkelstein and Ussishkin 1994; Rohl 1995; Talshir 1996; Herzog and Gichon 1997.

9. Albright 1925, 26, 32–34; Aharoni 1976; Aharoni 1977, 831; Kempinski 1989, 13; Aharoni et al. 1993, map 113; Finkelstein and Ussishkin 1994, 36.

10. Breasted 1906, 348–51; Mazar 1957; Redford 1973, 10–12; Kitchen 1986, 432–47; Mazar 1986; Na'aman 1992, 79–86; Rohl 1995, 124–28.

11. Mazar 1957, 1986. See also Aharoni 1979, 324–27; Rohl 1995, 124–28; Herzog and Gichon 1997, 127–28.

12. Kitchen 1986, 443–45; Na'aman 1992, 79–81.

13. Cf. Aharoni 1979, 324–27; Na'aman 1992, 79–81; Rohl 1995, 124–28; Herzog and Gichon 1997, 127–28.

14. Noth 1938, 283–89; Herrmann 1964, 55–79; Kitchen 1986, 296–300, 432–47, fig. 9. Cf. Ussishkin 1980, 7.

15. Kitchen 1986, 294–95.

16. The translation follows Kitchen 1989, 32–33. Cf. Redford 1973, 10; Na'aman 1992, 84.

17. Ussishkin 1990, 72–73. Cf. Na'aman 1992, 84 n. 11.

18. Fisher 1929, 16; Guy 1931, 47–48; Lamon and Shipton 1939, 3–4; Loud 1948, 43–46, fig. 99; Davies 1986, 96; Yadin 1970, 75, 95; Yadin 1980, 20–21; Ussishkin 1980, 5, 7; Ussishkin 1990, 73–74.

19. Redford 1973, 11; Kitchen 1986, 287, 302; Ussishkin 1990, 74.

20. For the following description and discussion of the coup, I am indebted to the accounts found in Whiston 1957; Napier 1959; Miller and Hayes 1986; Rogerson 1985; Rofé 1988; Williamson 1991; Aharoni et al. 1993; White 1994; Schneider 1995, 1996.

21. Rogerson 1985, 156; Miller and Hayes 1986, 254–55; Rofé 1988; White 1994.

22. The translation follows Whiston 1957, 270; cf. White 1994, 66.

23. Napier 1959, 370–71; Rogerson 1985, 156; Miller and Hayes 1986, 284–85; Aharoni et al. 1993, text to map 131.

24. Schneider 1995; Schneider 1996, 101–3, 107.

25. Rogerson 1985, 156; Miller and Hayes 1986, 285.

26. Napier 1959, 371; Rogerson 1985, 156; Miller and Hayes 1986, 285.

27. Biran and Naveh 1993, 95; Halpern 1994, 70; Biran and Naveh 1995, 11, 17–18; Schniedewind 1996, 83–85; Na'aman 1997, 125–27.

28. The translation follows Schniedewind 1996, 77–78; Na'aman 1997, 126.

29. Biran and Naveh 1995, 18; Schniedewind 1996, 83.

30. Halpern 1994; Biran and Naveh 1995, 18; Schniedewind 1996, 83–85; Na'aman 1997, 125.

31. Ussishkin and Woodhead 1992, 53; Ussishkin and Woodhead 1997, 64–66; Na'aman 1997, 125–27; Finkelstein 1998, 208; Finkelstein 1999, 61, 63.

32. Miller and Hayes 1986, 261, 285–86; Schneider 1995, 26, 29.

33. The translation of the Black Obelisk incscription follows Luckenbill 1926, paragraph 590. Cf. discussions in Miller and Hayes 1986, 285–86, 287; Schneider 1995, 26, 30–31; Schneider 1996, 105–6.

34. Aharoni et al. 1993, text to maps 146, 148; Herzog and Gichon 1997, 197, map 25.

35. The translation and reconstruction follow Na'aman 1993, 105–6. Cf. Tadmor 1994, 81–83, 221, 235, 279–82; Na'aman 1995, 271–72.

36. Aharoni et al. 1993, text to maps 149, 151, 155–156; Herzog and Gichon 1997, 197, map 25.

37. Aharoni 1977, 831; Rogerson 1985, 137; Davies 1986, 98; Miller and Hayes 1986, 296–97, 318; Kempinski 1989, 13; Aharoni et al. 1993, text to map 148; Finkelstein and Ussishkin 1994, 43; Na'aman 1995, 274; Ussishkin 1995, 261–62; Peersman 2000; Halpern 2000.

38. Davies 1986, 97–98; Finkelstein and Ussishkin 1994, 43; Peersman 2000. But Kempinski (1989, 10, 100) sees the Tiglath-Pileser III conquest in the destruction of Stratum IIIB rather than Stratum IVA.

39. Cross and Freedman 1953, 56–57; Na'aman 1991.

40. For the following description and discussion of the events, I am indebted to the accounts found in Binns 1917; Welch 1925; Boehmer 1933; Malamat 1950; Cross and Freedman 1953; Yadin 1963; Frost 1968; Malamat 1968; Pfeifer 1969; Malamat 1973, 1974, 1975; Spieckermann 1982; Williamson 1982; Nelson 1983; Davies 1986; Kempinski 1986; Begg 1987; Williamson 1987; Hobbs 1989; Na'aman 1991; Aharoni et al. 1993; Finkelstein and Ussishkin 1994; Talshir 1996; Herzog and Gichon 1997; Malamat 1999.

41. Welch 1925; Boehmer 1933; Malamat 1950; Noth 1958, 278–79; Malamat 1973, 1974, 1975; Nelson 1983, 188; Na'aman 1991; Talshir 1996; Herzog and Gichon 1997, 256–57; Malamat 1999, 36–38. Cf. Williamson 1982, 244; Davies 1986, 104–5; Cogan and Tadmor 1988, 300.

42. Cogan and Tadmor 1988, 300.

43. Halpern 1998, 501–3.

44. Frost 1968, 372–73; Talshir 1996, 213–14; Halpern 1998, 503.

45. Wiseman 1961, 18–19, 61–63; Pritchard 1969, 305; Williamson 1982; Begg 1987; Williamson 1987; Augustin 1988; Cogan and Tadmor 1988, 300–301; Talshir 1996, 213–16, 222.

46. Malamat 1950, 219–20; Yadin 1963, 311–12; Malamat 1973, 274–78; Herzog and Gichon 1997, 257.

47. Cf. Welch 1925, 255; Frost 1968, 376; Miller and Hayes 1986, 402; Cogan and Tadmor 1988, 302 n. 39; Talshir 1996, 219, 226–27, 236; Halpern 1998, 509.

48. Frost 1968, 372; Williamson 1982, 243–44; Augustin 1988, 138–39; Cogan and Tadmor 1988, 301; Na'aman 1991, 53–55; Talshir 1996, 219, 226–27, 236; Halpern 1998, 503, 509.

49. Talshir 1996, 234.

50. The translation follows Whiston 1957, 305.

51. Yadin 1976, 9–14; Feldman 1993, 122–23; Talshir 1996, 214–15; Malamat 1999, 37–38.

52. The translation follows Godley 1931, 472–73.

53. Binns 1917, 39–43; Malamat 1950, 220–21; Whiston 1957, 305 n. 297; Yadin 1963, 311–12; Malamat 1973, 274–76; Davies 1986, 104–5.

54. Wiseman 1961; Miller and Hayes 1986, 406–7.

55. Malamat 1973, 277; Herzog and Gichon 1997, 257.

56. Binns 1917, 38–39; Na'aman 1991, 51–52. Cf. Malamat 1973, 273 n. 23.

57. Welch 1925, 255–60; Boehmer 1933, 199–203; Noth 1958, 278–79; Helck 1971, 247; Nelson 1983, 188–89; Na'aman 1991, 51–58; Finkelstein and Ussishkin 1994, 43; Talshir 1996, 218.

58. Malamat 1973, 267, 274; Malamat 1975, 124–25; Nelson 1983, 187; Davies 1986, 104, 107; Kempinski 1986, 103–4; Finkelstein and Ussishkin 1994, 43.

59. Herzog and Gichon 1997, 258–59, map 29.

60. Davies 1986, 109–10; Kempinski 1989, 107.

CHAPTER 5

The epigraph translation follows Whiston 1957, 740–41.

1. For the following description and discussion of the battle, I am indebted to the accounts found in Abel 1952a; Huss 1976; Paton 1979; Elitzur 1985–88; Applebaum 1989; Shatzman 1991; Aharoni et al. 1993; Sherwin-White and Kuhrt 1993.

2. The translation follows Paton 1979, 172–75.

3. Allen 1997, 320–21; cf. Berquist 1995a, 1995b.

4. Fisher 1929, vii–viii.

5. Malamat 1973, 271–72; Malamat 1975, 124–25; Davies 1986, 104; Malamat 1999, 34, 36, 41.

6. Kitchener 1878, 161–63; Abel 1952a, 77–78; Elitzur 1985–88, 79–82; Shatzman 1991, 36; Aharoni et al. 1993, text to map 179.

7. Sherwin-White and Kuhrt 1993, 188–90.

8. Josephus *Antiquities of the Jews* 12.332, 13.191; Aharoni et al. 1993, map 191 and accompanying text, map 206 and accompanying text.

9. Josephus *Jewish War* 1.64; Josephus *Antiquities of the Jews* 13.275; Klausner 1972, 217–19; Aharoni et al. 1993, map 211 and accompanying text.

10. Josephus *Antiquities of the Jews* 13.395–97; Shatzman 1991, 75, 83; Aharoni et al. 1993, maps 213–14 and accompanying texts.

11. For the following description and discussion of the battle, I am indebted to the accounts found in Abel 1952a; Kanael 1957; Whiston 1957; Smallwood 1976; Shatzman 1991.

12. The translation follows Whiston 1957, 620. Cf. Abel 1952a, 295; Kanael 1957, 106; Smallwood 1976, 34–35; Shatzman 1991, 135.

13. The translation follows Whiston 1957, 416.

14. Smallwood 1976, 34–35 n. 46; Shatzman 1991, 135.

15. Schalit 1975, 45–46.

16. Stern 1975, 131–32.

17. Isaac and Roll 1982, 9. After the campaigns of 67 B.C., the Tenth and Fifteenth Legions traded places: the Fifth and Fifteenth Legions were stationed at Caesarea, while the Tenth Legion was based in Scythopolis.

18. Josephus *Jewish War* 2.572; Josephus *Life of Josephus* 185; Shatzman 1991, 260; Aharoni et al. 1993, text to map 257.

19. Josephus *Jewish War* 4.1; Smallwood 1976, 309–10; Aharoni et al. 1993, text to map 257.

20. For the following description and discussion of the battle, I am indebted to the accounts found in Abel 1952a; Whiston 1957; Smallwood 1976.

21. Kitchener 1878, 161–63; Smallwood 1976, 310; Shatzman 1991, 260.

22. The translation follows Whiston 1957, 740–41.

23. Whiston 1957, 741n.

24. Netzer 1991; Magness 1992.

25. Clausewitz 1942, 55. Cf. Clausewitz 1942, 37–38; Clausewitz 1976, 353–54.

26. Clausewitz 1976, 348, 354, 538.

27. Huang 1993, 83.

28. Avi-Yonah 1976, 36; Avi-Yonah 1977, 114, 141; Aharoni 1977, 831; Kennedy 1980, 307; Isaac and Roll 1982, 9–10; Davies 1986, 110; Kempinski 1986, 16; Ussishkin 1995, 262. See Rosenthal and Mozeson 1990, 114, on a debated gathering of rebellious Egyptian and Galilean Jewish troops in the Jezreel Valley in A.D. 116; cf. also discussion in Smallwood 1976, 425–27.

29. Schumacher 1908, 175, 188; Smallwood 1976, 436–37; Avi-Yonah 1977, 114, 141, 185–86; Isaac and Roll 1982, 11; Davies 1986, 110; Tsuk 1988–89, 96–97.

30. Avi-Yonah 1977, 122–23, 141; Isaac and Roll 1982, 11; Davies 1986, 110.

Chapter 6

1. Abel 1952b, 394–96; Gibb 1960, 208; Spuler 1969, 19; Friedmann 1992, 185–88.

2. Gibb 1960, 208; Donner 1981, 129; Gil 1992, 41–42.

3. For the following description and discussion of the battles, I am indebted to the accounts found in Canard 1951, 1971; Bacharach 1975, 1991; Gil 1992.

4. Bacharach 1975, 586, 594; Bianquis 1988, 178; Bacharach 1991, 411; Gil 1992, 316–17.

5. Bacharach 1975, 598–99; Bikhazi 1983, 140–41; Bacharach 1984, 63; Bacharach 1991, 411; Gil 1992, 318.

6. Bacharach 1975, 599–600; Gil 1992, 318.

7. Bacharach 1975, 600; Gil 1992, 318.

8. Bacharach 1975, 600; Bianquis 1988, 179; Gil 1992, 318.

9. Canard 1971, 127; Bianquis 1988, 179; Gil 1992, 319; Bianquis 1997, 105.

10. Canard 1971, 129; Bacharach 1975, 609; Bikhazi 1981, 614–16; Bikhazi 1983, 152–53; Bacharach 1984, 63; Bacharach 1991, 411; Bianquis 1997, 105.

11. Canard 1951, 586 n. 20; Bikhazi 1981, 619, 648–49 n. 43; Gil 1992, 319–20 n. 92.

12. Bikhazi 1981, 619, 648–49 n. 43.

13. Canard 1971, 129; Bikhazi 1981, 619; Bacharach 1984, 63–64; Bianquis 1988, 179; Bianquis 1997, 105.

14. It is not known who arrived first or second in the battle of A.D. 940 fought between the Ikhshidids and the Abbasids, which ended in a tie anyway, while the conflict between Saladin and the Crusaders at 'Ayn Jalut in A.D. 1183 also ended in a draw. The battles in which the last party to arrive was the victor were those of the Philistines versus Saul and Jonathan ca. 1016 B.C.; Necho II versus Josiah in 609 B.C.; Antiochus III versus Ptolemy IV in 218 B.C.; Gabinius versus Alexander, son of Aristobulus II, in 55 B.C.; Vespasian versus the Jewish rebels in A.D. 67; Saladin versus the Crusaders at Forbelet in A.D. 1182; the Mamlukes versus the Mongols in A.D. 1260; Zahir al-'Umar versus the Nablus-Saqr alliance ca. A.D. 1735; Napoleon versus the Ottomans in A.D. 1799; and Allenby versus the Ottomans in A.D. 1918.

15. For the following description and discussion of the campaign, I am indebted to the accounts found in Schlumberger 1896; Jenkins 1966; Holt 1986; Dostourian 1993; Treadgold 1995.

16. The translation follows Dostourian 1993, 29–31. See also discussions in Schlumberger 1896, 394; Jenkins 1966, 298; Holt 1986, 167–68; Treadgold 1995, 36–37, 212.

17. The battles in which the invading force was the victor were those of Pepi I

versus the Canaanites ca. 2350 B.C.; Thutmose III versus the Canaanites in 1479 B.C.; Amenhotep II versus the Canaanites ca. 1430 B.C.; Deborah and Barak versus Sisera ca. 1125 B.C.; Shoshenq I (Shishak) versus Megiddo in 925 B.C.; Jehu versus Joram and Ahaziah ca. 841 B.C.; John I Tzimisces versus the Fatimids in A.D. 975; Maudud of Mosul versus the Crusaders in A.D. 1113; Saladin versus the Daburiyans in A.D. 1182; Saladin versus the Crusaders in A.D. 1187; Ayyub versus the Crusaders in A.D. 1247; Baibars versus the Hospitallers in A.D. 1263; the Hospitallers/Templars versus the Mamlukes in A.D. 1264; Zahir al-'Umar versus Lejjun in A.D. 1773; and the Israelis versus Zarin, Lejjun, and Megiddo in A.D. 1948.

18. Clausewitz 1976, 370.
19. Clausewitz 1976, 360.
20. Jenkins 1966, 298–99; Holt 1986, 168; Treadgold 1995, 37.

CHAPTER 7

The epigraph translation follows Babcock and Krey 1943, 493–94.

1. The translation follows McGinty 1941, 69.
2. For the following description and discussion of the battle, I am indebted to the accounts found in Smail 1956; Cahen 1969; Fink 1969; Benvenisti 1970.
3. Smail 1956, 55; Fink 1969, 402; Benvenisti 1970, 358. The monks returned and restored the ruined monasteries a few years later.
4. Smail 1956, 207; Cahen 1969, 169; Fink 1969, 402–3.
5. For the following description and discussion of the battles, I am indebted to the accounts found in Archer and Kingsford 1894; Lane-Poole 1898; Stevenson 1907; Babcock and Krey 1943; Runciman 1952; Smail 1956; Baldwin 1969; Ehrenkreutz 1972; Lyons and Jackson 1982; Kedar 1992; Jones and Ereira 1995.
6. The translation follows Babcock and Krey 1943, 469.
7. Babcock and Krey 1943, 470; Lyons and Jackson 1982, 167.
8. Lyons and Jackson 1982, 168.
9. Babcock and Krey 1943, 472–74; Lyons and Jackson 1982, 169.
10. The translation follows Babcock and Krey 1943, 474.
11. Lyons and Jackson 1982, 169.
12. Babcock and Krey 1943, 474–75; Lyons and Jackson 1982, 169.
13. Ehrenkreutz 1972, 183; Lyons and Jackson 1982, 204, 206.
14. Stevenson 1907, 232; Babcock and Krey 1943, 497; Lyons and Jackson 1982, 206.
15. Lane-Poole 1898, 177; Stevenson 1907, 232; Runciman 1952, 437–38; Lyons and Jackson 1982, 206.
16. The translation follows Babcock and Krey 1943, 494–95.

17. Lane-Poole 1898, 177; Lyons and Jackson 1982, 206–7; Kedar and Pringle 1985, 164.

18. The translation of William of Tyre follows Babcock and Krey 1943, 498. See also Babcock and Krey 1943, 495; Lyons and Jackson 1982, 207.

19. The translation of William of Tyre follows Babcock and Krey 1943, 498. See also Babcock and Krey 1943, 496; Runciman 1952, 439; Smail 1956, 154.

20. Stevenson 1907, 233; Lyons and Jackson 1982, 208.

21. Babcock and Krey 1943, 497–98; Runciman 1952, 439; Smail 1956, 155–56; Baldwin 1969, 600; Lyons and Jackson 1982, 208; Jones and Ereira 1995, 148.

22. Smail 1982; Newby 1983, 115–35; Kedar 1992, 189–207; Jones and Ereira 1995, 159–60.

23. Benvenisti 1970, 323, 359; Humphreys 1977, 136; Broadhurst 1980, 83; Lyons and Jackson 1982, 268.

24. Donovan 1950, 35; Runciman 1954, 148–49.

25. The translation of the proclamation follows Riley-Smith and Riley-Smith 1981, 120–21. See also Donovan 1950, 33; Gibb 1969, 697; Van Cleve 1969, 378–79, 389–91; Benvenisti 1970, 358–62; Humphreys 1977, 136–37; Broadhurst 1980, 153, 156; Powell 1986, 131; Marshall 1992, 21–22, 26, 69.

26. For the following description and discussion of the Fifth Crusade, I am indebted to the accounts found in Röhricht 1876, 1891; Smith 1931; Donovan 1950; Runciman 1954; Gibb 1969; Hardwicke 1969; Van Cleve 1969; Benvenisti 1970; Peters 1971; Humphreys 1977; Broadhurst 1980; Sweeney 1981; Holt 1986; Powell 1986; Marshall 1992; Thorau 1992.

27. The translation of Oliver of Paderborn follows Peters 1971, 53–54. See also Donovan 1950, 32–34; Runciman 1954, 148; Gibb 1969, 698; Hardwicke 1969, 538–39; Van Cleve 1969, 389–91; Humphreys 1977, 156–57; Broadhurst 1980, 164–65; Sweeney 1981, 479; Powell 1986, 127, 130–31.

28. Donovan 1950, 35–36; Runciman 1954, 148–49; Van Cleve 1969, 393–94; Peters 1971, 56; Sweeney 1981, 479; Powell 1986, 132–34.

29. The translation of Oliver of Paderborn follows Peters 1971, 54–55. See also Donovan 1950, 34–35; Runciman 1954, 148; Van Cleve 1969, 391–92; Benvenisti 1970, 359; Humphreys 1977, 157–58; Powell 1986, 131–32; Marshall 1992, 226.

30. Donovan 1950, 34–35; Runciman 1954, 148; Van Cleve 1969, 392; Benvenisti 1970, 359; Humphreys 1977, 157–58; Powell 1986, 132; Marshall 1992, 228, 239–40.

31. Gibb 1969, 698; Van Cleve 1969, 392; Benvenisti 1970, 359–60; Humphreys 1977, 159; Broadhurst 1980, 181; Powell 1986, 132.

32. Runciman 1954, 223–27; Runciman 1969, 561–64; Benvenisti 1970, 360; Holt 1986, 65–66.

33. For the following description and discussion of the battle, I am indebted to the accounts found in Runciman 1954, 1969; Benvenisti 1970; Humphreys 1977; Holt 1986; Thorau 1992.

34. Runciman 1954, 228–29; Runciman 1969, 564; Humphreys 1977, 293; Thorau 1992, 20.

35. Benvenisti 1970, 360; Riley-Smith 1967, 135, 413–17; Lyons and Lyons 1971, 199–200 n. 1; Holt 1986, 66; Marshall 1992, 65, 97.

CHAPTER 8

For variations on the quotations in the epigraph, which are quite possibly erroneously attributed to Napoleon, cf. Lindsey 1970, 152–53; White 1977, 190–91; White 1983, 175–76; and numerous Web pages on Armageddon.

1. For the following description and discussion of the battle, I am indebted to the accounts found in Howorth 1888; Levi della Vida 1935; Glubb 1967, 1973; Saunders 1971, 1977; Jackson 1980; Smith 1984; Chambers 1985; Thorau 1985; Irwin 1986; Morgan 1986; Keegan 1993; Amitai-Preiss 1991; Thorau 1992; Amitai-Preiss 1995; Jones and Ereira 1995.

2. Morgan 1985, 232–34; Morgan 1986, 156; Amitai-Preiss 1995, 28.

3. The translation follows Glubb 1973, 60.

4. Smith 1984, 309; Thorau 1985, 236; Irwin 1986, 32; Keegan 1993, 210; Amitai-Preiss 1995, 27, 29, 39–40.

5. Glubb 1967, 267; Glubb 1973, 60; Lewis 1987, 85–86; Amitai-Preiss 1995, 36.

6. Amitai-Preiss 1995, 37–38.

7. Quotation from Irwin 1986, 33. See also Howorth 1888, 167; Smith 1984, 308, 311–12; Keegan 1993, 210–11; Amitai-Preiss 1995, 36.

8. Cf. Amitai-Preiss 1991, 123 n. 14.

9. Glubb 1973, 62; Smith 1984, 326; Amitai-Preiss 1995, 40.

10. Howorth 1888, 167; Chambers 1985, 154; Amitai-Preiss 1995, 394.

11. Cf. Howorth 1888, 167–68; Saunders 1971, 232 n. 94; Smith 1984, 326–28; Thorau 1985, 236, 237–39; Irwin 1986, 34; Lewis 1987, 84–89; Jones and Ereira 1993, 235–36; Amitai-Preiss 1995, 40–44.

12. This last, desperate stand by the Mongols probably took place not down the road at Beisan (Beth Shean), as al-Maqrizi states, but rather as a second phase of the battle at ʿAyn Jalut itself. There seems to have been an error of transmission on the part of al-Maqrizi: cf. Glubb 1973, 63; Amitai-Preiss 1995, 42.

13. Chambers 1985, 154–55.

14. The translation follows Howorth 1888, 168; cf. Saunders 1971, 232 n. 94.

15. Amitai-Preiss 1991, 143.

16. Amitai-Preiss 1995, 47.

17. Morgan 1986, 156.

18. Jackson 1980, 510–11; Smith 1984, 328; Irwin 1986, 34; Morgan 1986, 156–57; Amitai-Preiss 1995, 1.

19. Holt 1986, 94; Irwin 1986, 47.

20. For the following description and discussion of the conflicts in A.D. 1263 and 1264, I am indebted to the accounts found in Runciman 1954, 1969; Benvenisti 1970; Lyons and Lyons 1971; Holt 1986; Irwin 1986; Marshall 1992; Thorau 1992.

21. Quotation from Runciman 1969, 575. See also Runciman 1954, 317–18; Riley-Smith 1967, 125; Runciman 1969, 574–75; Benvenisti 1970, 251, 360; Lyons and Lyons 1971, 199–200 n. 1, 204 n. 1; Irwin 1986, 47; Marshall 1992, 195–96; Thorau 1992, 136–37, 147. Note that the "Lizon" mentioned by Runciman and Riley-Smith should be "Lejjun."

22. Edhem 1916, 16, 26–27, 37 n. 14; Salmon 1921, 95–98; Jansky 1926, 237–39. Cf. el-Aref 1975, 334; Isaac and Roll 1982, 14, 24 n. 92.

23. For the following description and discussion of the conflicts, I am indebted to the accounts found in Holt 1966; Rafeq 1966; Joudah 1971; Cohen 1973; Heyd 1976; Abu Dayya 1986; Joudah 1987; Khalidi 1992; Doumani 1995.

24. Holt 1966, 124–28; Rafeq 1966, 9–10; Cohen 1973, 15–16, 30–31; Joudah 1987, 7, 24–29; Doumani 1995, 41–42.

25. Heyd 1942, 19–20; Joudah 1987, 22, 27–28; Doumani 1995, 41–42.

26. Heyd 1942, 19–20; Joudah 1971, 37; Cohen 1973, 90; Joudah 1987, 28–29, map 1.

27. Joudah 1971, 37; Joudah 1987, 28.

28. Silberman 1989, 228–43; Doumani 1995, 31.

29. Joudah 1971, 137–38, 168; Abu Dayya 1986, 51; Khalidi 1992, 335; Doumani 1995, 34, 42–43, 95–96.

30. Rafeq 1966, 307–8; Haddad 1967; Cohen 1973, 19.

31. Watson 1917, 20–21, 27.

32. For the following description and discussion of the battle, I am indebted to the accounts found in Berthier [1799] 1990; Napoleon 1870; Jonquière 1904; Watson 1917; Herold 1962; Chandler 1966; Esposito 1969; Thiry 1973; Bernoyer in Tortel 1976; Laurens 1988, 1989; Derogy and Carmel 1992; Duncan and Opatowski 1998; Schur 1999.

33. Berthier [1799] 1990; Bonaparte 1870; Bonaparte 1872. Kléber's report to Napoleon is reproduced in the original French in Laurens 1988, 448–52.

34. Kléber in Laurens 1988, 449; Schur 1999, 108–10.

35. Millet 1903, 104; Laurens 1988, 449; Schur 1999, 110–11.

36. Chandler 1966, map on 232–33; Thiry 1973, 345; Tortel 1976, 158; Schur 1999, 111 and map on 107. Cf. Bernoyer's map, which cannot be correct, in Tortel 1976, map 3.

37. Nicholas the Turk as translated in Wiet 1950, 57. Cf. Lavallette 1831, 311; Bonaparte 1870, 48–51; Bonaparte 1872, 86–88; Wiet 1950, 57; Herold 1962, 293; Laurens 1988, 450.

38. Watson 1917, 27–28; Chandler 1966, map on 239; Thiry 1973, 345–46; Tortel 1976, 158–59; Duncan and Opatowski 1998, 89; Schur 1999, 111–14.

39. Bernoyer in Tortel 1976, 159; Laurens 1989, 192.

40. Jonquière 1904, 216–27; Schur 1999, 111–12.

41. Schur 1999, 112.

42. Millet 1903, 105; translation in Herold 1962, 294. Cf. also Schur 1999, 113.

43. Berthier 1799, 57; Herold 1962, 293; Chandler 1966, 239; Thiry 1973, 346; Laurens 1988, 450; Laurens 1989, 192; Duncan and Opatowski 1998, 89; Schur 1999, 113.

44. Clausewitz 1976, 234.

45. Translations by the present author, following Bonaparte 1870, 49; Bonaparte 1872, 88; and Tortel 1976, 159. Cf. also Chandler 1966, 239; Schur 1999, 113.

46. Herold 1962, 294–95; Thiry 1973, 347–49; Schur 1999, 114–16.

47. The translation is mine, from the original French presented by Bernoyer in Tortel 1976, 165–66.

48. Wavell 1941, 35–36, 38, 60–61; Wavell 1944, 10; Savage 1926, 25, 48.

CHAPTER 9

The epigraph translation follows the official document posted on the Website of the Israel Ministry of Foreign Affairs, under Foreign Relations, Historical Documents, volumes 1–2: 1947–1974, II.6.

1. Dupuy 1978, 24; Kurzman 1992, 123–25.

2. For the following description and discussion of the battle, I am indebted to the accounts found in Lorch 1961; Dupuy 1978; Herzog 1984; Morris 1987; Kurzman 1992; Duncan and Opatowski 1998.

3. Lorch 1961, 93; Dupuy 1978, 24; Herzog 1984, 23, 29; Morris 1987, 111–17; Kurzman 1992, 123; Duncan and Opatowski 1998, 120.

4. Lorch 1961, 93; Dupuy 1978, 24; Herzog 1984, 27–29; Kurzman 1992, 123–24.

5. Lorch 1961, 93; Dupuy 1978, 24; Kurzman 1992, 124.

6. Lorch 1961, 93; Dupuy 1978, 24; Herzog 1984, 27–29; Kurzman 1992, 126.

7. Lorch 1961, 93–94; Bauer 1970, 146–47, 185–91; Dupuy 1978, 24–25; Herzog 1984, 27–29; Schiff 1985, 18; Morris 1987, 115–16; Kurzman 1992, 126–28.

8. Lorch 1961, 93–94; Dupuy 1978, 24–25; Herzog 1984, 27–29; Kurzman 1992, 127–28.

9. Translation following Kurzman 1992, 128; cf. also Lorch 1961, 94–95.

10. Translation following Kurzman 1992, 128; cf. also Lorch 1961, 93–94; Dupuy 1978, 24–25; Herzog 1984, 27–29; Kurzman 1992, 127–29.

11. Quotes following Kurzman 1992, 129; cf. also Morris 1987, 116–17, 158–59; Khalidi 1992, 332.

12. Lorch 1961, 95; Herzog 1984, 29.

13. Lorch 1961, 170–71; Dupuy 1978, 51; Herzog 1984, 58; Khalidi 1992, 339–40; Duncan and Opatowski 1998, 121.

14. Lorch 1961, 171; Khalidi 1992, 337–39.

15. Lorch 1961, 171; Duncan and Opatowski 1998, 121.

16. Lorch 1961, 171; Khalidi 1992, 335–36.

17. Lorch 1961, 172; Dupuy 1978, 51; Herzog 1984, 58.

18. Dupuy 1978, 85–86; Ilan, Franklin, and Hallote 2000.

19. For the following description and discussion of the events, I am indebted to the accounts found in Dupuy 1978; Herzog 1984; Hammel 1992; Duncan and Opatowski 1998.

20. Dupuy 1978, 286; Hammel 1992, 290, 364.

21. Dupuy 1978, 286–87, 306, 308; Hammel 1992, 433.

22. Dupuy 1978, 247; Herzog 1984, 153; Cohen 1993, 220, 235.

23. Dupuy 1978, 308–9; Hammel 1992, 364.

24. Dupuy 1978, 247; Cohen 1993, 235–36.

25. Dupuy 1978, 465.

CHAPTER 10

The epigraph transcription follows Roosevelt 1925, 317.

1. Aharoni 1977, 831; Kempinski 1989, 15, 107; Finkelstein and Ussishkin 1994, 28; Mounce 1998, 301 and n. 55.

2. Ladd 1972, 7; White 1986, 170; deSilva 1992, 303–20; Metzger and Murphy 1994, 363 NT; Mounce 1998, 8–21.

3. Sneen 1978, 15–17, 20, 23–24; Minear 1981, 15–19.

4. White 1977; Jeffrey 1988; Walvoord 1990; Dobson 1997.

5. LaRondelle 1985, 24; Dobson 1997, 136. Cf. Yamauchi 1991, 50.

6. Mounce 1992, 103.

7. Hindson 1986, 57; Kline 1996, 213–22.

8. Cf. Hindson 1986, 58.

9. Scofield 1945, 1348–49 n. 4; Lindsey 1970, 152–54; White 1977, 190–91; Chandler 1981, 20; LaSor 1982, 135–36, 144–45; White 1983, 175–76; Walvoord 1984, 35–36; Halsell 1988, 28–29; Jeffrey 1988, 147; Kline 1996, 207; Dobson 1997, 135–36.

10. Torry 1938, 237–48; Ladd 1972, 216; Shea 1980, 159–60; LaSor 1982, 144; LaRondelle 1985, 31; Loasby 1989, 130–32; Kline 1996, 207–8, 212–13; Mounce 1998, 301–2.

11. I gained this geological information from a personal communication with Baruch Halpern.

12. Frost 1968, 375; Davies 1986, 104–5; Kempinski 1989, 15.

13. Halpern 2000.

14. E.g., Lindsey 1970; White 1977, 1983; Walvoord 1984, 1990; Dobson 1997.

Bibliography

Abel, F.-M. 1952a. *Histoire de la Palestine: Depuis la Conquête d'Alexandre jusqu'a L'invasion Arabe.* Vol. 1, *De la Conquête d'Alexandre jusqu'a la Guerre Juive.* Paris: Librairie Lecoffre.

———. 1952b. *Histoire de la Palestine: Depuis la Conquête d'Alexandre jusqu'a L'invasion Arabe.* Vol. 2, *De la Guerre Juive a L'invasion Arabe.* Paris: Librairie Lecoffre.

Abu Dayya, Musa, ed. 1986. *Zahir al-ʿUmar wa hukkam jabal Nablus, 1771–1773* (Zahir al-ʿUmar and the Rulers of Mount Nablus). Nablus: al-Najah University, Center for Documentation and Research. (Edited and annotated text of a manuscript by Ibrahim al-Danafi al-Samiri [d. 1790].)

Adamthwaite, M.R. 1991. Labʾaya's Connection with Shechem Reassessed. *Abr-Nahrain* 30:1–19.

Aharoni, Y. 1960. Some Geographical Remarks concerning the Campaigns of Amenhotep II. *JNES* 19:177–83.

———. 1967. Anaharath. *JNES* 26:212–15.

———. 1971. The Settlement of Canaan. In *The World History of the Jewish People,* vol. 3, *Judges,* ed. B. Mazar, 94–128. Jerusalem: Masada Press.

———. 1976. The Solomonic Districts. *Tel Aviv* 3:5–15.

———. 1977. Megiddo. In *Encyclopedia of Archaeological Excavations in the Holy Land,* vol. 3, ed. M. Avi-Yonah and E. Stern, 830–47. Jerusalem: Israel Exploration Society and Masada Press.

———. 1979. *The Land of the Bible: A Historical Geography.* Ed. A.F. Rainey. Rev. and enl. ed. Philadelphia: Westminster Press.

Aharoni, Y., M. Avi-Yonah, A.F. Rainey, and A. Safrai. 1993. *The Macmillan Bible Atlas.* 3d ed. New York: Macmillan.

Ahituv, S. 1978. Economic Factors in the Egyptian Conquest of Canaan. *IEJ* 28:93–105.

Albright, W.F. 1925. The Administrative Divisions of Israel and Judah. *JPOS* 5:2–54.

———. 1936. The Song of Deborah in the Light of Archaeology. *BASOR* 62:26–31.

———. 1937. Further Light on the History of Israel from Lachish and Megiddo. *BASOR* 68:22–26.

———. 1940. Reply to Engberg, "Historical Analysis or Archaeological Evidence: Megiddo and the Song of Deborah." *BASOR* 78:7–9.

———. 1944. A Prince of Taanach in the Fifteenth Century B.C. *BASOR* 94:12–27.

———. 1947. Review of *Stüdien over de el-Amarnabrieven en het Oude-Testament inzonderheid uit historisch Oogpunt*, by J. De Koning. *JNES* 6:58–59.

———. 1994. *Yahweh and the Gods of Canaan: A Historical Analysis of Two Contrasting Faiths*. Winona Lake, IN: Eisenbrauns.

Allen, M.J. 1997.*Contested Peripheries: Philistia in the Neo-Assyrian World-System*. Ann Arbor: University Microfilms International.

Amitai-Preiss, R. 1991. ʿAyn Jalut Revisited. *Tarih* 2:119–50.

———. 1995. *Mongols and Mamluks: The Mamluk-Ikhanid War, 1260–1281*. Cambridge: Cambridge University Press.

Applebaum, S. 1989. *Judaea in Hellenistic and Roman Times: Historical and Archaeological Essays*. Leiden: E.J. Brill.

Archer, T.A., and C.L. Kingsford. 1894. *The Crusades: The Story of the Latin Kingdom of Jerusalem*. London: T. Fisher Unwin.

Augustin, M. 1988. The Literary Form of the "Constructed War Chronicle with Theological Interpretation" in the Book of Chronicles. In *Proceedings of the Ninth World Congress of Jewish Studies, Panel Sessions: Bible Studies and Ancient Near East*, ed. M. Goshen-Gottstein, 133–40. Jerusalem: Magnes Press.

Avi-Yonah, M. 1976. *The Jews of Palestine: A Political History from the Bar Kokhba War to the Arab Conquest*. Oxford: Basil Blackwell.

———. 1977. *The Holy Land, from the Persian to the Arab Conquests (536 B.C. to A.D. 640): A Historical Geography*. Rev. ed. Grand Rapids, MI: Baker Book House.

Babcock, E.A., and A.C. Krey, eds. and trans. 1943. *William, Archbishop of Tyre's A History of Deeds Done beyond the Sea*. Vol. 2. New York: Columbia University Press.

Bacharach, J.L. 1975. The Career of Muhammad Ibn Tughj al-Ikhshid, a Tenth-Century Governor of Egypt. *Speculum* 50:586–612.

———. 1984. Palestine in the Policies of Tulunid and Ikhshidid Governors of Egypt (A.H. 254–358/868–969 A.D.). In *Egypt and Palestine: A Millennium of Association (868–1948)*, ed. A. Cohen and G. Baer, 51–65. New York: St. Martin's Press.

———. 1991. Muhammad B. Tughdj. In *The Encyclopaedia of Islam*, vol. 7, ed. C.E. Bosworth et al., 411. New ed. Leiden: E.J. Brill.

Bal, M. 1988. *Murder and Difference: Gender, Genre, and Scholarship on Sisera's Death*. Trans. M. Gumpert. Bloomington: Indiana University Press.

Baldwin, M.W. 1969. The Decline and Fall of Jerusalem, 1174–1189. In *A History of the Crusades*, vol. 1, *The First Hundred Years*, ed. M.W. Baldwin, 590–621. Madison: University of Wisconsin Press.

Barnes, W.H. 1991. *Studies in the Chronology of the Divided Monarchy of Israel.* Harvard Semitic Monographs, no. 48. Atlanta: Scholars Press.

Bauer, Y. 1970. *From Diplomacy to Resistance: A History of Jewish Palestine, 1939–1945.* Philadelphia: Jewish Publication Society of America.

Begg, C.T. 1987. The Death of Josiah in Chronicles: Another View. *VT* 37:1–8.

Benvenisti, M. 1970. *The Crusaders in the Holy Land.* Jerusalem: Israel Universities Press.

Berquist, J.L. 1995a. *Judaism in Persia's Shadow: A Social and Historical Approach.* Minneapolis: Fortress Press.

———. 1995b. The Shifting Frontier: The Achaemenid Empire's Treatment of Western Colonies. *Journal of World-Systems Research* 1, no. 17: 1–38.

Berthier, L-A. [1799] 1990. *Narrative of the French Expedition into Syria, 1799, together with letters from General Bonaparte and Sir Wm. Sidney Smith.* Reprint, Felling, England: Worley Publications.

Bianquis, T. 1988. Egypt from the Arab Conquest until the End of the Fatimid State (1171). In *General History of Africa,* vol. 3, *Africa from the Seventh to the Eleventh Century,* ed. M. Elfasi, 163–93. Berkeley: University of California Press.

———. 1997. Sayf al-Dawla. In *The Encyclopaedia of Islam,* vol. 9, ed. C.E. Bosworth et al., 103–10. New ed. Leiden: E.J. Brill.

Bikhazi, R.J. 1981. *The Hamdanid Dynasty of Mesopotamia and North Syria, 254–404/868–1014.* 3 vols. Ann Arbor: University Microfilms International.

———. 1983. The Struggle for Syria and Mesopotamia (330–58/941–69) as Reflected on Hamdanid and Ikhshidid Coins. *American Numismatic Society Museum Notes* 28:137–86.

Binns, L.E. 1917. The Syrian Campaign of Necho II. *JTS* 18:36–47.

Biran, A., and J. Naveh. 1993. An Aramaic Fragment from Tel Dan. *IEJ* 43:81–98.

———. 1995. The Tel Dan Inscription: A New Fragment. *IEJ* 45:1–18.

Boehmer, J. 1933. König Josias Tod. *Archiv für Religionswissenschaft* 30:199–203.

Boling, R.G. 1975. *Judges: Introduction, Translation, and Commentary.* Anchor Bible Series, vol. 6A. New York: Doubleday and Company.

Bonaparte, N. 1870. *Correspondance de Napoléon Ier: Oeuvres de Napoléon I à Sainte-Hélène.* Vol. 30. Paris: J. Dumaine.

———. 1872. *Campagnes d'Italie, d'Ègypte et de Syrie,* vol. III. Paris: Hachette and Company.

Breasted, C. 1943. *Pioneer to the Past: The Story of James Henry Breasted, Archaeologist.* New York: Charles Scribner's Sons.

Breasted, J.H. 1906. *Ancient Records of Egypt.* 6 vols. Chicago: University of Chicago Press.

Broadhurst, R.J.C. 1980. *A History of the Ayyubid Sultans of Egypt.* Boston: G.K. Hall and Company.

Cahen, C. 1969. The Turkish Invasion: The Selchükids. In *A History of the Crusades*, vol. 1, *The First Hundred Years*, ed. Kenneth Setton and Marshall W. Baldwin, 135–76. Madison: University of Wisconsin Press.

Campbell, E.F. 1964. *The Chronology of the Amarna Letters, with Special Reference to the Hypothetical Coregency of Amenophis III and Akhenaten.* Baltimore: Johns Hopkins University Press.

Canard, M. 1951. *Histoire de la Dynastie des H'amdanides de Jazira et de Syrie.* Algiers: Jules Carbonel, Réunies.

———. 1971. Hamdanids. In *The Encyclopaedia of Islam,* vol. 3, ed. B. Lewis et al., 126–31. New ed. Leiden: E.J. Brill.

Caquot, A. 1986. Les tribus d'Israel dans le cantique de Débora (Juges 5, 13–17). *Semitica* 36:47–70.

Chambers, J. 1985. *The Devil's Horsemen: The Mongol Invasion of Europe.* New York: Athenaeum.

Chandler, D.G. 1966. *The Campaigns of Napoleon.* New York: Macmillan.

Chandler, R. 1981. Profits of Doom. *Baptist Reformation Review* 10, no. 2: 19–23. Reprinted from the *Roanoke Times,* 10 May 1981.

Clausewitz, C. von. 1942. *Principles of War.* Ed. and trans. H.W. Gatzke. Harrisburg, PA: Military Service Publishing Company.

———. 1976. *On War.* Ed. and trans. M. Howard and P. Paret. Princeton: Princeton University Press.

Clayton, P.A. 1994. *Chronicle of the Pharaohs: The Reign-By-Reign Record of the Rulers and Dynasties of Ancient Egypt.* New York: Thames and Hudson.

Cline, E.H. 1994a. Hatshepsut. In *Historic World Leaders,* vol. 1, ed. A. Commire and D. Klezmer, 218–21. Detroit and London: Gale Research.

———. 1994b. Thutmose III. In *Historic World Leaders,* vol. 1, ed. A. Commire and D. Klezmer, 655–58. Detroit and London: Gale Research.

———. 1998. In Pharaoh's Footsteps: History Repeats Itself in General Allenby's 1918 March on Megiddo. *Archaeology Odyssey* 1, no. 2: 32–41.

———. 1999a. Once More into the Breach. *Archaeology Odyssey* 2, no. 2: 10–12.

———. 1999b. Review of *War in the Holy Land,* by A. Duncan and M. Opatowski. *BAR* 25, no. 3: 56–57.

Cogan, M., and H. Tadmor. 1988. *II Kings: A New Translation with Introduction and Notes.* Anchor Bible Series, vol. 11. Garden City, NY: Doubleday and Company.

Cohen, A. 1973. *Palestine in the Eighteenth Century: Patterns of Government and Administration.* Jerusalem: Magnes Press.

Conder, C.R. 1873. The Survey of Palestine. VII. The Plain of Esdraelon. *PEFQS,* January 1873, 3–10.

Crawley, R. trans. 1910. *Thucydides: The Peloponnesian War.* New York: E.P. Dutton.

Cross, F.M., and D.N. Freedman. 1953. Josiah's Revolt against Assyria. *JNES* 12:56–58.

Davies, G.I. 1986. *Megiddo*. Grand Rapids, MI: William B. Eerdmans Publishing Company.

der Manuelian, P. 1987. *Studies in the Reign of Amenophis II*. Hildesheim: Gerstenberg Verlag.

Derogy, J., and H. Carmel. 1992. *Bonaparte en Terre sainte*. Paris: Librairie Arthème Fayard.

deSilva, D.A. 1992. The Social Setting of the Revelation of John: Conflicts Within, Fears Without. *WTJ* 54:303–20.

Dobson, E. 1997. *Fifty Remarkable Events Pointing to The End: Why Jesus Could Return by A.D. 2000*. Grand Rapids, MI: Zondervan Publishing House.

Donner, F.M. 1981. *The Early Islamic Conquests*. Princeton: Princeton University Press.

Donovan, J.P. 1950. *Pelagius and the Fifth Crusade*. Philadelphia: University of Pennsylvania Press.

Dostourian, A.E. 1993. *Armenia and the Crusades, Tenth to Twelfth Centuries: The Chronicle of Matthew of Edessa*. New York: University Press of America.

Dothan, T. 1982. *The Philistines and Their Material Culture*. Jerusalem: Israel Exploration Society.

Doumani, B. 1995. *Rediscovering Palestine: Merchants and Peasants in Jabal Nablus, 1700–1900*. Berkeley: University of California Press.

Duncan, A., and M. Opatowski. 1998. *War in the Holy Land: From Meggido* [sic] *to the West Bank*. Gloucestershire: Sutton Publishing.

Dupuy, T.N. 1978. *Elusive Victory: The Arab-Israeli Wars, 1947–1974*. New York: Harper and Row.

Edhem, H. 1916. *Tagebuch der ägyptischen Expedition des Sultans Selim I*. Weimar: Verlag Gustav Riepenheuer.

Ehrenkreutz, A.S. 1972. *Saladin*. Albany: State University of New York Press.

el-Aref, A. 1975. The Closing Phase of Ottoman Rule in Jerusalem. In *Studies on Palestine during the Ottoman Period*, ed. M. Ma'oz, 334–40. Jerusalem: Magnes Press.

Elitzur, Y. 1985–88. The Meaning of in ἐπι λουγου Polybius' Writing and Its Effect on the Location of the Town Tabor. *Scripta Classica Israelica* 8–9:79–82.

Engberg, R.M. 1940. Historical Analysis or Archaeological Evidence: Megiddo and the Song of Deborah. *BASOR* 78:4–7.

Eph'al, I. 1983. On Warfare and Military Control in the Ancient Near Eastern Empires: A Research Outline. In *History, Historiography, and Interpretation*, ed. H. Tadmor and M. Weinfeld, 88–106. Jerusalem: Magnes Press.

Epstein, C. 1963. A New Appraisal of Some Lines from a Long-Known Papyrus. *JEA* 49:49–63.

Esposito, Brigadier General V.J. 1969. *Military History and Atlas of the Napoleonic Wars*. New York: Frederick A. Praeger.

Falls, C. 1930. *Military Operations: Egypt and Palestine; from June 1917 to the End of the War*. London: H.M. Stationery Office.

———. 1964. *Armageddon: 1918*. Philadelphia: J.B. Lippincott Company.

Faulkner, R.O. 1942. The Battle of Megiddo. *JEA* 28:2–15.

Feldman, L.H. 1982. Josephus' Portrait of Saul. *HUCA* 53:45–99.

———. 1986. Josephus' Portrait of Deborah. In *Hellenica et Judaica: Hommage À Valentin Nikiprowetzky*, ed. A. Caquot, M. Hadas-Lebel, and J. Riaud, 116–28. Louvain: Éditions Peeters.

———. 1993. Josephus' Portrait of Josiah. *Louvain Studies* 18:110–30.

Fink, H.S. 1969. The Foundation of the Latin States, 1099–1118. In *A History of the Crusades*, vol. 1, *The First Hundred Years*, ed. Kenneth Setton and Marshall W. Baldwin, 368–409. Madison: University of Wisconsin Press.

Finkelstein, I. 1996. The Stratigraphy and Chronology of Megiddo and Beth-Shean in the Twelfth–Eleventh Centuries B.C.E. *Tel Aviv* 23:170–84.

———. 1998. Notes on the Stratigraphy and Chronology of Iron Age Ta'anach. *Tel Aviv* 25: 208–18.

———. 1999. Hazor and the North in the Iron Age: A Low Chronology Perspective. *BASOR* 314:55–70.

Finkelstein, I., and D. Ussishkin. 1994. Back to Megiddo. *BAR* 20, no. 1: 26–43.

Fisher, C.S. 1929. *The Excavation of Armageddon*. Oriental Institute Communications, no. 4. Chicago: University of Chicago Press.

Freedman, D.N. 1975. Early Israelite History in the Light of Early Israelite Poetry. In *Unity and Diversity: Essays in the History, Literature, and Religion of the Ancient Near East*, ed. H. Goedicke and J.J.M. Roberts, 3–35. Baltimore: Johns Hopkins University Press.

Friedmann, Y. 1992. *The History of al-Tabari*. Vol. 12, *The Battle of al-Qadisiyyah and the Conquest of Syria and Palestine*. Albany: State University of New York Press.

Frost, S.B. 1968. The Death of Josiah: A Conspiracy of Silence. *JBL* 87:369–82.

Fuller, J.F.C. 1954. *A Military History of the Western World: From the Earliest Times to the Battle of Lepanto*. New York: Minerva Press.

Gal, Z. 1994. Iron I in Lower Galilee and the Margins of the Jezreel Valley. In *From Nomadism to Monarchy: Archaeological and Historical Aspects of Early Israel*, ed. I. Finkelstein and N. Na'aman, 35–46. Jerusalem: Israel Exploration Society.

Gardiner, A. 1961. *Egypt of the Pharaohs*. Oxford: Clarendon Press.

Gardner, B. 1965. *Allenby*. London: Cassell.

Gibb, H.A.R. 1960. Adjnadayn. In *The Encyclopaedia of Islam*, vol. 1, ed. H.A.R. Gibb et al., 208–9. New ed. Leiden: E.J. Brill.

———. 1969. The Aiyubids. In *A History of the Crusades*, vol. 2, *The Later Crusades, 1189–1311*, ed. Kenneth Setton, Robert L. Wolff, and Harry W. Hazard, 693–714. Madison: University of Wisconsin Press.

Gil, M. 1992. *A History of Palestine, 634–1099*. Cambridge: Cambridge University Press.

Giles, F.J. 1997. *The Amarna Age: Western Asia*. Warminster: Aris and Phillips.

Glubb, J.B. 1967. *The Lost Centuries*. Englewood Cliffs: Prentice-Hall.

———. 1973. *Soldiers of Fortune: The Story of the Mamluks*. New York: Stein and Day.

Godley, A.D., trans. 1931. *Herodotus: Books I and II*. Cambridge, MA: Harvard University Press.

Gonen, R. 1987. Megiddo in the Late Bronze Age: Another Reassessment. *Levant* 19:83–100.

Grimal, N. 1992. *A History of Ancient Egypt*. Trans. I. Shaw. Oxford: Basil Blackwell.

Guy, P.L.O. 1931. *New Light from Armageddon*. Oriental Institute Communications, no. 9. Chicago: University of Chicago Press.

Haddad, G.M. 1967. The Chronicle of Abbud al-Sabbagh and the Fall of Daher al-ʿUmar of Acre. *al-Abhath* 20:37–44.

Halpern, B. 1983a. Doctrine by Misadventure: Between the Israelite Source and the Biblical Historian. In *The Poet and the Historian: Essays in Literary and Historical Biblical Criticism,* ed. R.E. Friedman, 41–73. Chico, CA: Scholars Press.

———. 1983b. The Resourceful Israelite Historian: The Song of Deborah and Israelite Historiography. *HTR* 76:379–401.

———. 1988. *The First Historians: The Hebrew Bible and History*. San Francisco: Harper and Row.

———. 1994. The Stela from Dan: Epigraphic and Historical Consideratons. *BASOR* 296:63–80.

———. 1998. Why Manasseh is Blamed for the Babylonian Exile: The Evolution of a Biblical Tradition. *VT* 48:473–514.

———. 2000. Centre and Sentry: Megiddo's Role in Transit, Administration, and Trade. In *Megiddo III: The 1992–96 Seasons,* ed. I. Finkelstein, D. Ussishkin, and B. Halpern, 534–75. Monograph Series of the Institute of Archaeology, Tel Aviv University. Tel Aviv: Tel Aviv University.

Halsell, G. 1988. Courting Armageddon: The Politics of Christian Zionism. *The Other Side,* January/February, 28–31.

Hammel, E. 1992. *Six Days in June: How Israel Won the 1967 Arab-Israeli War*. New York: Charles Scribner's Sons.

Hanson, V.D. 1998. *Warfare and Agriculture in Classical Greece*. Rev. ed. Berkeley: University of California Press.

Hardwicke, M.N. 1969. The Crusader States, 1192–1243. In *A History of the Crusades,* vol. 2, *The Later Crusades, 1189–1311,* ed. Kenneth Setton, Robert L. Wolff, and Harry W. Hazard, 522–56. Madison: University of Wisconsin Press.

Hayes, W.C. 1953. *The Scepter of Egypt*. Vol. 1, *From the Earliest Times to the End of the Middle Kingdom*. New York: Harper and Brothers.

Helck, W. 1971. *Die Beziehungen Ägyptens zu Vorderasien im 3. Und 2. Jahrtausend v. Chr*. Wiesbaden: Harrassowitz.

Herold, J.C. 1962. *Bonaparte in Egypt*. London: H. Hamilton.

Herrmann, S. 1964. Operationen Pharao Schoschenks I. Im östlichen Ephraim. *ZDPV* 80:55–79.

Herzog, C. 1984. *The Arab-Israeli Wars: War and Peace in the Middle East from the War of Independence through Lebanon*. New York: Vintage Books.

Herzog, C., and M. Gichon. 1997. *Battles of the Bible*. London: Greenhill Books.

Hess, R.S. 1993. *Amarna Personal Names*. Winona Lake, IN: Eisenbrauns.

Heyd, U. [1942] 1976. *Dahir al-Umar: Ruler of Galilee in the Eighteenth Century* (in Hebrew). Reprint, Jerusalem: Reuben Mass Press.

Hindson, E. 1986. Libya: A Part of Ezekiel's Prophecy? *Fundamentalist Journal* 5:57–58.

Hobbs, T.R. 1989. *A Time For War: A Study of Warfare in the Old Testament*. Wilmington, DE: Michael Glazier.

Hogarth, D.G. 1914. *The Ancient East*. London: Williams and Norgate.

Holt, P.M. 1966. *Egypt and the Fertile Crescent, 1516–1922: A Political History*. London: Longmans, Green, and Company.

———. 1986. *The Age of the Crusades: The Near East from the Eleventh Century to 1517*. London: Longman Publishing Co.

Horowitz, W. 1996. An Inscribed Clay Cylinder from Amarna Age Beth Shean. *IEJ* 46:208–17.

Howorth, H. 1888. *History of the Mongols*. Vol. 3, *The Mongols of Persia*. New York: Burt Franklin.

Huang, J.H. 1993. *Sun Tzu: The New Translation*. New York: William Morrow.

Hughes, G.R., and C.P. Nims. 1954. *Reliefs and Inscriptions at Karnak*. Vol. 3, *The Bubasite Portal*. Oriental Institute Publications, no. 84. Chicago: University of Chicago Press.

Hughes, M. 1996. General Allenby and the Palestine Campaign, 1917–18. *JSS* 19, no. 4: 59–88.

Humphreys, R.S. 1977. *From Saladin to the Mongols: The Ayyubids of Damascus, 1193–1260*. Albany: State University of New York Press.

Huss, W. 1976. *Untersuchungen zur Aussenpolitik Ptolemaios' IV*. Munich: Verlag C.H. Beck.

Ilan, D., N. Franklin, and R.S. Hallote. 2000. The Excavation of Area F. In *Megiddo III: The 1992–96 Seasons*, ed. I. Finkelstein, D. Ussishkin, and B. Halpern, 75–103. Monograph Series of the Institute of Archaeology, Tel Aviv University. Tel Aviv: Tel Aviv University.

Irwin, R. 1986. *The Middle East in the Middle Ages: The Early Mamluk Sultanate, 1250–1382*. Carbondale, IL: Southern Illinois University Press.

Isaac, B., and I. Roll. 1982. *Roman Roads in Judaea*. Vol. 1, *The Legio-Scythopolis Road*. BAR International Series, 141. Oxford: British Archaeological Reports.

Izre'el, S. 1990. A New Translation of the Amarna Letters. *BibOr* 47, nos. 5–6: 577–604.

Jackson, P. 1980. The Crisis in the Holy Land in 1260. *EHR* 95:481–513.

Jansky, H. 1926. Die Eroborung Syriens durch Sultan Selim I. *Mitteilungen Zur Osmanischen Geschichte* 2:173–241.

Jeffrey, G.R. 1988. *Armageddon: Appointment with Destiny*. Toronto: Frontier Research Publications.

Jenkins, R. 1966. *Byzantium: The Imperial Centuries, A.D. 610–1071*. London: Weidenfeld and Nicolson.

Jones, T., and A. Ereira. 1995. *Crusades*. New York: Facts on File Publications.

Jonquière, C. de la. 1904. *L'Expedition en Egypte, 1798–1801*. 5 vols. Paris.

Joudah, A.H. 1971. *A History of the Movement of Shaykh Zahir al-'Umar Al-Zaydani (1690?–1775)*. Ann Arbor: University Microfilms International.

———. 1987. *Revolt in Palestine in the Eighteenth Century: The Era of Shaykh Zahir al-'Umar*. Princeton: Kingston Press.

Kanael, B. 1957. The Partition of Judea by Gabinius. *IEJ* 7:98–106.

Kaufmann, Y. 1985. *The Biblical Account of the Conquest of Canaan*. 2d ed. Jerusalem: Magnes Press.

Kedar, B.Z. 1992. The Battle of Hattin Revisited. In *The Horns of Hattin: Proceedings of the Second Conference of the Society for the Study of the Crusades and the Latin East, Jerusalem and Haifa, 2–6 July 1987*, ed. B.Z. Kedar, 190–207. Jerusalem: Israel Exploration Society.

Kedar, B.Z., and D. Pringle. 1985. La Fève: A Crusader Castle in the Jezreel Valley. *IEJ* 35:164–79.

Keegan, J. 1993. *A History of Warfare*. New York: Alfred A. Knopf.

Kempinski, A. 1989. *Megiddo: A City-State and Royal Centre in North Israel*. Munich: Verlag C.H. Beck.

Kennedy, D.L. 1980. Legio VI Ferrata: The Annexation and Early Garrison of Arabia. *HSCP* 84:283–309.

Kenyon, K. 1969. The Middle and Late Bronze Age Strata at Megiddo. *Levant* 1:25–60.

Khalidi, W., ed. 1992. *All That Remains: The Palestinian Villages Occupied and Depopulated by Israel in 1948*. Washington, D.C.: Institute for Palestine Studies.

Kitchen, K.A. 1986. *The Third Intermediate Period in Egypt (1100–650 B.C.)*. 2d ed., rev. Warminster: Aris and Phillips.

———. 1989. Shishak's Military Campaign in Israel Confirmed. *BAR* 15, no. 3: 32–33.

Kitchener, H.H. 1878. Survey of Galilee. *PEFQS*, October 1878, 159–75.

Klausner, J. 1972. John Hyrcanus I. In *The World History of the Jewish People*. Vol. 6, *The Hellenistic Age*, ed. A. Schalit, 211–21. New Brunswick: Rutgers University Press.

Klein, R.W. 1983. *Word Biblical Commentary*. Vol. 10, *1 Samuel*. Waco, TX: Word Books.

Kline, M.G. 1996. Har Magedon: The End of the Millennium. *JETS* 39, no. 2: 207–22.

Kochavi, M. 1965. The Site of the Battle of Deborah in the Light of Recent Archaeological Evidence. In *Doron: Essays in Honor of Professor Abraham J. Katsh,* ed. I.T. Naamani and D. Rudavsky. 90–95. New York: National Association of Professors of Hebrew in American Institutions of Higher Learning.

Kurzman, D. 1992. *Genesis 1948: The First Arab-Israeli War.* New York: Da Capo Press.

Ladd, G.E. 1972. *A Commentary on the Revelation of John.* Grand Rapids, MI: William B. Eerdmans Publishing Company.

Lamon, R.S., and G.M. Shipton. 1939. *Megiddo I: Seasons of 1925–34.* Oriental Institute Publications, no. 42. Chicago: University of Chicago Press.

Lane-Poole, S. 1898. *Saladin and the Fall of the Kingdom of Jerusalem.* London: G.P. Putnam's Sons.

Lapp, P. 1967. Taanach by the Waters of Megiddo. *BA* 30:2–27.

LaRondelle, H.K. 1985. The Biblical Concept of Armageddon. *JETS* 28, no. 1: 21–31.

Larson, J.A. 1990. Egypt in Israel: The Discovery of the "Shishak Stela Fragment" at Megiddo. *Oriental Institute News and Notes* 124:2–3.

LaSor, W.S. 1982. *The Truth about Armageddon.* New York: Harper and Row.

Laurens, H. 1988. *Kléber en Égypte, 1798–1800.* Vol. 2, *Kléber et Bonaparte, 1798–1799.* Paris: Institut Français d'Archéologie Orientale.

———. 1989. *L'Expédition d'Égypte, 1798–1801.* Paris: Armand Colin.

Lavallette, A.-M. Chamans, Comte de. 1831. *Mémoires et souvenirs.* Vol. 1. Paris: H. Fournier.

Leonard, A., Jr., and E.H. Cline. 1998. The Aegean Pottery at Megiddo: An Appraisal and Reanalysis. *BASOR* 309:3–39.

Levi della Vida, G. 1935. L'Invasione dei Tartari in Siria nel 1260 nei ricordi di un testimone oculare. *Orientalia* 4:253–76.

Lewis, B. 1987. *Islam: From the Prophet Muhammad to the Capture of Constantinople.* Vol. 1, *Politics and War.* Oxford: Oxford University Press.

Lichtheim, M. 1973. *Ancient Egyptian Literature: A Book of Readings.* Vol. 1, *The Old and Middle Kingdoms.* Berkeley: University of California Press.

Liddell Hart, B.H. 1934. *History of the First World War.* London: Cassell.

Lindars, B. 1995. *Judges 1–5: A New Translation and Commentary.* Ed. A.D.H. Mayes. Edinburgh: T & T Clark.

Lindsey, H. [1970] 1990. *The Late Great Planet Earth.* Reprint, New York: Bantam Books.

Loasby, R.E. 1989. "Har-Magedon" according to the Hebrew in the Setting of the Seven Last Plagues of Revelation 16. *AUSS* 27, no. 2: 129–32.

Lorch, N. 1961. *The Edge of the Sword: Israel's War of Independence, 1947–1949.* New York: G.P. Putnam's Sons.

Loud, G. 1948. *Megiddo II: Seasons of 1935–39.* Oriental Institute Publications, no. 62. Chicago: University of Chicago Press.

Luckenbill, D.D. 1926. *Ancient Records of Assyria and Babylonia.* Vol. 1. Chicago: University of Chicago Press.

Lyons, M.C., and D.E.P. Jackson. 1982. *Saladin: The Politics of the Holy War.* Cambridge: Cambridge University Press.

Lyons, U., and M.C. Lyons. 1971. *Ayyubids, Mamlukes, and Crusaders: Selections from the Tarikh al-Duwal wa'l- Muluk of Ibn al-Furat.* Vol. 2, *The Translation.* Cambridge: W. Heffer and Sons.

Magness, J. 1992. Masada: Arms and the Man. *BAR* 18, no. 4: 58–67.

Maisler, B. [B. Mazar]. 1953. Beth She'arim, Gaba, and Harosheth of the Peoples. *HUCA* 25:75–84.

Malamat, A. 1950. The Last Wars of the Kingdom of Judah. *JNES* 9:218–27.

———. 1953. The War of Gideon and Midian: A Military Approach. *PEFQ* 1953:61–65.

———. 1961. Campaigns of Amenhotep II and Thutmose IV to Canaan. In *Scripta Hierosolymitana,* vol. 3, *Studies in the Bible,* ed. C. Rabin, 218–31. Jerusalem: Magnes Press.

———. 1968. The Last Kings of Judah and the Fall of Jerusalem. *IEJ* 18:137–56.

———. 1971a. The Period of the Judges. In *The World History of the Jewish People,* vol. 3, *Judges,* ed. B. Mazar, 129–63. Jerusalem: Masada Press.

———. 1971b. Syro-Palestinian Destinations in a Mari Tin Inventory. *IEJ* 21:31–38.

———. 1973. Josiah's Bid for Armageddon: The Background of the Judean-Egyptian Encounter in 609 B.C. *JANES* 5:267–78.

———. 1974. Megiddo, 609 B.C.: The Conflict Re-examined. *Acta Antiqua* 22:445–49.

———. 1975. The Twilight of Judah in the Egyptian-Babylonian Maelstrom. *VT* supp. 28:123–45.

———. 1999. Caught between the Great Powers. *BAR* 25, no. 4: 34–41, 64.

Malul, M. 1996. Was David Involved with the Death of Saul on the Gilboa Mountain? *Revue Biblique* 103:517–45.

Margalit, B. 1995. Observations on the Jael-Sisera Story (Judges 4–5). In *Pomegranates and Golden Bells: Studies in Biblical, Jewish, and Near Eastern Ritual, Law, and Literature in Honor of Jacob Milgrom,* ed. D.P. Wright, D.N. Freedman, and A. Hurvitz, 629–41. Winona Lake, IN: Eisenbrauns.

Marshall, C. 1992. *Warfare in the Latin East, 1192–1291.* Cambridge: Cambridge University Press.

Masterman, E.W.G. 1917. Palestine: Its Resources and Suitability for Colonization. *Geographical Journal* 50:12–32.

Mauchline, J. 1971. *First and Second Samuel.* Greenwood, SC: Attic Press.

Maunsell, F.R. 1908. The Hejaz Railway. *Geographical Journal* 32:570–85.

Mayes, A.D. 1969. The Historical Context of the Battle against Sisera. *VT* 19:353–60.

Mazar, B. 1957. The Campaign of Pharaoh Shishak to Palestine. *VT* supp. 4:57–66.

———. 1986. Pharaoh Shishak's Campaign to the Land of Israel. In *The Early Biblical Period: Historical Studies,* ed. S. Ahituv and B.A. Levine, 139–50. Jerusalem: Israel Exploration Society.

McGinty, M.E. 1941. *Fulcher of Chartes: Chronicle of the First Crusade.* Philadelphia: University of Pennsylvania Press.

Metzger, B.M., and R.E. Murphy. 1994. *The New Oxford Annotated Bible.* New Revised Standard Version. New York: Oxford University Press.

Miller, J.M., and J.H. Hayes. 1986. *A History of Ancient Israel and Judah.* Philadelphia: Westminster Press.

Millet, P.-J.-S. 1903. *Le Chasseur P. Millet: Souvenirs de la campagne d'Egypt, 1898–1901.* Paris.

Minear, P.S. 1981. *New Testament Apocalyptic.* Nashville: Abingdon Press.

Moran, W.L. 1992. *The Amarna Letters.* Baltimore: Johns Hopkins University Press.

Morgan, D.O. 1985. The Mongols in Syria, 1260–1300. In *Crusade and Settlement: Papers Read at the First Conference of the Society for the Study of the Crusades and the Latin East and Presented to R.C. Smail,* ed. P.W. Edbury, 231–35. Cardiff: University College Cardiff Press.

———. 1986. *The Mongols.* Oxford: Basil Blackwell.

Morris, B. 1987. *The Birth of the Palestinian Refugee Problem, 1947–1949.* Cambridge: Cambridge University Press.

Mounce, R.H. 1992. *What Are We Waiting For? A Commentary on Revelation.* Grand Rapids, MI: William B. Eerdmans Publishing Company.

———. 1998. *The Book of Revelation.* Rev. ed. Grand Rapids, MI: William B. Eerdmans Publishing Company.

Myres, J.L. 1911. *Dawn of History.* London: Williams and Norgate.

Na'aman, N. 1981. Economic Aspects of the Egyptian Occupation of Canaan. *IEJ* 31:172–85.

———. 1988. Pharaonic Lands in the Jezreel Valley in the Late Bronze Age. In *Society and Economy in the Eastern Mediterranean (c. 1500–1000 B.C.),* ed. M. Heltzer and E. Lipinski, 177–85. Louvain: E.J. Brill.

———. 1990. Literary and Topographical Notes on the Battle of Kishon (Judges IV–V). *VT* 40:423–36.

———. 1991. The Kingdom of Judah under Josiah. *Tel Aviv* 18:3–71.

———. 1992. Israel, Edom, and Egypt in the Tenth Century B.C.E. *Tel Aviv* 19:71–93.

———. 1993. Population Changes in Palestine following Assyrian Deportations. *Tel Aviv* 20:104–24.

———. 1994. The "Conquest of Canaan" in the Book of Joshua and in History.

In *From Nomadism to Monarchy: Archaeological and Historical Aspects of Early Israel*, ed. I. Finkelstein and N. Na'aman, 218–81. Jerusalem: Israel Exploration Society.

———. 1995. Tiglath-Pileser III's Campaigns against Tyre and Israel (734–732 B.C.E.). *Tel Aviv* 22:268–78.

———. 1997. Historical and Literary Notes on the Excavation of Tel Jezreel. *Tel Aviv* 24:122–28.

Napier, B.D. 1959. The Omrides of Jezreel. *VT* 9:366–78.

Nelson, H.H. [1913] 1920. *The Battle of Megiddo*. Reprint, Chicago: University of Chicago Press.

Nelson, R. 1983. Realpolitik in Judah (687–609 B.C.E.). In *Scripture in Context*, vol. 2, ed. W.W. Hallo, J.C. Moyer, and L.G. Perdue, 177–89. Winona Lake, IN: Eisenbrauns.

Netzer, E. 1991. The Last Days and Hours at Masada. *BAR* 17, no. 6: 20–32.

Newby, P.H. 1983. *Saladin in His Time*. London: Faber and Faber.

Newell, J.Q.C. 1991. Learning the Hard Way: Allenby in Egypt and Palestine, 1917–19. *JSS* 14, no. 3: 363–87.

Noth, M. 1938. Die Wege der Pharaonenheere in Palästina und Syrien. IV. Die Schoschenkliste. *ZDPV* 61:277–304.

———. 1960. *The History of Israel*. 2d ed., revised. New York: Harper.

O'Connor, D., and E.H. Cline. 1998. *Amenhotep III: Perspectives on His Reign*. Ann Arbor: University of Michigan Press.

Paton, W.R., trans. 1979. *Polybius: The Histories*. Cambridge: Harvard University Press.

Peersman, J. 2000. Assyrian Magiddu: The Town Planning of Stratum III. In *Megiddo III: The 1992–96 Seasons*, ed. I. Finkelstein, D. Ussishkin, and B. Halpern, 523–33. Monograph Series of the Institute of Archaeology, Tel Aviv University. Tel Aviv: Tel Aviv University.

Peters, E. 1971. *Christian Society and the Crusades, 1198–1229: Sources in Translation, including the Capture of Damietta by Oliver of Paderborn*. Philadelphia: University of Pennsylvania Press.

Petrie, W.M.F. 1896. *A History of Egypt*. Vol. 2, *A History of Egypt during the XVIIth and XVIIIth Dynasties*. 1st ed. London: Methuen and Company.

———. 1898. *A History of Egypt*. Vol. 2, *A History of Egypt during the XVIIth and XVIIIth Dynasties*. 2d ed., with additions. London: Methuen and Company.

———. 1904. *A History of Egypt*. Vol. 2, *A History of Egypt during the XVIIth and XVIIIth Dynasties*. 4th ed., with additions. London: Methuen and Company.

Pfeifer, G. 1969. Die Begegnung zwischen Pharao Necho und König Josia bei Megiddo. *MIO* 15:297–307.

Pirie-Gordon, H. 1919. *A Brief Record of the Advance of the Egyptian Expeditionary Force under the Command of General Sir Edmund H.H. Allenby, G.C.B.,*

G.C.M.G., July 1917 to October 1918. 2d ed. London: H. M. Stationery Office.

Powell, J.M. 1986. *Anatomy of a Crusade, 1213–1221.* Philadelphia: University of Pennsylvania Press.

Pritchard, J.B. 1969. *Ancient Near Eastern Texts Relating to the Old Testament.* 3d ed., with supp. Princeton: Princeton University Press.

Rafeq, A-K. 1966. *The Province of Damascus, 1723–1783.* Beirut: Khayats Publishers.

Rainey, A.F. 1973. Amenhotep II's Campaign to Takhsi. *JARCE* 10:71–75.

———. 1978. *El Amarna Tablets 359–379: Supplement to J.A. Knudtzon "Die el-Amarna Tafeln."* 2d ed., revised. Neukirchener: Verlag Butzon and Bercker Kevelaer.

———. 1981. The Military Camp Ground at Taanach by the Waters of Megiddo. *Eretz-Israel* 15:61*–66*.

———. 1983. Toponymic Problems (Cont.): Harosheth-Hagoiim. *Tel Aviv* 10:46–48.

Rast, W.E. 1978. *Taanach I: Studies in the Iron Age Pottery.* Cambridge, MA: American Schools of Oriental Research.

Redford, D.B. 1973. Studies in Relations between Palestine and Egypt during the First Millennium B.C. II. The Twenty-Second Dynasty. *JAOS* 93:3–17.

Reviv, H. 1966. The Government of Shechem in the el-Amarna Period and in the Days of Abimelech. *IEJ* 16:252–57.

Riley-Smith, J. 1967. *The Knights of St. John in Jerusalem and Cyprus, c. 1050–1310.* London: Macmillan.

Riley-Smith, L., and J. Riley-Smith. 1981. *The Crusades: Idea and Reality, 1095–1274.* London: Edward Arnold.

Rofé, A. 1988. The Vineyard of Naboth: The Origin and Message of the Story. *VT* 38:89–104.

Rogerson, J. 1985. *Atlas of the Bible.* New York: Facts on File Publications.

Rohl, D.M. 1995. *Pharaohs and Kings: A Biblical Quest.* New York: Crown Publishers.

Röhricht, R. 1876. Der Kreuzzug des Königs Andreas II von Ungarn 1217. *Forschungen zur Deutschen Geschichte* 16:139–56.

———. 1891. *Studien zur Geschichte des fünften kreuzzuges.* Innsbruck: Wagner GmbH.

Roosevelt, T. 1925. *Social Justice and Popular Rule: Essays, Addresses, and Public Statements Relating to the Progressive Movement (1910–1916).* New York: Charles Scribner's Sons. (Reprint, New York: Arno Press, 1974.)

Rosenthal, M., and I. Mozeson. 1990. *Wars of the Jews: A Military History from Biblical to Modern Times.* New York: Hippocrene Books.

Runciman, S. 1952. *A History of the Crusades.* Vol. 2, *The Kingdom of Jerusalem and the Frankish East, 1100–1187.* Cambridge: Cambridge University Press.

———. 1954. *A History of the Crusades.* Vol. 3, *The Kingdom of Acre and the Later Crusades.* Cambridge: Cambridge University Press.

————. 1969. The Crusader States, 1243–1291. In *A History of the Crusades*, vol. 2, *The Later Crusades, 1189–1311*, ed. Kenneth Setton, Robert L. Wolff, and Harry W. Hazard, 557–98. Madison: University of Wisconsin Press.

Russell, C.T. 1920. *Studies in the Scriptures*. Vol. 4, *The Battle of Armageddon*. Brooklyn: International Bible Students Association.

Salmon, W.H. 1921. *An Account of the Ottoman Conquest of Egypt in the Year A.H. 922 (A.D. 1516)*. London: Royal Asiatic Society.

Saunders, J.J. 1971. *The History of the Mongol Conquests*. London: Routledge and Kegan Paul.

————. 1977. The Mongol Defeat at Ain Jalut and the Restoration of the Greek Empire. In *Muslims and Mongols: Essays on Medieval Asia*, ed. G.W. Rice, 67–76. Christchurch, NZ: University of Canterbury.

Savage, R. 1926. *Allenby of Armageddon*. Indianapolis: Bobbs-Merrill Company.

Schalit, A. 1975. The End of the Hasmonean Dynasty and the Rise of Herod. In *The World History of the Jewish People*, vol. 7, *The Herodian Period*, ed. M. Avi-Yonah and Z. Baras, 44–70. New Brunswick: Rutgers University Press.

Schiff, Z. 1985. *A History of the Israeli Army, 1874 to the Present*. New York: Macmillan.

Schlumberger, G. 1896. *L'Epopée Byzantine a la fin du dixième siècle*. Vol. 1. Paris: Hachette and Company.

Schneider, T. 1995. Did King Jehu Kill His Own Family? *BAR* 21, no. 1: 26–33, 80.

————. 1996. Rethinking Jehu. *Biblica* 77, no. 1: 100–107.

Schniedewind, W.M. 1996. Tel Dan Stela: New Light on Aramaic and Jehu's Revolt. *BASOR* 302:75–90.

Schumacher, G. 1908. *Tell el-Mutesellim I*. Leipzig: Haupt.

Schur, N. 1999. *Napoleon in the Holy Land*. London: Greenhill Books.

Scofield, C.I., ed. 1945. *The Scofield Reference Bible*. New York: Oxford University Press.

Shatzman, I. 1991. *The Armies of the Hasmonaeans and Herod: From Hellenistic to Roman Frameworks*. Tübingen: J.C.B. Mohr.

Shea, W.H. 1980. The Location and Significance of Armageddon in Rev. 16:16. *AUSS* 18, no. 2: 157–62.

Sherwin-White, S., and A. Kuhrt. 1993. *From Samarkhand to Sardis: A New Approach to the Seleucid Empire*. London: Gerald Duckworth and Company.

Shipton, G.M. 1939. *Notes on the Megiddo Pottery of Strata VI–XX*. Chicago: University of Chicago Press.

Silberman, N.A. 1989. *Between Past and Present: Archaeology, Ideology, and Nationalism in the Modern Middle East*. New York: H. Holt.

Silberman, N.A., I. Finkelstein, U. Ussishkin, and B. Halpern. 1999. Digging at Armageddon: Where Biblical History and Legend Meet. *Archaeology* 52, no. 6: 32–39.

Singer, I. 1988. Megiddo Mentioned in a Letter from Bogazköy. In *Documentum*

Asiae Minoris Antiquae (Festschrift Heinrich Otten), ed. E. Neu and Ch. Rüster, 327–32. Wiesbaden: Harrassowitz.

———. 1988–89. The Political Status of Megiddo VIIA. *Tel Aviv* 15–16:101–12.

Smail, R.C. 1956. *Crusading Warfare (1097–1193)*. Cambridge: Cambridge University Press.

———. 1982. The Predicaments of Guy of Lusignan, 1183–87. In *Outremer: Studies in the History of the Crusading Kingdom of Jerusalem Presented to Joshua Prawer*, ed. B.Z. Kedar, H.E. Mayer, and R.C. Smail, 159–76. Jerusalem: Yad Izhak Ben-Zvi Institute.

Smallwood, E.M. 1976. *The Jews under Roman Rule*. Leiden: E.J. Brill.

Smith, G.A. 1894. *The Historical Geography of the Holy Land*. 1st ed. New York: Hodder and Stoughton.

———. 1919. *The Historical Geography of the Holy Land*. 18th ed. New York: Hodder and Stoughton.

———. 1931. *The Historical Geography of the Holy Land*. 25th ed. New York: Hodder and Stoughton.

Smith, J.M., Jr. 1984. 'Ayn Jalut: Mamluk Success or Mongol Failure? *HJAS* 44:307–45.

Sneen, D. 1978. *Visions of Hope: Apocalyptic Themes from Biblical Times*. Minneapolis: Augsburg Publishing House.

Spalinger, A. 1983. The Historical Implications of the Year 9 Campaign of Amenophis II. *JSSEA* 13:89– 101.

Spieckermann, H. 1982. *Juda unter Assur in der Sargonidenzeit*. Göttingen: Vandenhoeck and Ruprecht.

Spuler, B. 1969. *The Age of the Caliphs*. Trans. F.R.C. Bagley. Princeton: Markus Wiener Publishers.

Stager, L.E. 1988. Archaeology, Ecology, and Social History: Background Themes to the Song of Deborah. *VT* supp. 40:221–34.

———. 1989. The Song of Deborah: Why Some Tribes Answered the Call and Others Did Not. *BAR* 15, no. 1: 50–64.

Stern, M. 1975. The Herodian Dynasty and the Province of Judea at the End of the Period of the Second Temple. In *The World History of the Jewish People*, vol. 7, *The Herodian Period*, ed. M. Avi-Yonah and Z. Baras, 124–78. New Brunswick: Rutgers University Press.

Stevenson, W.B. 1907. *The Crusaders in the East: A Brief History of the Wars of Islam with the Latins in Syria during the Twelfth and Thirteenth Centuries*. Cambridge: Cambridge University Press.

Sweeney, J.R. 1981. Hungary in the Crusades, 1169–1218. *International History Review* 3:467–81.

Tadmor, H. 1994. *The Inscriptions of Tiglath-Pileser III, King of Assyria: Critical Edition, with Introductions, Translations, and Commentary*. Jerusalem: Israel Academy of Sciences and Humanities.

Talshir, Z. 1996. The Three Deaths of Josiah and the Strata of Biblical Historiography (2 Kings XXIII 29–30; 2 Chronicles XXXV 20–5; 1 Esdras I
23–31). *VT* 46:213–36.

Thiry, Baron J. 1973. *Bonaparte en Égypte*. Paris: Berger-Levrault.

Thorau, P. 1985. The Battle of ʿAyn Jalut: A Re-examination. In *Crusade and Settlement: Papers Read at the First Conference of the Society for the Study of the Crusades and the Latin East and Presented to R.C. Smail*, ed. P.W. Edbury,
236–41. Cardiff: University College Cardiff Press.

———. 1992. *The Lion of Egypt: Sultan Baybars I and the Near East in the Thirteenth
Century*. Trans. P.M. Holt. London and New York: Longman Publishing
Co.

Tolkowsky, S. 1925. Gideon's Three Hundred. *JPOS* 5:69–74.

Torry, C.C. 1938. Armageddon. *HTR* 31:237–48.

Tortel, Ch., ed. 1976. *François Bernoyer's avec Bonaparte en Egypte et en Syrie
1798–1800: 19 Lettres Inedites*. Abbeville: Les Presses Françaises.

Treadgold, W. 1995. *Byzantium and Its Army*. Stanford: Stanford University
Press.

Trotter, C. 1894. Review of *Historical Geography of the Holy Land*, by G.A. Smith,
1st ed. *Geographical Journal* 4:450–53.

Tsuk, T. 1988–89. The Aqueduct to Legio and the Location of the Camp of the
Sixth Roman Legion. *Tel Aviv* 15–16:92–97.

Tsevat, M. 1979. The Emergence of the Israelite Monarchy: Eli, Samuel, and
Saul. In *The World History of the Jewish People*, vol. 4, part 1, *The Age of the
Monarchies: Political History*, ed. A. Malamat, 61–75. Jerusalem: Masada
Press.

Ussishkin, D. 1980. Was the "Solomonic" City Gate at Megiddo Built by King
Solomon? *BASOR* 239:1–18.

———. 1990. Notes on Megiddo, Gezer, Ashdod, and Tel Batash in the Tenth
to Ninth Centuries B.C. *BASOR* 277/278:71–91.

———. 1995. The Destruction of Megiddo at the End of the Late Bronze Age
and Its Historical Significance. *Tel Aviv* 22:240–67.

Ussishkin, D., and J. Woodhead. 1992. Excavations at Tel Jezreel, 1990–1991:
Preliminary Report. *Tel Aviv* 19:3–56.

———. 1997. Excavations at Tel Jezreel, 1994–1996: Third Preliminary
Report. *Tel Aviv* 24:6–72.

Van Cleve, T.C. 1969. The Fifth Crusade. In *A History of the Crusades*, vol. 2, *The
Later Crusades, 1189–1311*, ed. Kenneth Setton, Robert L. Wolff, and
Harry W. Hazard, 377–428. Madison: University of Wisconsin Press.

Walvoord, J.F. 1984. Russia, King of the North. Part 1. *Fundamentalist Journal*
3:34–38.

———. 1990. *Armageddon, Oil, and the Middle East Crisis*. Rev. ed. Grand Rapids,
MI: Zondervan Publishing House.

Watson, Colonel Sir C.M. 1917. Bonaparte's Expedition to Palestine in 1799. *PEFQ* 1917, 17–35.

Wavell, A.P. 1929. *The Palestine Campaigns*. 2d ed. London: Constable and Company.

———. 1941. *Allenby: A Study in Greatness*. New York: Oxford University Press.

———. 1944. *Allenby in Egypt (Being Volume II of Allenby: A Study in Greatness)*. New York: Oxford University Press.

———. 1948. *The Good Soldier*. London: Macmillan.

Weinstein, J.M. 1981. The Egyptian Empire in Palestine: A Reassessment. *BASOR* 241:1–28.

Welch, A.C. 1925. The Death of Josiah. *ZAW* 43:255–60.

Whiston, W. 1957. *The Life and Works of Flavius Josephus*. Philadelphia: John C. Winston Company.

White, J.B. 1986. *From Adam to Armageddon: A Survey of the Bible*. Belmont, CA: Wadsworth Publishing Company.

White, J.W. 1977. *WW III: Signs of the Impending Battle of Armageddon*. Grand Rapids, MI: Zondervan Publishing House.

———. 1983. *Arming for Armageddon*. Milford, MI: Mott Media.

White, M. 1994. Naboth's Vineyard and Jehu's Coup: The Legitimation of a Dynastic Extermination. *VT* 44:66–76.

Whitelam, K.W. 1979. *The Just King: Monarchical Judicial Authority in Ancient Israel*. Sheffield: JSOT Press.

Whitley, C.F. 1957. The Sources of the Gideon Stories. *VT* 7:157–64.

Wiet, G., ed. and trans. 1950. *Nicolas Turc: Chronique d'Égypte, 1798–1804*. Cairo: Institut Français d'Archéologie Orientale.

Williamson, H.G.M. 1982. The Death of Josiah and the Continuing Development of the Deuteronomic History. *VT* 32:242–47.

———. 1987. Reliving the Death of Josiah: A Reply to C.T. Begg. *VT* 37:9–15.

———. 1991. Jezreel in the Biblical Texts. *Tel Aviv* 18:72–92.

Wiseman, D.J. 1961. *Chronicles of Chaldean Kings (626–556 B.C.) in the British Museum*. London: Trustees of the British Museum.

Yadin, Y. 1960. *Military and Archaeological Aspects of the Conquest of Canaan in the Book of Joshua*. New York: Jewish Education Committee of New York.

———. 1963. *The Art of Warfare in Biblical Lands, in the Light of Archaeological Discovery*. London: Weidenfeld and Nicolson.

———. 1970. Megiddo of the Kings of Israel. *BA* 33:66–96.

———. 1976. The Historical Significance of Inscription 88 from Arad: A Suggestion. *IEJ* 26:9–14.

———. 1980. A Rejoinder. *BASOR* 239:19–23.

Yamauchi, E. 1991. Updating the Armageddon Calendar: A Review of Walvoord's *Armageddon, Oil, and the Middle East Crisis*. *Christianity Today*, 29 April, 50–51.

Yeivin, Sh. 1967. Amenophis II's Asianic Campaigns. *JARCE* 6:119–28.

Index